CRITICAL PERSPECTIVES ON WORK AND ORGANISATIONS

Series editors:

David Knights, Manchester School of Management, UMIST
Paul Thompson, Department of Management, University of Edinburgh
Chris Smith, School of Management, Royal Holloway, University of London
Hugh Wilmott, Manchester School of Management, Umist

This series offers a range of titles examining the broad areas of work and organisation within a national and global arena. Each book in the series is written by leading experts and covers a topic chosen to appeal to students and academics. Originating out of the International Labour Process Conference, the series will be informative, topical and leading edge.

Published:
Paul Thompson and Chris Warhurst *Workplaces of the Future*

Forthcoming:
Alan Felstead and Nick Jewson *Global Trends in Flexible Labour*

Workplaces of the Future

Edited by
Paul Thompson and Chris Warhurst

MACMILLAN
Business

First published 1998 by
MACMILLAN PRESS LTD
Houndmills, Basingstoke, Hampshire RG21 6XS
and London
Companies and representatives
throughout the world

ISBN 0–333–72799–1 hardback
ISBN 0–333–72800–9 paperback

A catalogue record for this book is available
from the British Library.

This book is printed on paper suitable for recycling and
made from fully managed and sustained forest sources.

10 9   8   7   6   5   4   3   2   1
07 06 05 04 03 02 01 00 99 98

Printed in Great Britain by Antony Rowe Ltd, Chippenham, Wiltshire

Contents

Preface

As is usual in this Series, most of the chapters are drawn from papers contributed to the Annual International Labour Process Conference. Indeed the main impetus for the book came from a feeling that the Series needed a volume that returned to some of the 'classical' roots of labour process writings. This does not imply anything negative about the new directions and issues dealt with in recent volumes, but represents a positive desire to enable contributors writing in a critical tradition to focus on some of the core themes of changes in the nature of work itself, which was after all the motivating force of early labour process analysis.

This is particularly pertinent in the current period. As the millennium approaches popular discourse is deluged with futurist babble. When work is not ending, it is beginning anew, transformed by fresh challenges and visions: smart, flexible, committed employees replacing the sullen, disengaged factory hands and office drudges of industrial society. But what is the office, the factory or the hospital of the future? We hope that the eleven chapters in this book can help answer that question and provide a more accurate picture than that filtered through the 'popular'.

This is also our purpose in our introductory chapter. But we want to engage *with* those popular images of change more than engage *in* another review of the literature and debates. It is important to engage and, whenever possible, supplant erroneous mainstream accounts of the future of the workplace. To do otherwise would be to repeat those mistakes of social science that Braverman sought to rectify. However this is not a sterile exercise in maintaining a legacy. Mainstream accounts have far too much leverage on public perceptions and the deliberations of policy makers. It is a task for all of us to attempt to enjoin and make a positive contribution to those perceptions and deliberations about the future of the workplace. Our introductory chapter therefore starts with an exposition of those popular themes before exploring the issues through an examination of the key sectors of waged work: routine, technical, professional and managerial.

We have tried to bring together a collection of papers that covers key developments in all the main sectors of work, but, inevitably, given the sources available, some areas are covered more than others. It is, additionally, about waged work rather than all types of work activity. Though the internationalisation of the political economy is the context for many of the contributions, the empirical focus is primarily Europe and the US.

Finally, empirically-informed theoretical analysis has always been the aim of the Labour Process Conference and Series. This volume is squarely in that tradition. Though the theoretical perspectives sometimes differ, the chapters as a whole provide a sceptical, research-led antidote to much that is misinformed or misunderstood about the 'new workplace'.

Two hard-pressed colleagues whom the authors would particularly like to thank in the preparation of this volume are Kirsteen Daly and Janie Ferguson for their secretarial and library resource support respectively.

Paul Thompson
Chris Warhurst

Notes on the Contributors

PETER BAIN is Lecturer in the Department of Human Resource Management at the University of Strathclyde. His published work encompasses trade union recruitment, labour history and office work and sick building syndrome. His current areas of interest include health and safety in the airline industry and employment conditions and relations in call centres.

CHRISTOPHER BALDRY is Senior Lecturer in Industrial Relations in the Department of Human Resource Management at the University of Strathclyde. He has researched and written on aspects of technological change and work organisation, and European employment systems. Most recently he has been working with his colleagues on a study of sick building syndrome in office workers, exploring the relationship between occupational health, the labour process and the built environment.

MARTIN BEIRNE is Senior Lecturer in Organisational Behaviour and Director of Undergraduate Management Programmes at the University of Glasgow. His research interests and publications focus on the theory and practice of employee participation schemes, with particular current attention to nursing management and the impact of quality improvement initiatives on computing work. The latter recently included an ESRC-funded project on the social organisation of software development.

ANDY DANFORD is Senior Lecturer in Personnel at the Bristol Business School, University of the West of England. He gained his PhD in Sociology at the University of Bristol studying the impact of Japanese management techniques on employees in British firms. He has worked in the engineering industry for over twenty years, including ten years as a senior representative and lay official with the Manufacturing Science and Finance Union.

MIKE DENT is Reader in Sociology at the University of Staffordshire. He has published a number of articles and a book – *Professions, Information Technology and Management in Hospitals* – on the medical and nursing professions, health care organisation and information technology. Currently, he is researching comparative changes in health care organisation and professions in various European countries.

JÖRG FLECKER is Head of FORBA – Forschungs-und Beratungsstelle Arbeitswelt (Working Life Research Centre), Vienna. He is also a part-time lecturer at the University of Economics and Business Administration, Vienna.

Prior to 1991 he held posts as post-graduate student and researcher at the Institute for Advanced Studies in Vienna. His research and publications focus on the areas of work organisation, industrial relations, internationalisation and organisation studies.

JOAN GREENBAUM is Professor of Computer Information Systems at LaGuardia Community College (City University of New York) and Visiting Professor of Informatiks at the University of Oslo. She has been involved in research, teaching and practice about the development of computer systems with particular emphasis on participation of users as workers in the design of workplace technology. Among her many publications, her recent books include: *Windows on the Workplace* in 1995 and *Design at Work* co-edited in 1991 with Morten Kyng.

JOHANNA HOFBAUER studied Social Sciences in Innsbruck, Austria, and was a post-graduate student and researcher at the Institute for Advanced Studies in Vienna. Since 1991 she has been a University Assistant at the Institute of Sociology at the University of Economics, Vienna. Her research, publications and teaching focus on the areas of industrial sociology, organisation studies, and women studies.

MIGUEL MARTINEZ LUCIO is a Lecturer in Industrial and Labour Studies at Leeds University Business School, University of Leeds. He has taught and researched at various institutions in the UK and Spain. He has published in the areas of politics, industrial relations and human resource management. He has also worked on the impact of managerialism in the public sector and the micro-political construction of markets. His current research focuses on the changing parameters of worker representation in the context of political and organisational change.

RUTH MILKMAN teaches Sociology at UCLA and frequently writes on workplace issues. Her most recent book is *Farewell to the Factory* (1997). She is also the author of *Japan's California Factories* (1991) and *Gender at Work* (1987), which was awarded the Joan Kelly Memorial Prize for History by the American Historical Association. She is now at work on a study of immigrant unionisation in California.

KATE MULHOLLAND is a Research Fellow at Warwick Business School. She is presently researching change management in the utilities from a critical perspective. She has previously researched and published on the links between gender, class and ethnicity with reference to the creation and ownership of family capitalism. Her research interests also include gender and workplace relations.

ANDRONIKI PANTELI received her doctorate from Warwick Business School in 1995. She then joined the University of Glasgow as a Research Assistant in the Department of Management Studies analysing the social organisation issues of computer software development. Other research examines the role of women in the UK software industry. From 1997, she has worked as Lecturer in Management in the Department of Management Studies at the University of Aberdeen.

HARVIE RAMSAY is Professor of International Human Resource Management at the University of Strathclyde. He has conducted research and published widely on worker participation and employee involvement, labour organisation in mult:national companies, profit-sharing and participative computing systems design. He is continuing to research managerial strategies towards software development, including work on gender divisions in computing labour markets and processes.

PAUL STEWART is a Research Fellow in the sociology of work and employment at the University of Wales, Cardiff. He has written widely on the labour process and trade unions in the automotive industry. He is the author of *Working Smarter Not Harder: The New Sociology of the Car Industry* and co-authored *The Nissan Enigma* (with Philip Garrahan). He is currently researching the relationship between gender, ethnicity and new forms of employment in South Wales.

PHIL TAYLOR lectures in Industrial Relations in the Department of Management and Organisation at the University of Stirling. His research interests include sick building syndrome and occupational health, students and patterns of part-time employment, call centres and the white-collar labour process and HRM in the electronics industry.

STEVE TAYLOR studied at the universities of Nottingham Trent, Warwick and Durham. He is currently Senior Lecturer in Sociology within the School of Social Sciences at the University of Teesside. His current research interests include: emotion and organisations; labour process theory; culture and identity at work.

PAUL THOMPSON is Professor of Management in the Department of Business Studies at the University of Edinburgh. He has co-organised three Labour Process Conferences and is an Editor with the associated series *Critical Perspectives on Work and Organisations*. The author of *The Nature of Work*, *Working the System* (with Eddie Bannon), and *Work Organisations* (with David McHugh), he is currently completing a new book, *Organisational Misbehaviour* with Stephen Ackroyd. His current research interests focus on work with colleagues at

Edinburgh and St Andrews universities on an ESRC-funded project concerning workplace innovation in the Scottish spirits industry.

CHRIS WARHURST is Lecturer in Organisational Behaviour in the Department of Management Studies at the University of Glasgow. His research and teaching interests focus on management and labour issues within the international economy. A textbook on these issues is currently being written (with Al Rainnie and Jane Hardy). He has published widely on the kibbutz and the transformation of its industry, with *Between Market, State and Kibbutz* published in 1997. With colleagues from the University of Strathclyde, a new research project is underway examining 'aesthetic labour' in the service economy. He has co-organised a number of Labour Process Conferences.

1 Hands, Hearts and Minds: Changing Work and Workers at the End of the Century

Chris Warhurst and Paul Thompson

Images of Change

Charles Handy has argued that we do not have 'hands' in today's organisations. The popular view is that organisations are opting, by choice or necessity, to engage with hearts and minds instead. It sits slightly oddly with a recent report on the fastest growing US occupations in the decade from 1994, which include home and health service aides, varieties of therapists, corrections officers and security guards. It seems that the future is care or constraint. Actually, there is a considerable amount of common ground among popular business and academic commentators about what the trends in work and workplace are. That commonality starts from a relabelling of the big picture. We are now living in a post-industrial, information or knowledge economy. As one recent study put it, 'Future prosperity is likely to hinge on the use of scientific and technical knowledge, the management of information and the provision of services. The future will depend more on brains than brawn' (Barley, 1996:xvii).

The rise of the service sector and the decline of manufacturing is associated with a technological dynamism epitomised by announcements of the end of the *machine age* and the emergence of an *information age* (Hamel and Prahalad, 1996), within which work is no longer about the production of tangible goods but concerned with the centrality of knowledge and manipulation of symbols (Drucker, 1986).[1] This abrupt, and dramatic, shift in the nature of the economy and work requires an equally categorical response from organisations in terms of their structures and practices. Success for organisations, Quah insists, rests not on 'having built the largest factory ... or the longest assembly line ... [but] on knowing how to locate and juxtapose critical pieces of information, how to organise understanding into forms that others will understand' (1997:4).

Beneath the over-arching descriptions, the engine of change is held to be driven by two interrelated transformations in the technical division of labour and the structure of the organisation. Like many commentators, Robert Reich argues

1

that the workplace is no longer a pyramid or bureaucracy, but a 'web of enterprise'. Such webs have an internal and external dimension.

In terms of the overall structure, ownership and control, use of advanced information technology allows the firm's boundaries to become blurred, even to the point of the much-vaunted 'virtual organisation'; while its functions are increasingly disaggregated into complex mixtures of profit centres, franchises, small firms and subcontractors. As disaggregation is combined with downsizing and delayering, we will move, according to Charles Handy (1995), towards a 20–80 society with only a small core directly employed by the organisation. A growing number will become 'portfolio people' offering their skills to a collection of clients and customers, and leading flexilives between home and workplace. Reich echoes this when stating that few people in the 'high-value enterprise' will have steady jobs with fixed salaries (1993: 90).

Internally, the web will result in the replacement of hierarchies by networks. Put another way, the old vertical division of labour will be replaced by horizontal co-ordination. This is driven by the nature of knowledge work itself, which is essentially concerned with problem solving, problem identifying and strategic brokering between the two processes. The key employees of the information age will therefore be what Reich calls 'symbolic analysts' who trade globally in the manipulation of symbols, such as engineers, consultants and advertising executives. Such work is too complex, domain-specific and esoteric to be subject to vertical control. Instead, and facilitated by information technology, co-ordination can be based on collaboration between technical and professional groups who retain authority over their own work (Barley, 1996). Indeed, knowledge workers, working for their own interest rather than that of the company, are 'less inclined to think of themselves as loyal soldiers and more inclined to think of themselves as sought-after faculty members' (Hamel and Prahalad, 1996:238). With the diffusion of information and resources, and control of knowledge workers by managers illusory, the 'corporate campus' requires a form of management that is 'more collegial than supervisory, shar[ing] information, delegat[ing] responsibility and encourag[ing] upward and horizontal communication' (Despres and Hiltrop, 1995:19).

Such horizontal co-ordination is replicated at lower levels through the increased use of teamworking to involve workers in problem solving and continuous improvement. Frenkel *et al.* (1995:786) note that, 'The trend away from routine work towards more creative, information and people-focused activity ... leads management to cede more control over the work process to employees and requires management to ensure reciprocated trust.'

For such commentators, the implications for managers and workers are immense. Old-style command and control management is out, to be replaced by co-ordination based on managing ideas. Much of middle management can be eliminated because they were co-ordinating functions which have disappeared or processing knowledge which can be directly accessed. Once perceived as the indispensable functionaries of organisations; the standard bearers of rationality, technocratic efficiency and the embodiment of a corporate ideology that says managers know best, they are now no longer seen as the solution to organisational problems.

Within such reconfigured organisations the old tension between professional autonomy and bureaucratic control will diminish. Even at the bottom, empowered production and service employees will be 'working smarter not harder'. For those workers who can contract into the new workplace through their education, experiences and amenability, the workplace of the future offers new possibilities for creative expression, greater satisfaction, more security and enhanced personal growth (Osterman, 1991). Assets rather than liabilities, these employees can make 'major contributions of strategic and long-term importance' to their companies (Despres and Hiltrop, 1995:13).

Future knowledge workers of all kinds will be selected, rewarded and promoted according to competencies, values and individual performance rather than seniority, formal skill or rate-for-the-job. Stable career patterns will be a thing of the past. Rather than climb the reduced rungs of the organisational ladder, knowledge workers will hawk their skills around organisations, moving 'toward the centre of an occupational community rather than the pinnacle of an organisation' (Barley, 1996:47). In this respect, having a 'job' reverts to its etymological origin in that it once again refers to a task or piece of work rather than permanent employment.

Handy (1995:6–7) describes the outcome as 'fewer jobs for better people in the core', while admitting that 'there will be many casualties in the new dispersed organisations' among those who cannot add value. Such unfortunates will be pushed to the organisational and social margins. Recognition that all is not likely to be well in the garden is welcome, but how realistic is this overall picture of the 'new' workplace?

Don't Let the Facts Get in the Way of a Good Argument

Optimistic predictions of the development of work and the workplace are nothing new, and claims of an emerging knowledge economy are in a tradition of proclamations of third waves, information societies and computopia. Certainly, occupational shifts have been and are taking place, with a long-term rise in non-manual employment (Routh, 1987). Within this trend, the creation of new tertiary occupations and the expansion of older ones, for example in financial services, medicine, education, leisure and technical services, is particularly notable. So is the growth of the retail sector. Britain may never have been a nation of shopkeepers, but the continued expansion of multiple stores is pushing employment in the retail distribution and service sector close to 4.5m, only just behind total manufacturing (*Labour Market Trends*, 1996).

However, official classifications of the occupational structure focus upon the form of jobs rather than the content of labour. If we examine lists of so-called knowledge workers – ranging from librarians to musicians, bankers and insurance workers (Handy, 1995: 4) – the sheer banality of the description and links become clear. That workers are now more highly educated does not necessarily indicate a higher level of knowledge inherent in the jobs in which these people are employed. Kumar (1996) is right to suggest that the rise in credentialism results in a misleading appearance of the growth of more knowledgeable workers – a point further complicated by the growing tendency to relabel job titles so that travel agents become travel consultants, or plumbers become heating engineers.

This phenomenon seems widespread. The *OECD Jobs Study* (1994) notes that there are now a substantial number of workers and managers throughout the developed economies who are vastly over-qualified for their jobs. In addition, the survey shows that particularly in the US, an 'unbundling' process can be identified in which the jobs created are in no small part accounted for by manufacturing restructuring through subcontracting and outsourcing. Here again, the fragility of the accounting process that delineates industry and service sectors is highlighted. In analysing the decline of manufacturing jobs and increase in service jobs, the study points out that 'temporary workers, classified as service workers, were hired by manufacturing firms who were trying to retain flexibility and cut costs. If these temporary workers working in manufacturing firms were counted as manufacturing workers, the loss of manufacturing jobs since 1991 would be cut by two-thirds' (157–9).

Of course there have been more serious attempts to capture the extent of skill change from survey data. Reporting on the ESRC's *Social Change and Economic Life Initiative*, Gallie argues that, 'the upward shift in the occupational structure did indeed 'reflect the expansion of higher skilled jobs, even when a different range of indicators of skill were used' (1991: 349). This may indeed be the case and it is surely time to move beyond the dominant 'optimists versus pessimists' scenario reproduced by Gallie. The expanded range of indicators moved beyond conventional categories, such as qualifications and training, to the question of whether individuals considered their current job to have had a significant increase or decrease in levels of skill and responsibility compared to five years ago. But it remains the case that such methods provide a very blunt instrument for telling us much about what is happening to different types of work, particularly when employees may be comparing their present job to a completely different one! With this in mind, we move to an examination of changes in the labour process of each major sector of waged work, engaging with key issues and debates along the way.

Routine Workers – Look No Hands?

Despite Handy's 'no hands' scenario, the content of much contemporary work remains highly routinised. Despite his emphasis on the key role of symbolic analysts, this is recognised by Reich (1993), who estimates that repetitive and highly specified production and in-service jobs account for 55 per cent of the US economy. Statistics from the US Bureau of Labor Statistics show that those who could be classified as 'symbolic analysts', that is those who in some way manipulate symbols and ideas, comprise only seven per cent of current employment in the US (Henwood, 1996). Indeed, proponents of the knowledge economy fail to appreciate that most tertiary sector growth has occurred not in knowledge work but in the low-paid 'donkey work' of serving, guarding, cleaning, waiting and helping in the private health and care services, as well as hospitality industries.

We find that much of the 'knowledge' work, for example in financial services, requires little more of workers than information transfer. This includes the inputting of customer details on to pre-programmed screens and software, as Leidner (1993) shows in his examination of work in the insurance industry. Non-standard responses and requests are referred to supervisors or 'exceptions claims handlers'. Much of the growth in service work has been in the more explicitly 'interactive' categories such as telesales or call-centres. As Taylor shows in Chapter 5, it too has its own routine in that the process is likely to be governed by scripted interactions, and monitored for deviance by supervisors. For Ritzer, this is an extension of his McDonaldisation thesis. This version of the carefully calculated, simplified and predictable 'McJob' adds in the familiar Taylorist element of incorporation of workers' skills – this time verbal and interactive rather than manual – into a management 'technology': 'just as management has long "conceived" what employees are supposed to do, it now "conceives" what they are supposed to say and how they are supposed to say it, and in both action and interaction employees have little choice but to "execute" management's demands' (1997:11).[2] While there have been some pretty silly applications of Ritzerian imagery – the 'McUniversity' springs immediately to mind – this argument has real force. Companies like to argue that it is the human element that now adds value to the provision of services. Hence the appearance of a 'quality' agenda in sectors such as hotels and hospitality. But there is a contradiction at the heart of the service encounter. The very uncertainty that inevitably accompanies the human element, in itself often provided by relatively unqualified labour, drives management to try and *standardise* the encounter as a means of ensuring 'quality' or at least consistency (Thompson *et al.*, 1996).

The routinisation of clerical and white-collar work has been a long-observed phenomenon. Baldry *et al.*'s case studies in Chapter 9 do nothing to dispel that image. Despite gleaming new buildings and open-plan offices, employees 'endlessly repeat familiar routines' around rigidly structured tasks and peformance schedules. A manager in one of the organisations referred to clerical work as 'basically a production line process'. This corresponds with the view of an increasing number of commentators that service work is now characterised by an 'industrial logic' (Segal-Horn, 1993). But this carries an assumption that factory work has some traditional or immutable character. What if that 'logic' is different?

Changing the logic: innovation and its limits

It is not necessary to accept an epochal shift argument to recognise the increased competitive pressures on management to improve the quality and quantity of labour's input. This *has* led many companies to put into question aspects of the traditional Taylorist division between thinking and doing, as well as the rigidities characteristic of a Fordist production regime.

This argument has been around since the mid-1980s, if not earlier, but the practice did not necessarily match the rhetoric. For example, quality circles and employee involvement were characteristic of early stages of work transformation, but were not intrinsically built into a different technical division of labour. The introduction of teamworking in a context of an expanded array of lean production techniques, facilitates a much more substantial restructuring geared towards innovation and continuous improvement. This is not a return, or indeed advance, to craft or professional labour given that task structures largely remain unaltered. But the collective skill of the group requires an increased emphasis on cognitive and behavioural abilities geared towards multi-skilling, problem solving and decision making. As a result, employees are increasingly drawn into what Milkman in Chapter 2 refers to as the 'micro-management of production'.

So far, so (relatively) consensual, given that there are only a few diehards clinging to the view that nothing really has changed and that it is still just the same old capitalist labour process. But it is a curious feature of contemporary debate that the same developments can be interpreted to form entirely different views of the nature of the future workplace.

We have already seen the relatively optimistic account managerial commentators – ranging from advocates of HRM, to enthusiasts of lean production and the information age – have produced of the nature of modern work and organisations. It is surprising just how much their radical equivalents share that agenda, at least in terms of an acceptance of some kind of paradigm break, as well as shifts away from traditional forms of bureaucratic control and division of labour towards the high commitment workplace based on dispersed, delegated authority, combined with electronic or cultural controls.

With their accounts of captured subjectivity and labour trapped in totalising institutions combined with new, oppressive forms of regulation and surveillance through JIT, TQM and corporate culture, it is as if contemporary management theory has produced its own dystopian offspring (see for example, Willmott, 1993; Delbridge, Turnbull and Wilkinson, 1992; Casey, 1995). As McKinlay and Taylor (1997:3) observe, such writers 'have inverted the euphoric rhetoric of HRM to produce gloomy analyses of emerging factory regimes in which workers lose even the awareness of their own exploitation'. They note the pervasive and particular influence of Foucault, and it is true that British universities at least are producing generations of graduate students who can spot a panopticon, a disciplinary practice or a power/knowledge discourse at fifty paces. While critical of (mis)interpretations of Foucault, McKinlay and Taylor's own empirical work on Phoneco's plant in Scotland appears to travel well down the dystopian path: 'It is difficult to overstate Phoneco's ambition in its attempt to go beyond the rhetorics of flexibility, commitment and quality: to achieve nothing less than the total colonisation of the EasterInch workforce' (1997:9). At the heart of the shopfloor strategy was the introduction of peer review, a form of 'mutual control' where employees accept responsibility for self-discipline and assessment of each other.

They accepted that peer review is seldom seen outside Japanese transplants. But in Chapter 3 we have Danford's case studies of Japanese companies in South Wales in which it really does not appear at all. Reading Danford we get a very different picture of the contemporary workplace. As he observes, the descriptions of repetitive tasks, fixed cycle times and tightly policed operatives do not differ much from ethnographies of the assembly line in previous decades. Though the management was particularly adept at squeezing and regulating labour, the devil was in the detail rather than in any grand innovative work design or ambitious cultural controls.

So, which is the 'factory of the future'? Or are they simply different lenses on the same thing? To answer this question it is necessary to start from a recognition of the need for forms of analysis that can capture the balance between continuity and change, convergence and variability. Take the issue of knowledge as an example. It is important not to lose sight of the elements of continuity. All workers are, of course, knowledgeable about their work – and always have been. At the turn of the twentieth century owner-managers were keenly aware of the knowledge workers possessed and how important that was to the development of their companies. As Jacques reveals in his sweeping historical account of management knowledge, it has long been management's job to make capital out of the originality of what labour knows and does. Indeed, 'It could be said indeed that the knowledge of workers was a key concern at this juncture in the development of industrial capitalism, providing the "constitutive problem" of capital–labour relations throughout the twentieth century' (1996:143). The knowledgeable worker is therefore not a post-industrial phenomenon but rather an integral part of the development of industrial capitalism. However, if throughout this century management has attempted to appropriate this knowledge or accommodated the residual knowledge of workers in the form of informal working practices, now management is keen to introduce organisational structures and practices which facilitate initiative in the form of creativity and learning.

With this in mind, it might be useful to jettison the overly-broad notion of *knowledge workers* in favour of a more realistic appreciation of the growth of *knowledgeability in work*. The managerial instruments to register and if possible capture employee knowledge have some innovative forms in teamworking and off-line problem-solving groups. But we should not lose sight of the role played by the development of traditional Taylorist techniques. Wright and Lund (1996) chart the introduction of new engineering standards systems – which they dub 'computerised Taylorism' – which result in real-time monitoring of highly variable work processes in Australian grocery distribution. As the ex-work study engineer, Oswald Jones (1997) demonstrates, more sophisticated forms of work measurement necessarily underpin a TQM-style regime, though workgroups are increasingly encouraged to contribute to job analysis. This kind of activity has been dubbed 'democratic Taylorism' by the more honest and critical advocates of lean production (Adler, 1993; Adler and Cole, 1995). The idea that Taylorism is itself innovative or can contribute to innovation should come as no surprise to any student of industrial history who has followed the earlier path-breaking work of the Gilbreths, Henry Gantt and many others. But the point is lost on those who present Scientific Management as a static, historically-bound system.

A recognition of continued variability in workplace trends is also important. The banal but simple truth is that there is no simple or universal direction. Look in detail at case study research across companies and countries and we find the usual suspects of mediation by institutional factors; notably national industrial relations systems and labour markets, as well as strategic choices by firms themselves. This should be obvious, but runs counter to the investment in high theory and epochal breaks by those whose job description is to draw the 'big picture', resulting in too many commentators continuing to insist on a coherent transformation package.

For example, whether one focuses on the technical, governance or normative dimensions of teamworking, research reveals that companies vary significantly in the extent to which their practices focus on or facilitate flexibility, normative attachments or delegated responsibilities (Mueller, 1994; Sandberg, 1995; Thompson and Wallace, 1996). In fact, the very same skill requirements in leaner production can lead to a preference for different labour inputs in particular countries or companies. With respect to the UK, readers will be unsurprised to know that there is evidence that British managers frequently choose to use the current state of the market and weakening of union strength to redefine their skill needs away from craft to semi-skilled labour (Thompson *et al.*, 1995). As Ackroyd and Proctor (1996:11) note, 'there is little evidence that the emasculation of traditional skills is being counter-acted by the emergence of new comprehensive systems of education and training to produce the "polvalent employee". What evidence there is of new forms of training points towards the use of cut-down 'on-the-job' company-based skill appraisal and training schemes.'

Agreements for workers to acquire more skills and knowledge are often circumscribed by management as Clark's (1995) detailed case study example of Pirelli Cables illustrates. A massive financial investment in Aberdare, South

Wales, was intended to produce the 'all singing, all dancing' factory of the future with full task flexibility and worker autonomy. However, flexibility was within rather than across occupational groups and managerial action to cap the acqusition of 'skill modules' further constrained progress. Shop floor innovation is also constrained by continuing evidence that most managements simply do not trust their workforce. British companies are still less likely to initiate and implement progressive human resource policies than other European companies, according to academic sources such as the *Second Company Level Industrial Relations Survey* (Edwards *et al.*, 1996) and consultants (Ingersoll Engineers, 1996).

Nor is Britain alone. In Chapter 2 Milkman gathers a variety of evidence from her own and other studies to demonstrate that most companies in the US remain traditionally managed, wedded to a low-trust, low-skill, authoritarian route to competitiveness. As she notes, there are a few 'true exemplars' of the high road strategy, though a cautious reading need not necessarily be a gloomy one – institutional analysis of national trends and characteristics does not preclude there being instances of more innovative and progressive practices in some sectors.

If much management remains *traditional*, it should also make us more wary of claims of radical departures in control technologies. Some organisations have invested in expanded means of monitoring and surveillance. But while digital smart cards that track employee movements on site and discreet video surveillance that allows managers and security personnel to remotely view workers make good publicity and lecture material, the 'electronic ball and chain' (as one trade union official put it[3]), remains the exception (Lyon, 1994). Social scientists have a particular susceptibility to being dazzled by the potential of technological or other managerial devices without fully investigating how or even whether they are being utilised. There are indeed enhanced controls operating in the contemporary workplace, but they are more likely to be based on monitoring and evaluation through processes such as internal benchmarking, customer appraisal or financial targets.

Underneath all the rhetoric about new-wave management, the most important trend appears to be people working harder. Pressures on the effort-bargain are, of course, a constant feature of market relations. But the combination of increased competitive pressures for cost reduction on private and public sector organisations, with expanded means for reducing and recording 'idle time', are leading to substantial work intensification, whether through reductions in manning levels and job demarcation, or other means (Elger, 1991; Nichols, 1991). The nature and effects of such intensification are consistent themes in the studies in this volume. But the hollow laugh received when mentioning the word 'empowerment' in most organisations is the true test that employees at many levels experience this 'great innovation' less as the opportunity to exercise extra discretion and more as the necessity to undertake more tasks. The extent to which people feel change fatigue and 'worn down' by increased expectations in downsized structures is registering firmly in popular consciousness. Even in Japan – *karoshi*, or death by overwork, has become a matter of policy debate (Kyotani, 1996). Actually, there is more consensus on this issue than might appear. Most managers would be far too embarassed by the evidence of their own eyes and ears to repeat the 'working smarter not harder' mantra. These days 'lean and mean' is an accepted, if regretted, part of the organisational landscape (Harrison, 1994).

Captured hearts or hardened arteries?

If minds are more engaged and bodies are tired, what about the third of our managerial objects – hearts? There can be no argument that many organisations have been trying to engender more commitment, no doubt influenced by the popular managerial nostrum that being competititive today requires more than instrumental compliance. What managers refer to as 'buying into the message', academics prefer to relabel the 'internalisation of values'. On one level this is the most controversial area of current change, both because issues of subjectivity are the most complex to theorise, and because of the strength of claims by corporate culture theorists and radical commentators alike that new regimes have succeeded in reshaping the affective domain.

This apparent success is, of course, heavily disputed (see particularly Thompson and Ackroyd, 1995). Yet, once again, we should not lose sight of the common ground about contemporary trends towards 'capitalising on subjectivity', as Flecker and Hofbauer put it in Chapter 6. There are two widely acknowledged aspects to this process. The first – that of emotional labour – has moved from the rather exotic illustrations of Hochschild's (1983) studies of airline attendants and debt collectors to mainstream studies of retail and service work in a variety of settings. As we observed earlier, the interactions between employees and customers are likely to be highly scripted, but the former are increasingly exhorted, indeed trained, to manage and mobilise their feelings in pursuit of higher quality and increased productivity. That may be linked to a wider process in which employees are encouraged to be 'enterprising subjects' – more self-reliant, risk-taking and responsible as part of a contemporary discourse of organisational and political change (du Gay, 1996; Flecker and Hofbauer, Chapter 6 this volume).

The second aspect focuses on the extension of normative controls, this time not restricted to the service sector. Management is increasingly specifying an extended repertoire of attitudes and behaviour deemed appropriate to job performance. To use the example of teamworking again, once this range of expanded 'skills' needed to become a 'team player' has been identified – for example co-operativeness and positive attitudes – logic is likely to dictate that they seek some means of measuring and regulating them. Workers are often well aware that efforts are being made to 'change your personality' (McKinlay and Taylor, 1997; and see Marks *et al.*, 1997). Hence the concept of normative controls is rightly used to help understand new forms of appraisal and selection.

Controversy nevertheless remains concerning the salience and effectiveness of both aspects of the 'winning hearts' process. Here we side with the sceptics. The high profile examples are more topical than typical. After all, there are few companies with as ambitious an agenda of head-fixing as Phoneco. This is compounded when cultural engineering is elevated from an aspect of managerial activity into *the* driving force of workplace transformation, when new managerial discourses simply *displace* old corporate realities as the focus of attention.

It is too easy in this area to confuse managerial ambition with outcome. But even where it gets beyond the mission statement or other change texts, engaging with employees' feelings and values is likely to be the most fragile of all managerial activities. In part this is because many, perhaps most, employees do not buy very far into the message. Case studies reveal considerable scepticism about the 'new' managerial agenda. Jones notes of a TQM programme, 'Hotpoint employees view these US-inspired changes with the cynicism of workers who recognise another management scam designed to ensure that they work harder' (1997:19). Even the most dystopian studies often reveal the rather more muddied realities when managerial schemes are filtered through employee attitudes and self-organisation. For instance the sting in McKinlay and Taylor's fascinating tale of Motorola is that the company with the grandest ambitions to 'govern the soul' found intense opposition to the disciplinary purposes of the system: 'Quietly and systematically peer review was dismantled by a combination of workforce resistance and tactical choices by a plant management under intense pressure for output' (1997:12). If we switch to a different reading of subjectivity, survey data, often generated by companies themselves about employee attitudes to change and change programmes, also tend to make for gloomy corporate reading (Coopey, 1995; Marks *et al.*, 1997). For example, in 1993 the results of the Royal Mail attitude survey indicated that 70 per cent of the employees were unhappy at work. 'Uncertainty over privatisation, reorganisation of the service, new technology and worries over job security – all contribute to rock-bottom morale' (Summers, 1993:8).

Academics can debate from now until the end of time whether this scepticism and distancing is 'authentic' resistance, or whether, as the Daleks used to proclaim – 'resistance is futile'. But it seems clear that in terms of what management set out to do, employees often *dis*engage and treat expanded demands as a form of additional calculative performance. Of course, employees are often responding to the gap between managerial words and deeds rather than rejecting the aims of better service and enhanced competitiveness, as other case studies amply demonstrate (Rosenthal, Hill and Peccei, 1997). Mobilising subjectivity is consistently put under strain by internal and external tensions. For example, as Taylor shows in Chapter 5 of this volume, employees frequently react adversely to being told to 'act natural' whilst being subject to the plethora of measuring and monitoring techniques to enforce compliance to standardised scripts or managerial controls. Equally, Flecker and Hofbauer illustrate how external demands on individuals generate 'superfluous subjectivity' which means that in managerial attempts to capitalise on subjectivity, 'workers' orientations, aspirations and ingenuity are neither tailor-made nor reserved' for organisational utility.

Subjectivity is a difficult subject matter to research with accuracy and sufficient complexity, and academics should always be careful about the strength of the claims they make (Thompson and Findlay, 1996). But we would make one cautious observation in reviewing these issues and debates. When management asks workers to be 'really' committed and emotionally engaged, it is likely to be asking for impossible outcomes from workers whose conditions of labour lack the necessary characteristics of autonomy and trust that would lead to making those 'investments'. This may well be different for employees further up the occupational ladder, to whom we now turn.

Technical and Professional Labour

A reading of the popular and academic literature indicates that technical and professional workers are best placed to benefit from these changes to the workplace. Certainly these 'new professionals' who represent the archetypal symbolic analysts or knowledge workers, such as scientists, engineers and marketeers, have expanded massively as an occupational group in the recent period (*OECD Jobs Study*, 1994). They now form the largest occupational group in the UK and indicate the highest projected growth rates towards the end of the century in the US (McRae, 1996). Their labour, as with salaried managers before them in the old 'new middle class thesis', provides the creative entrepreneurialism that can best assure the accumulation of capital in the twenty-first century.

More concretely, these workers, with their superior qualifications, creative work content and operational autonomy are the typical pre-'information age' knowledge workers. Moreover, 'technicisation' – that is, an infusion of theoretical knowledge into previously tacit knowledge-only jobs – would further indicate that the nature of work for service and production workers is changing as abstract thinking and theorisation attain increasing centrality (Frenkel *et al.*, 1995). Technical labour is inherently uncertain and ambiguous, requiring an artful management of 'creative, and rather intelligent and autonomous individuals' (Jain and Triandis, 1990:xiv). The most immediate outcome of this management is reciprocated trust relations and an operational autonomy through which they can determine the techniques and timing of much of their work. As the earlier outlines of the management and organisation of the 'new workplace' indicated, it is precisely this form of operational autonomy that is advocated for all workers by commentators of the knowledge economy. In this sense technical and professional labour's experience of work could be argued to be the *new benchmark* for all employees in the workplace.

Suggestions that technical and professional labour represents the new model worker, however, rests on a gross over-simplification of their current working experience and organisational status. The extent of the autonomy of these workers can be exaggerated. The dominant characteristic features of their labour does not exclude these occupational groups from management intervention or control, nor is professional status with its characteristic terms and conditions of employment immutable. Although still relatively highly paid (see, for example, *Labour Market Trends*, 1996), in organisations with less defined boundaries, the claim to and strategies of ensuring occupational closure and exclusivity expected by professionals is undermined. Horizontal co-ordination which combines flexibility with the pooling and sharing of information, can produce a trend towards 'de-professionalisation' because, as Kanter argues, 'the organisation that produces a great deal of innovation must by definition be less category-conscious' (1983:32). Indeed, in Chapter 7 Greenbaum notes how some professional work has been absorbed by routine white-collar workers such as bank clerks. Ironically, these latter workers are then expected to 'act professionally' in their work, which beneath the rhetoric offers organisations the opportunity for fewer supervisory staff if those employees internalise the new expectations and self-controls.

If the knowledge of technical and professional labour is diffused to a much wider group of organisational members, their working practices are also vulnerable to managerial control. Randle's (1995) study of technical workers in the pharmaceutical industry highlights the tightening of management control through performance related pay and promotion systems in which 'targets' attained determine salary levels and career trajectories. Discretionary activity, such as the 'ten per cent time' or one half day per week to provide 'a greater degree of creative and independent thinking', frequently became subsumed into ordinary working time on 'goals emphasised by line managers' (13 & 14). These constraints create tensions between management on the one hand, and technical and professional labour on the other. In the Pirelli case discussed earlier the senior accountants, citing commercial priority, effectively arrested the technical innovations being made to the labour process by systems engineers. With the retreat from the intended factory of the future, a number of these engineers were aggrieved enough to resign their posts (Clark, 1995).

Furthermore, they may be the casualties of organisational restructuring. For example, there is some indication of less rather than more occupational mobility within external and internal labour markets. Instead of technical labour being more footloose as it comes to assert its organisational value, labour turnover in the R&D sections of the pharmaceutical industry is low as recruitment is curtailed by management in order to control labour costs, the result of which is diminished promotion prospects and frustrated workers. The outcome is a 'capping' on the number of current entrants into this occupational category which is surprising given that laboratory technicians are one of the occupations forwarded as indicative of knowledge workers. As competition for promotion intensifies, these workers, it has been noted by Perin (1991:259), then become reluctant to adopt more flexible temporal and spatial patterns of work, believing that presence brings visibility and influence so 'that being absent would be disadvantageous to their careers'.[4]

As we have noted earlier, a key theme of the literature is the extension of collegiality. There is no doubt that technical and professional labour does require some features of this ethos and practice. But it is rather foolish to start calling commercial work environments 'campuses' when universities themselves are becoming far less collegial! Under the impact of the quasi-marketisation of higher education and increased bureaucratic regulation through a variety of 'quality' audit procedures, university academics are subject to tighter work specification, intensification of labour and vertical 'line management' complementing if not replacing horizontal co-ordination. As Wilson (1991:254) explains; 'most higher education systems [within the industrialised countries] are experiencing similar trends towards management assertiveness, far greater use of casualised labour ... devolution of budgetary responsibility ... within tight institutional guidelines and greater sensitivity to market forces'. As a result, there are deteriorating terms and conditions of employment, a weakening of the academic ethos, and low-trust relations emerging between university management and academics.

There have also been demands for medical doctors to shift their loyalties away from their profession to the employing organisation (Brindle, 1994). As Dent notes in Chapter 11, a struggle is apparent for control of medical work. In 1996, the British Association of Medical Managers recommended a contractual obligation on all doctors to inform on poorly performing colleagues. The 'shop-a-doc' proposal caused anger amongst members of the British Medical Association with its council chair claiming that the initiative was 'totally contrary ... to the concept of the profession ... and utterly unacceptable' (Turner, 1997:11). Nevertheless, in this regard, a number of professors and heads of departments in higher education are now indeed required to take on budgetary responsibility and the performance evaluation of colleagues, and may even be incorporated into management strategies.

Taking these factors into account, the traditional tension between bureaucracy and professionalism has been recast rather than eliminated. Senior management still requires the capacity for creativity and intuitive exploration, but there is greater pressure in both public and private sectors for marketable outcomes and competitive working practices, and therefore less 'space' for individual initiative and ingenuity as 'there is a ceiling on managerial approval of informal interactions and expressions of [software] developer autonomy' Beirne, Ramsay and Panteli note in Chapter 8. Going further, there can also be tighter bureaucratic controls on software developers, downsizing resulting in work intensification as fewer workers do more work and some software companies routinise work with the use of 'standardised adaptations of generic systems for clients'.

Nevertheless, it would be wrong to assume that the impact of the changes has been evenly experienced by technical and professional labour. There are divisions and hierarchies within this, as any other set of occupational categories. Such labour can be divided with, for example, the use of different employment contracts as Greenbaum indicates or through the technical and / or a gendered division of labour as Beirne, Ramsay and Panteli note of information systems workers; an occupational category, they note, in which women are mainly located in non-managerial posts such as programmers, and men more likely to be project leaders and consultants. Similarly we need to grasp the dynamics of change over time as the labour process is constantly redivided and reassembled – in the current period as a result of 'management practices co-ordinated by computer systems' as Greenbaum argues in Chapter 7 – but which still reflect a managerial desire for control. Greenbaum also suggests that moves towards the new workplace have resulted in little more than work intensification for some professionals, such as computer systems analysts. Other technical workers, however, can informally reskill themselves Beirne, Ramsay and Panteli discovered as, through trial and error, these workers correct and improve flawed software systems – indicating that managerial control is neither absolute nor, in some situations, efficacious. All these processes can have contradictory aspects. For example there has been increasing formal opportunity for upskilling in previous 'teaching only' universities in the UK as staff are encouraged to develop research profiles. But given the squeeze on existing resources and the expansion of student numbers, such opportunities are either impossible to operationalise or lead only to even greater workloads and burned-out staff.

In conclusion therefore, it is more accurate to say that some of the benchmarks set for routine workers are more likely to be applied to technical and professional labour. Certainly they do not offer a cohesive and coherent occupational group which is in a position to assume organisational and economic dominance. Commentators need to be more cautious in their mapping of these varied groups into an assumed model of their labour within the contemporary workplace.

Management and the Middle Layers

If there are substantial constraints on employees further down the organisational hierarchy, what about those in the middle? It has been suggested that it is possible and desirable to delayer management levels within organisations because there are alternative means of co-ordination. Middle management are often described as a prime obstacle to change. In fact in recent years, as Scarbrough and Burrell observe, they have been redefined *as* the problem:

> They are costly, resistant to change, a block to communication both upwards and downwards. They consistently underperform; they spend their time openly politicking rather than in constructive problem-solving. They are reactionary, undertrained and regularly fail to act as entrepreneurs. (1996:178)

However, we should be extremely cautious concerning tales of the death of the middle manager. The early 1990s' recession hit not only manufacturing employees, as in the early 1980s' recession, but also this time service sector employees. It is true that recession and restructuring have hit those industries within the service sector that offered a 'job for life' with good remuneration and promotion prospects, such as the civil service and the media. But only 14 per cent of managers, professionals and white-collar employees generally had experienced unemployment in the five years to 1995. The figure for unskilled manual workers was more than double at 29 per cent (Smith, 1997). More typically, the proportion of managers within the British employment structure has increased in both the public and private sectors throughout the post-war period and shows no sign of slowing down. By the early 1990s, there were 2.75 million managers in the UK with a further 90 000 new managers swelling that number every year (Thomas, 1993). While some layers have been taken out, others have been added, particularly to collect and process information connected to the already discussed growth in monitoring performance, quality and outputs. The burgeoning bureaucracy in the British National Health Service is a case in point. Between 1989 and 1994 the NHS lost 50 000 nurses and midwives but gained over 18 000 managers, an increase of 400 per cent (Milhill, 1996). Management, business and related courses now have the largest student enrolments in British higher education (*Department for Education and Employment, 1996*). As any survey of occupational earning demonstrates, the pay of managers is still relatively high compared to other groups of employees (see, for example again *Labour Market Trends, 1996*).

Nevertheless, evidence does indicate some important changes with regard to managers and management. A managerial version of the search for greater innovation and cost-effectiveness among routine workers is compelling organisations to attack some of the traditional forms of functional responsibilities, 'organisational chimneys' and hierarchical decision making: 'The traditional ... approach was to manage through levels and tasks, now the intention is to manage across levels and projects' (Starkey and McKinlay, 1994:986). 'Delayering' is a reality in many companies. Nationally British Telecom have reduced their management layers from twelve to six, at branch level WH Smith from four to two, GM (Saturn plant) from six to four and Pirelli (Aberdare plant) have collapsed eight levels into three. This frequently involves new titles and responsibilities. As a result of reorganisation at the British retail group WH Smith, branch managers are 'team leaders' and 'coaches' (*IRS Employment Trends, 1995*). Co-ordinators and conduits of information between production and senior managers may be rendered superfluous by greater organisational transparency via information technology or delegated decision making. Retail sales data that can be collected through EPOS systems means that senior managers can have real time information about the performance of stores and make rapid responses. As a result decisions previously taken by store managers – pricing, space allocation and promotion for example – are displaced to head office (*ibid.*).

However, we would argue that current perspectives misunderstand both the nature and the number of managerial jobs involved. The prime mistake of those promoting the post-bureaucratic organisation is to believe that new horizontal forms of co-ordination have replaced rather than complemented more traditional vertical divisions of labour and command structures. Many, although not all, of the tasks and functions of middle managers have remained, and organisations are still reliant upon their experience and understanding. Managers continue to exist even if their job titles are changed as supervisors become team-leaders, functional managers become project managers and branch managers become customer care champions. Such developments, are, however, more than plays on words. What *is* happening in many workplaces is the emergence of a dual structure which combines the search for innovation with enhanced financial and operational accountability. Methods of co-ordination and accountability therefore become more complex, but vertical structures remain the backbone of organisations. Given that the horizontal forms are largely project-based and temporary in nature, we prefer to refer to them as a *shadow division of labour*, that cuts across and supplements vertical structures and hierarchies. Managerial and professional labour that communicates and co-ordinates across functions is therefore *at the same time* subject to increased monitoring of performance, financial targets and penalties (Edwards *et al.*, 1996).

It is also difficult to be as unambiguously enthusiastic as business commentators about such developments. Though, as we have indicated, 'delayering' and 'downsizing' are primarily aimed at routine workers, shifts in the nature of managerial hierarchies have made the working lives of many professionals and managers more stressful. An *Observer Business*/Gallup survey in 1994 demonstrated that 70 per cent of public and private sector managers reported that their organisations had recently restructured with staff cutbacks and cost reduction initiatives, resulting in greater workloads, increased and often unpaid responsibilities, longer hours and less job security. The practice of 'presenteeism', that is working extra long hours to demonstrate commitment and indispensability, is now common amongst middle managers. Twenty per cent of managers were working more than fifty hours a week in 1995, that figure rising to thirty per cent the following year. With no extra reward for middle managers, job satisfaction is dwindling in restructured companies. Worldwide, 85 per cent of managers are now more concerned about the need to lead a balanced life than at the start of the decade, according to Herriot and Pemberton (1995). Attempts to motivate disaffected managers with performance-related pay has also often backfired due to its lack of objectivity and under-funded schemes that circumscribe the levels of pay settlements. The lack of promotion opportunities in flatter organisations further lowers morale amongst managers previously expectant of upward career trajectories.

As a consequence of such developments Herriot and Pemberton go on to argue that if, in the past, managers had an employment *relationship* based upon mutual trust and commitment rather than *contract* with their companies, this relationship is now being replaced by a *transaction* based on mutual instrumentality involving a simple effort–reward bargain. The relative fragility of the new employment relationship is indicated by the frequency with which even senior managers have to reapply for their own jobs or be evaluated through assessment centres – as managers in a variety of manufacturing and service companies such as LucasVarity, British Gas and House of Fraser can testify.

However, as Mulholland explores in Chapter 10, managers are not a homogeneous group – even middle managers – and the experiences of these different managers within the restructuring of organisations also varies. There are, of course, both various vertical levels and horizontal occupational groupings of managers, each with differing functions and organising logics. Organisational change may be driven by any of these levels or groups of managers, though not without the form and logic informing that restructuring being contested amongst those levels and groupings. Similarly, different levels or groups of managers can both benefit from and become victims of that organisational restructuring.

Finally, it is worth noting an increasing recognition in business and the business press that we may have reached the limits of managerial delayering and downsizing. In the US, companies are realising that experience and organisational memory is being lost in an exercise that has done little to really improve productivity. As early as 1994 one British management recruitment consultant was commenting that[5]:

> Other than sales and marketing, middle management recruitment is probably the area that is experiencing the most significant growth at present ... This seems to indicate that many companies have overdone the cutting out of so-called deadwood, and are finding that any pick-up at all in their business has left them deficient in many areas of middle management.

Conclusion

> When I was growing up, we used to read that by the year 2000 everyone would have to work only 30 hours a week and that the rest would be leisure time. But as we approach the year 2000, it seems likely that half of us will work 60 hours a week and the rest of us will be unemployed (Bridges, 1995b:20).

Little is heard about work in contemporary policy debates. The days when leisure opportunities and job enrichment were the stuff of official government and business reports are mostly long gone. Getting a job is, understandably, a priority and the 1990s' reports are much more likely to be on labour market flexibility or insecurity.

Nevertheless, the experience of work and workplace remains a central one in most people's lives. We have tried to capture the complexity of current trends. Powerful forces *have* been reshaping the world of work; notably intensified competition within a more global political economy, expanded technological and informatic resources, new managerial ideologies and practices, and the spread of market relations within the state sector and large private firms. Interacting with the limits to old Taylorist and Fordist forms, an imperative to organisational innovation has been created which is the prime source of initiatives to change the nature of labour utilisation and work co-ordination. In order to retain some vertical structure of command and accountability, managers have sought to develop a variety of organisational coping mechanisms in the form of cross-functional and on-line teams, thus creating a shadow division of labour.

References to the 'new workplace', then, are not out of place, if kept firmly *in* place. For this is not the 'paradigm shift' beloved of academics and commentators looking for a conceptual peg to launch their latest publication. Continuity is as pervasive as change, if for no other reason than because new ideas and practices are by definition built on the legacy of the old. Despite the bewildering number of change programmes and grand new titles for people and practices, the 'new workplace' is still easily recognisable for the vast majority who too often remain poorly motivated, overworked and undervalued. There is, however, no single or simple future work/place. Variation by firm, sector or country co-exists with the powerful structural tendencies to standardise through business-defined 'best practice', as workplace actors struggle to adapt to the constraints and opportunities of their own environments.

In developing the arguments in this chapter, we are aware that they are somewhat 'against the grain'. The world of work has always been something that can be portrayed in terms of high drama. For every popular commentator such as Drucker or Handy that talks soothingly about a future where work for the majority will be more autonomous, creative and professionalised, there is a doom merchant proclaiming that work, at least as we know it, is dead and buried. So Rifkin in *The End of Work* (1995) is the latest to predict the wipe-out of employment by the march of technology; while Bridges in *Jobshift* (1995a) focuses more realistically on the threat to the traditional employment package we call a 'job'.

Jobshift touches on important themes – job insecurity, the blurred edges between employment and self-employment as a 'contract culture' develops and the stunted career paths available in large organisations. Certainly, redundancy is a standard feature of 'employment' for an increasing number of workers; manual, non-manual, professional and managerial. Over five million people have been made redundant in Britain since 1990. In financial services, for example, there have been massive job losses, over 80 000 in banking alone between 1990 and 1994 (Sinden, 1996). Many banks no longer pretend that they offer a career structure, let alone a 'job for life'. But Bridges spoils a good argument in search of *the* future trend, asserting that 'everyone' is now a contingent worker and that all employees must act like people in business for themselves, maintaining self-development career plans. We are back on the territory of Handy's portfolio people.

Our territory in this book is the labour process rather than the labour market, so we have not had the space to consider in detail the extent and character of shifts in employment.[6] But from looking inside the workplace such claims do not mirror the experience of most of the workforce. In truth most workers are struggling to survive in and make sense of routine jobs and there are few employees communicating from electronic cottages or happily hawking their portfolios around companies. Full-time work still dominates employment, accounting for 76 per cent of all jobs and declining only 2.2 per cent over the ten years to 1993 (Ash and Rainnie, 1995).

If anyone has become a portfolio person it is more likely that he or she is a conscript of organisational restructuring than a new breed of entrepreneurs. Becoming the victims of downsizing, subcontracting, out-sourcing, contingent contracts and other forms of organisational restructuring is not a situation favoured by most, and given the opportunity such workers – manual, non-manual and managerial – would happily return to the ranks of full-time permanent employment in the big battalions.

This chapter has only been able to touch on some of these issues through the interfaces between the labour process and the employment relationship, but we recognise that people's experience of work develops from what they bring to it in orientations from the wider social structure and what they take out of it in terms of rewards and an employment package. Nevertheless, practices in the labour process shape that wider picture. As Martinez Lucio and Stewart illustrate in Chapter 4, a new politics of production can develop as issues of health and safety and work organisation are foregrounded as capital and labour attempt to reconfigure industrial relations in the image of the 'new workplace'.

It is important to get the trends right, because accurate, realistic knowledge can inform policy choices. Politicians too often take their agendas from 'policy entrepeneurs', management gurus and think-tankers who have a vested interest in the sweeping statement, popular slogan and digestible knowledge-gobbitt, regardless of how inconsistent with or embedded in existing bodies of knowledge (Thompson and du Gay, 1997). But that is hardly surprising when academics, particularly in Britain, absent themselves from the policy arena in search of texts to deconstruct, or to keep their world-weary cynicism about politics and the public realm intact.

Choices are there whether academics keep their heads in the theoretical sand or not. For all the hassles and hardships at work, employees at all levels, when and where encouraged to participate and innovate in a climate of trust and reasonable security, welcome real change – a point made evident in the surveys conducted by Clark (1995) and raised too by Milkman in Chapter 2 of this volume. And there is ample evidence that management failure to implement their own rhetoric of better human resource policy, training or service quality is often used by staff as part of their armoury of tactics to improve workplace life. A new politics and policy agenda cannot, however, be confined to the workplace. It requires a supportive institutional environment. Reforming governments need to find ways of rewarding innovation and partnership in the workplace. Models are available from the way in which the Swedish Work Environment Fund or the Australian Productivity Commission have encouraged collaboration on workplace innovation between employers, unions and researchers (Mathews, 1994). Nor is this purely theoretical. Evidence from the US (Bluestone and Bluestone, 1992; Levine, 1995) demonstrates that it is stakeholding firms with strong unions and a 'mutual gains' agenda that are at the cutting edge of change, with a vested interest in ensuring competitiveness through investment in skills and equipment.

The existence of policy discussion implies that the future is not set or determined by impersonal forces whether technology or markets, or by overarching theoretical models. As we approach the end of the century it is time to take stock of the nature and future of work, and what options that creates for different kinds of workplace transformation. For those willing to take that opportunity, there are plenty of choices and places between utopia and dystopia.

References

Ackroyd, S. and Proctor, S.J. (1996) 'Identifying the New Flexible Firm: Technology, Labour and Organisation in Contemporary British Manufacturing', unpublished paper.

Adler, P.S. (1993) 'Time-and-Motion Regained', *Harvard Business Review*, January–February, 97–107.

Adler, P. and Cole, R. (1995) 'Designed for Learning: A Tale of Two Auto Plants' in Sandberg, A. (ed.) *Enriching Production*, Aldershot: Avebury.

Ash, S. and Rainnie, A. (1995) 'Stress Management and the End of the Full Time Job', paper to the *Restructuring of the Local Economy of Lancashire Conference*, University of Central Lancashire with Lancashire County Council.

Barley, S. (1996) *The New World of Work*, Pamphlet, British–North American Committee, London.

Bluestone, B. and Bluestone, I. (1992) *Negotiating the Future: A Labor Perspective on American Business*, New York: Basic Books.

Bridges, W. (1995a) *Jobshift: How to Prosper in a Workplace without Jobs*, London: Nicholas Brealey.

Bridges, W. (1995b) 'The Death of the Job', *Independent on Sunday*, 5 February, 19.

Brindle, D. (1994) '"Trusts First" NHS chief condemned', *Guardian*, 14 November, 2.

Casey, C. (1995) *Work, Self and Society: After Industrialism*, London: Routledge.

Clark, J. (1995) *Managing Innovation and Change*, London: Sage.

Cook, E. (1995) 'Bosses spy on time thieves', *Independent on Sunday*, 11 June, 23.

Coopey, J. (1995) 'Managerial Culture and the Stillbirth of Organisational Commitment', *Human Resource Management Journal*, 5:3, 56–76.

Delbridge, R., Turnbull, P. and Wilkinson, B. (1992) 'Pushing back the frontiers: management control and work intensification under JIT/TQM regimes', *New Technology, Work and Employment*, 7:2, 97–106.

Department for Education and Employment (1996) 'Education Statistics for the United Kingdom', London: The Stationery Office.

Despres, C. and Hiltrop, J-M. (1995) 'Human resource management in the knowledge age: current practice and perspectives on the future', *Employee Relations*, 17:1, 9–23.

Drucker, P. (1986) 'The Changed World Economy', *Foreign Affairs*, 64:4, 768–91.

du Gay, P. (1996) *Consumption and Identity at Work*, London: Sage.

Edwards, P., Armstrong, P., Marginson, P. and Purcell, J. (1996) 'Towards the Transnational Company?' in Crompton, R., Gallie, D. and Purcell, K. (eds) *Corporate Restructuring and Labour Markets*, London: Routledge.

Elger, T. (1991) 'Task Flexibility and the Intensification of Labour in UK Manufacturing in the 1980s' in Pollert, A. (ed.) *Farewell to Flexibility*, Oxford: Blackwell.

Frenkel, S., Korczynski, M., Donohue, L. and Shire, K. (1995) 'Re-constituting Work', *Work, Employment and Society*, 9:4, 773–96.

Gallie, D. (1991) 'Patterns of Skill Change: Upskilling, Deskilling or the Polarisation of Skills?' *Work, Employment and Society*, 5:3, 319–51.

Hamel, G. and Prahalad, C.K. (1996) 'Competing in the New Economy: Managing Out of Bounds', *Strategic Management Journal*, 17, 237–42.

Handy, C. (1995) *The Future of Work*, WH Smith Contemporary Papers 8.

Harris, M. (1997) 'Rethinking the virtual organisation', unpublished paper.

Harrison, B. (1994) *Lean and Mean: The Changing Landscape of Corporate Power in the Age of Flexibility*. New York: Basic Books.

Henwood, D. (1996) 'Work and its future', *Left Business Observer*, 72, Internet edition.

Herriot, P. and Pemberton, C. (1995) *New Deals*, Chichester: John Wiley & Sons.

Hochschild, A.R. (1983) *The Managed Heart*, Berkeley: University of California Press.

Ingersoll Engineers (1996) *The Way We Work*, London.

IRS Employment Trends (1995) 'Putting the customer first: organisational change at WH Smith', 596, 5–9.

Jacques, R. (1996) *Manufacturing the Employee*, London: Sage.

Jain, R.K. and Triandis, H.C. (1990) *Management of Research and Development Organisations*, Chichester: John Wiley & Sons.

Jones, O. (1997) 'Changing the Balance? Taylorism, TQM and Work Organisation', *New Technology, Work and Employment*, 12:1, 13–24.

Kanter, R.M. (1983) *The Change Masters*, New York: Simon & Schuster.

Kumar, K. (1996) *From Post-Industrial to Post-Modern Society*, Oxford: Blackwell.

Kyotani, E. (1996) 'The Bright and Dark Sides of the Japanese Labour Process', unpublished paper.

Labour Market Trends (1996) May, London: Great Britain Office for National Statistics.

Lash, S. and Urry, U. (1994) *Economies of Sign and Space*, London: Sage.

Leidner, R. (1993) *Fast Food, Fast Talk: Service Work and the Routinisation of Everyday Life*, Berkeley, CA: University of California Press.

Levine, D. (1995) *Reinventing the Workplace*, The Brookings Institute, Washington DC.

Lyon, D. (1994) *The Electronic Eye*, Oxford: Polity Press.

Marks, A., Findlay, P., Hine, J., McKinlay, A. and Thompson, P. (1997) 'Whisky Galore: Teamworking and Workplace Transformation in the Scottish Spirits Industry', paper to the *15th International Labour Process Conference*, University of Edinburgh.

Mathews, J. (1994) *Catching the Wave: Workplace Reform in Australia*, New York: ILR Press.

McKinlay, A. and Taylor, P. (1997) 'Foucault and the Politics of Production' in McKinlay, A. and Starkey, K. (eds) *Foucault, Management and Organisation*, London: Sage.

McRae, H. (1996) 'You can't treat a skill-force like a workforce', *Independent on Sunday*, Business Section, 3 March, 4.

Milhill, C. (1996) 'NHS managers up 400pc on 1989', *Guardian*, 18 January, 6.

Mueller, F. (1994) 'Teams Between Hierarchy and Commitment: Change Strategies and the Internal Environment', *Journal of Management Studies*, 31:3, 383–403.

Nichols, T. (1991) 'Labour Intensification, Work Injuries and the Measurement of the Percentage Utilisation of Labour (PUL)', *British Journal of Industrial Relations*, 29:3, 569–92.

Observer Business / Gallup Poll (1994) 'The Workplace Revolution' *Observer*, 25 September.

OECD (1994) *Jobs Study: Evidence and Explanations* Pts 1 & 2, Paris: OECD.

Osterman, P. (1991) 'Impact of IT on Jobs and Skills' in Morton, M.S.S. (ed.) *The Corporation of the 1990s*, Oxford: Oxford University Press.

Quah, D. T. (1997) 'Weightless economy packs a heavy punch', *Independent on Sunday*, 18 May, 4.

Perin, C. (1991) 'The Moral Fabric of the Office: PanopticAn Discourse and Schedule Flexibilities', *Research in the Sociology of Organisations*, 8, London: JAI Press.

Randle, K. (1995) 'The Whitecoated Worker: Professional Autonomy in a Period of Change', paper to the *13th Annual International Labour Process Conference*, University of Central Lancashire, Preston.

Reich, R. (1993) *The Work of Nations*, London: Simon & Schuster.

Rifkin, J. (1995) *The End of Work: the Decline of the Global Labour Force and the Dawn of the Post-Market Era*, New York: G.P. Putnam's Sons.

Ritzer, G. (1997) 'McJobs: McDonaldization and Its Relationship to the Labour Process' in Ritzer, G. (ed.) *The McDonaldisation Thesis*, London: Sage.

Rosenthal, P., Hill, S. and Peccei, R. (1997) 'Checking Out Service: Evaluating Excellence, HRM and TQM in Retailing', *Work, Employment and Society*, forthcoming.

Routh, G. (1987) *Occupations of the People of Great Britain 1801–1981*, Basingstoke: Macmillan.

Sandberg, A. (ed.) (1995) *Enriching Production*, Aldershot: Avebury.

Scarbrough, H. and Burrell, G. (1996) 'The Axeman Cometh: the Changing Roles and Knowledges of Middle Managers' in Clegg, S.R. and Palmer, G. (eds) *The Politics of Management Knowledge*, London: Sage.

Seaton, M, (1995) 'Destructive dismissal', *Independent on Sunday*, 15 October, 10.

Segal-Horn, S. (1993) 'The Internationalisation of Service Firms', *Advances in Strategic Management*, 9, 31–55.

Sinden, A. (1996) 'The Decline, Flexibility and Geographical Restructuring of Employment in British Retail Banks', *The Geographical Journal*, 162:1, 25–40.

Smith, D. (1997) 'Job insecurity and other myths', *Management Today*, May, 38–41.

Starkey, K. and McKinlay, A. (1994) 'Managing for Ford', *Sociology*, 28:4, 975–90.

Summers, D. (1993) 'Management – the Right Attitude – Staff Surveys Are Popular, But Can Be Fraught With Pitfalls', *Financial Times*, 14 June, 8.

Thomas, A.B. (1993) *Controversies in Management*, London: Routledge.

Thompson, P. and Ackroyd, S. (1995) 'All Quiet on the Workplace Front? A Critique of Recent Trends in British Industrial Sociology', *Sociology*, 29:4, 1–19.

Thompson, P. and du Gay, P. (1997) 'Future Imperfect', *Renewal*, 5:1, 3–8.

Thompson, P. and Findlay, P. (1996) 'The Mystery of the Missing Subject', paper to the *14th International Labour Process Conference*, University of Aston, Birmingham.

Thompson, P., Jones, C., Nickson D. and Wallace, T. (1996) 'Internationalisation and Integration: A Comparison of Manufacturing and Service Firms', paper to *The Globalisation of Production and Regulation of Labour Conference*, University of Warwick.

Thompson, P. and Wallace, T. (1996) 'Redesigning Production Through Teamworking', *International Journal of Operations and Production Management*, Special Issue on Lean Production and Work Organisation', 16:2, 103–18.

Thompson, P., Wallace, T., Flecker, J. and Ahlstrand, R. (1995) 'It Ain't What You Do, It's the Way that You Do it: Production Organisation and Skill Utilisation in Commercial Vehicles', *Work, Employment and Society*, 9:4, 719–42.

Turner, S. (1997) 'Senior doctors slam medical managers' contractual "shop-a-doc" proposals', *BMA News Review*, August, 11.

Willmott, H. (1993) 'Strength is Ignorance; Slavery is Freedom: Managing Culture in Modern Organisation', *Journal of Management Studies*, 30:5 , 515–52.

Wilson, T. (1991) 'The proletarianisation of academic labour', *Industrial Relations Journal*, 22:4, 250–62.

Wright, C. and Lund, J. (1996) 'Best-Practice Taylorism: "Yankee Speed-Up" in Australian Grocery Distribution', *Journal of Industrial Relations*, 38:2, 196–212.

Notes

1   For a more academic version of the argument that there has been a move from capital and labour as commodities to an economy of signs, see Lash and Urry (1994).
2   In this piece, adapted from a paper given at the Labour Process Conference in 1995, Ritzer for the first time acknowledges the links between his own work and that of Braverman, between Weber's theory of rationalisation and Marx's theory of exploitation.
3   See Cook (1995).
4   Quoted and cited in Harris (1997).
5   Quoted in Herriot and Pemberton (1995: 5).
6   However there is a companion volume to this focusing on labour market issues – *Global Trends in Flexible Labour Markets*, edited by Nick Jewson and Alan Felstead (forthcoming).

2 The New American Workplace: High Road or Low Road?

Ruth Milkman

Introduction

Extravagant claims about workplace transformation have proliferated in the late twentieth-century US, as corporate experiments with various forms of worker participation have captured the imaginations of managers and social scientists alike. Traditional, top–down forms of organising work have increasingly been criticised in favour of such innovations as employee involvement, quality circles, pay-for-knowledge, multi-skilling, and teamwork. These techniques have spread from manufacturing to the service sector, and can be found in unionised as well as non-union settings. The new 'high-performance' workplace has been credited both with raising productivity (and thus competitiveness) and with enhancing the quality of workers' daily lives on the job. It is often portrayed as a means of alleviating the nation's economic malaise, and at the same time as a form of workplace democratisation, since the various participatory and skill-enhancing schemes it comprises include workers in processes and activities that were formerly monopolised by management. Indeed, evidence that workers themselves prefer the new forms of work organisation to more traditional ones is accumulating (although this remains an under-researched aspect of the phenomenon). Many observers see workplace reform as a key prerequisite for moving toward a high-skill, high-wage economy – the 'high road' for human resource management.

Yet a number of disturbing facts intrude on this idyllic scene. In precisely the same period in which these progressive human resource innovations have been introduced and celebrated, US workers' real wages have declined, job insecurity has reached new peaks in the wake of 'downsizing,' unionisation levels and union power have fallen precipitously, and the extent of economic inequality (in both income and wealth) has increased. These latter developments portend a dark future of declining living standards, even 'thirdworldisation,' as global competition drives wages lower and undermines union power – pointing in precisely the opposite direction to the high-wage, high-skill 'high road'.

How can we make sense of this contradictory picture? To what extent has the daily experience of workers actually changed in workplaces where participation-oriented innovations have been introduced? How extensively and intensively have such innovations spread? Under what conditions are they effective? What is the role of labour unions in workplace transformation? Are reforms being introduced in the same workplaces that are sites of recent downsizing, de-unionisation and declining real pay, or are individual firms choosing between two distinct 'high' and 'low' roads? These questions are only beginning to be systematically explored.

The critical literature on workplace transformation has focused primarily on exposing the exploitative aspects of the changes that have been introduced, arguing that what is touted as workplace democratisation is actually a new form of management manipulation and a threat to independent unionism. While there is much to be said for this critique, it generally ignores the fact that workers themselves do perceive benefits in the participatory innovations. This chapter pursues a somewhat different approach, namely to suggest that while the new forms of work organisation *do* offer positive benefits to workers, at least under certain conditions, thoroughgoing workplace reform has not diffused very widely through the US economy. Instead, most firms continue to employ top–down, authoritarian supervision which constructs workers as objects of suspicion rather than as active contributors to the welfare of the enterprise – a managerial approach that offers fertile soil for downsizing, reducing wages, and avoiding or eliminating unions, but which undermines the possibility of genuine worker participation. Moreover, many firms that *have* introduced employee involvement schemes or other workplace reforms are unable to reap the potential benefits of those innovations because they are simultaneously engaged in practices that threaten workers' immediate economic welfare. There are, of course, some true exemplars of the 'high road' that have avoided these pitfalls. Yet the disproportionate attention such showcase firms receive often obscures the fact that they are so atypical – even as it points to the viability of the alternative path they have forged.

The Call for Workplace Reform

Since the mid-1970s, as the pressure of international competition has intensified, and as new technologies have stimulated a wide range of organisational changes, US firms have increasingly introduced workplace reforms in a quest for improved productivity and quality. A vast literature documenting, analysing, and often advocating workplace transformation has emerged in the wake of these developments. Although the particular perspectives and emphases of different commentators vary widely, most of this literature suggests that participatory forms of work organisation offer benefits to both management and workers. On this basis, indeed, both parties are urged to set aside their traditional conflicts in favour of co-operation to advance their shared interest in greater competitiveness and an enhanced quality of work life. Throughout the literature, too, there is explicit acknowledgement of serious obstacles that must be overcome – most importantly, managerial reluctance to share power and the tradition of 'adversarial' labour relations – by firms that wish to travel on the 'high road' to a high-wage, high-skill, democratised workplace.

For example, in what is still perhaps the single most influential perspective on the topic, Piore and Sabel (1984) argued that the traditional, 'Fordist' mass production system had become less and less viable as a result of the growth of increasingly specialised markets and new information technologies. They pointed to an emergent system of 'flexible specialisation' which 'opens up long-term prospects for improvement in the condition of working life'. While noting that the transition to this new system could involve a severe loss in union power, they insisted that workers would still gain:

> Mass production is least attractive on the shop floor ... [It] invites an adversarial, hierarchal relation between workers and managers, and among the different units of an organisation. Mass production's extreme division of labour routinises and thereby trivialises work to a degree that often degrades the people who perform it. By contrast, flexible specialisation is predicated on collaboration. And the frequent changes in the production process put a premium on craft skills. Thus the production worker's intellectual participation in the work process is enhanced – and his or her role revitalised.(1984:278)

Thus Piore and Sabel urged management and public policy makers to recognise the potential benefits of flexible specialisation and to reorganise their activities accordingly, and they also implored organised labour to 'shake its attachment to increasingly indefensible forms of shop-floor control' so as not to impede such progress (307).

Many commentators have linked the rise of participative work systems to the new microprocessor-based technologies that were diffusing through the economy in the 1970s and 1980s, highlighting the potential benefits to both labour and management. New production technologies, in this view, can eliminate the most boring and dangerous jobs, while upgrading the skill and responsibility levels of those that remain. The key claim here is that new computer-based technologies are fundamentally different from earlier waves of industrial innovation. Whereas in the past, automation involved the use of special-purpose, 'dedicated' machinery to perform specific functions previously done manually, the new information-based technologies are flexible, allowing a single machine to be adapted to a variety of specific tasks. Thus Zuboff (1988) argued, for example, that new technologies often require workers to use 'intellective' skills. Rather than simply manipulating tools and other tangible objects, workers must respond to abstract, electronically presented information. For this reason, Zuboff suggested, computer technology offers the possibility of a radical break with the Taylorist tradition of work organisation, moving toward more skilled and rewarding jobs, and toward workplaces where learning is encouraged and rewarded. 'Learning is the new form of labour', she declared (395). Hirschhorn (1984) made similar claims about the computerised workplace, arguing that with new technology; 'the deskilling process is reversed. Machines extend workers' skill rather than replace it' (97; see also Block, 1990). Both Zuboff and Hirschhorn insisted that the potential productivity gains of the new technology can only be realised if managers cede more control over decision making to workers, and on this basis they argued that increased worker participation is in the best interest of the firm.

Other observers are less concerned with the enabling potential of technology and instead focus on the desirability of organisational change in its own right. They too make sweeping pronouncements about the potential benefits for management and workers alike of radical workplace transformation. Consultants Hammer and Champy's (1993) popular management guide to *Reengineering the Corporation*, for example, claims that with the introduction of more efficient 'process teams', the job fragmentation typical of traditional work organisation systems is eliminated:

> After reengineering, work becomes more satisfying, since workers achieve a greater sense of completion, closure, and accomplishment from their jobs ... work becomes more rewarding since people's jobs have a greater component of growth and learning ... People working in a reengineered process are, of necessity, empowered. As process teamworkers they are both permitted and required to think, interact, use judgment, and make decisions. (69–70)

Equally extravagant rhetoric along these lines comes from a team of auto industry analysts at the Massachusetts Institute of Technology, made up of Womack, Jones and Roos. Their best-selling book, *The Machine that Changed the World* (1990), popularised the term 'lean production' to describe the system first perfected by Toyota in Japan and later transplanted successfully to US auto plants (in both union and non-union settings). 'Lean producers employ teams of multiskilled workers at all levels of the organisation and use highly flexible, increasingly automated machines to produce volumes of products in enormous variety', they state (13; see also Monden, 1983). Although their research did not include any direct examination of the impact of this system on workers, the MIT team argues that lean production is a vast improvement on traditional Fordist mass production:

> While the mass-production plant is often filled with mind-numbing stress, as workers struggle to assemble unmanufacturable products and have no way to improve their working environment, lean production offers a creative tension in which workers have many ways to address challenges. This creative tension involved in solving complex problems is precisely what has separated manual factory work from professional 'think' work in the age of mass production ...
> Lean production is a superior way for humans to make things. It provides better products in wider variety at lower cost. Equally important, it provides more challenging and fulfilling work for employees at every level, from the factory to headquarters. It follows that the whole world should adopt lean production, and as quickly as possible. (Womack, Jones and Roos, 1990:101–2, 225)

As new technologies and organisational reform have transformed more and more workplaces, claims like these have won widespread public acceptance. They are, indeed, the basis for labour market projections that suggest a technologically-driven decline in demand for unskilled labour and the need for educational upgrading to produce future generations of workers capable of functioning in the factory and office of the computer age. As Hammer and Champy put it:

> If jobs are more satisfying, they are also more challenging and difficult. Much of the old, routine work is eliminated or automated. If the old model was simple tasks for simple people, the new one is complex jobs for smart people, which raises the bar for entry into the workplace. Few simple, routine, unskilled jobs are to be found in a reengineered environment. (1993:70)

Yet it is far from clear that the reality of work is actually changing in the ways that this optimistic scenario suggests. For one thing, it ignores the fact that employee involvement and participation schemes emerged historically as efforts to prevent unionism from taking root, and in a period of dramatic decline in union power. And crucially, proponents of this perspective tend to underestimate the formidable structural and cultural difficulties involved in creating a corporate environment that fosters genuine trust between managers and workers, even though they recognise that this is a precondition of successful workplace transformation.

Labour Unions and Workplace Transformation

Consider first the historical relationship of workplace reform to unionism. As Kochan, Katz and McKersie (1986) demonstrated over a decade ago, it was firms committed to 'union avoidance' that first developed the alternative approach to traditional industrial relations that has been the basis for most subsequent reforms. This new, non-union model of work organisation centred on enhanced communication between management and managed, and was more flexible and less 'adversarial' than the traditional system. Focusing mainly on the manufacturing sector the authors highlighted non-union 'team concept' plants that organised workers into flexible teams whose members were rewarded for mastering a variety of tasks and skills and who regularly participated in decision making. They also pointed to increasing experimentation with participative schemes in the unionised sector, as illustrated by Quality of Work Life (QWL) programmes. In both the non-union and union sectors, they predicted, efforts 'to foster greater employee participation and to adopt more flexible forms of work organisation will be a constant feature of workplace industrial relations in the future' (1986:239–40). This prognostication proved accurate as many unions have endorsed the idea of labour–management co-operation in the 1980s and 1990s.

Heckscher (1988) further explored the tension between traditional forms of union organisation and the emerging participative work systems, arguing that the only viable labour movement response to the accelerating crisis of de-unionisation was a new, flexible and decentralised form of collective bargaining that would replace traditional, 'adversarial' unionism with a more co-operative relationship with management rooted in greater worker involvement in decision making and skill upgrading. He argued passionately that worker participation without strong unionism was inadequate, since under these conditions the inequality between management and labour would lead to corporate despotism; at the same time he insisted that unions had to become more flexible to survive in the newly emerging economic order.

A recent book by Barry and Irving Bluestone (1992) extended this line of reasoning into an explicit appeal to the business community, arguing that unions must be at the centre of any workable strategy for economic revival. Like Heckscher, the Bluestones rejected unionism in its traditional, 'adversarial' form, instead embracing the idea of labour–management co-operation – particularly as exemplified by the General Motors Saturn plant. They pointed to the accumulating evidence that unionised workplaces have higher productivity and quality than non-unionised ones and on this basis expressed optimism that rational self-interest ultimately would lead employers to recognise unions as a critical ingredient in any successful strategy to restore US economic competitiveness (see also Eaton and Voos, 1992). Unions have indeed responded to the call to explore the path of co-operation with management and to put aside traditional work rules in the name of 'flexibility'. However, in unionised firms, worker participation typically has gone hand in hand with various forms of 'concession bargaining'. As unions were pressured to scale back their wage and benefit demands (or in some cases, to accept outright cuts in compensation) in the early 1980s, they also were induced to abandon many traditional work rules and to experiment with the worker participation schemes previously limited to the non-union sector. This took place in the context of a sharp plunge in union density, and in many cases unions were forced to agree to introduce 'participation' and other forms of labour–management 'co-operation' as a condition of their very survival. Thus there is an inextricable link between the collapse of union power in the 1980s and the trend toward employee involvement and participation. Authors like Heckscher and the Bluestones tend to gloss over this troubling history, yet it casts doubt on their characterisation of worker participation in unionised settings as a step toward workplace democracy. To their credit, they express deep scepticism about whether participation *can* be democratising in the absence of a union. However, they ignore the logical corollary, namely to question the democratising effect of participation in cases where it is linked to a decline in union power and influence.

Critics of Workplace Reform and the Workers' Perspective

The decline in labour's power is an underlying concern in the critical analyses of participation, the 'team concept,' and 'lean production' which have appeared in reaction to the literature advocating such changes. Critics such as Parker and Slaughter (1988) have argued eloquently that what appears as participation is really just a new form of exploitation. (See also Parker and Slaughter, 1994; Garrahan and Stewart, 1992; Graham, 1995; and Babson, 1995 for similar critiques.) They stress that innovations like the 'team concept' sharply increase the pace and pressures of work, despite the rhetoric of worker empowerment. In essence, they argue that such schemes are merely strategies to enhance managerial control, and allow workers to 'participate' mainly in the intensification of their own exploitation. 'The little influence workers do have over their jobs is that in effect they are organised to time-study themselves', Parker and Slaughter (1988:19) write, noting that participation serves only to mobilise workers' detailed knowledge of the labour process so as to help management speed up production and eliminate wasteful work practices. They label the team concept 'management by stress' and emphasise its potential for undermining union power.

This is a trenchant and deservedly influential critique. Yet it overlooks one crucial fact: namely, that workers themselves seem to have a favourable attitude toward the concept of participation. Workers who have experience with both the traditional, authoritarian management approach and with the new, participatory initiatives appear to strongly prefer the latter, even if they are critical of it in some respects. Even Parker and Slaughter admit that at NUMMI (New United Motor Manufacturing Inc., the GM–Toyota joint venture plant that was the focus of their pioneering analysis of the team concept), 'nobody says they want to return to the days when GM ran the plant' (1988:111). Workers (unionised or not) are often critical of management's failure to live up to its own rhetoric, particularly when it comes to genuine empowerment of lower-level employees. Most workers find the rhetoric itself intrinsically appealing and they are generally enthusiastic about any reforms that increase their autonomy and input into decision making at the workplaces to which they devote so much time and energy on a daily basis.

Under some conditions, at least, employee participation does seem to yield genuine workplace democratisation. At GM's Saturn plant, for example, workers participate not only in the micromanagement of production (to which at many workplaces, employee involvement and QWL often are limited), but also, through their union, in other aspects of managing the enterprise itself, such as product design, pricing, and personnel policies. Shaiken and his colleagues recently reported that Saturn workers express a high level of satisfaction with these arrangements, particularly when compared to the traditionally managed GM plants where they worked previously (Shaiken, Lopez and Mankita, 1997; see also Bluestone and Bluestone, 1992). Even in plants where participation-oriented reforms have been more modest, workers have been extremely receptive to them. At the GM plant I studied in Linden, New Jersey, for example, workers hated the traditional management system so intensely that they were more than willing to give such reforms a try (Milkman, 1997, especially Chapter 5).

But workplace participation by itself does nothing to reverse the reality that unions and workers have lost a great deal of power and influence in recent years, and this loss itself constitutes a sharp decline in workplace democracy. It seems obvious that in their current state of disarray, with private sector union density at only about ten per cent (US Department of Labor, 1996:212), American unions lack the power to foster workplace democratisation of any type; they are mostly engaged in a desperate struggle to survive. Even if the new AFL–CIO leadership's effort to rebuild the labour movement proves successful, it will be some time before unions can exert real leverage in most US workplaces. Implicitly recognising this, many of the advocates of workplace reform cited above rely on the *deux ex machina* of employer rationality to restore a central role for unions and for worker participation in a revived US economy. The lure of vast improvements in productivity and quality is dangled in front of managers in the hope that they might choose to travel the high road of participation and workplace democratisation. As virtually all advocates of reform agree, even when union co-operation has been secured, the economic payoffs of workplace transformation will only materialise if corporate organisations can foster a new 'high trust' culture in the workplace. But given the deeply rooted anti-union animus and authoritarian culture of US managers, the notion that they will voluntarily lay down their sword and shield and invite workers to participate more extensively in decision making may be wishful thinking – even if it would be in their firm's best interest.

The Problem of Management Resistance

Can traditionally authoritarian businesses really learn to encourage autonomy and intellectual development among workers? Zuboff, even while advocating this paradigm shift, acknowledges that 'sharing information and maximising opportunities for all ... to become more knowledgeable is felt [by managers] to be a kind of treason' (1988:238). Indeed, her own fieldwork includes many instances in which managers, fearful of losing their traditional monopoly of knowledge and power, suppress rather than encourage the empowering potential of new technologies. Her plea that managers allow rationality to triumph over their fear of losing power and control has a compelling logic but other research suggests that there is no guarantee that this will occur. As Thomas puts it, '"post-industrial possibilities" ... will remain precisely that as long as extant worldviews, evaluative criteria, and organisational structures remain unchallenged and unchanged ... Far more than the absorption of new technology must take place if organisations are to achieve the daring new forms and functions implied by flexible specialisation and lean production' (1994:243).

In practice US corporations have found it extremely difficult to instill the 'high road' spirit of enlightenment advocated by writers from Piore and Sabel, to Zuboff, to Hammer and Champy, through their multilayered management structures. While some firms have successfully implemented workplace reforms, in many others a huge gap has emerged between the rhetoric of participation and the reality of the factory or office floor. All too often, the participatory ideas are discussed intensively at the top of the organisation and with consultants, but then are implemented in a superficial, mechanical fashion. By the time they trickle down to low-level supervisors and the individual worker, there may not be much substance left. Managers who themselves have no job security and came of age under the old regime, where independent thinking was punished, often balk at suddenly shifting course and offering their own subordinates greater freedom and decision-making power.

At GM–Linden, for example, although rank-and-file workers were enthusiastic when management announced plans to introduce a more participative system in conjunction with a major technological modernisation, touted as the 'new Linden', their hopes for change were soon disappointed, as the following account drawing on Milkman (1997) indicates. A wide gulf opened up between the managerial rhetoric of participation and the reality of the shop floor. For example, workers were initially told that if they were unable to complete their assigned task in their own work station, they could and indeed *should* stop the line. However, as problems with the new technology led to slower than expected production, supervision came under pressure to increase output and workers who stopped the line were immediately reprimanded. 'They really didn't want to you to stop the line', reported one worker.

> Officially you were allowed to do it, but when you did, they came down real quick: 'Don't worry about the problem yet, let's get the line running, then we'll talk about it.' It was supposed to be, like, if you didn't have your parts or anything, you could stop the line. But they'd rather have a repair man go down there and put the parts on than you stop the line, 'cause every minute they're down, to them, all they see is dollar signs. So, they put it there, but they really didn't want you to use it at all.

Another worker agreed. 'They don't want that line to stop for any reason. When I'd stop the line, they got real mad and everything, started the line and said; "Don't do it again."' And a union official commented:

> The training was great. All that jazz, telling all the people we're going to have 'stop the line' and we're going to fix the car. And they did all that for a little while. But the little while didn't last too long. Some places, people are not allowed to stop the line, even though they said they were going to be. They got it set up so that when you press it, nothing happens, it's like bypassed. When they don't get the count, all the good talking stuff goes down the tube, and that's one of our problems in America.

Supervisors themselves confirmed that it was very difficult for them to adjust to the 'stop the line' idea. 'It took a while for us to get used to as managers, because we always wanted the line to continue running', one confessed. 'For twenty years that was what was always bred into us. Production was first!'

Some workers were also disappointed by the flip-flops in parking policy. For a brief period after the 'new Linden' campaign was launched, parking spaces formerly reserved for foremen had been opened up to workers on a first-come, first-served basis. Later, for reasons that are unclear, this policy was reversed. One worker was bitter:

> That parking lot, it used to be salaried, then with the big kissing affair going on, to show we're all equal, they opened it up. I get to work forty minutes before I have to be there, and so then I could park right up front. But now, I can't park there. The lot's empty, but I can't park there, because I'm not a foreman, I'm not supervision. I said, 'What happened to all this kissy-kiss shit?' I says, 'Is it back to the old ways?' He [manager] says, 'Nobody else is complaining.' I says, 'I don't know about that.' I said, 'I get here forty minutes ahead of work, and I got to park all the way over there, and then some shithead foreman can get here two minutes before the whistle blows and gets a prime spot.' I said, 'That sounds a little prejudicial to me.'

The same theme of broken promises resounded in workers' comments about the Employee Involvement Groups (EIGs) that were established as part of the 'new Linden'. The idea was appealing to many workers, but in practice numerous problems emerged, and after three years management effectively dropped the programme, by ending the previous policy of paying workers (at overtime rates) who attended the half-hour weekly meetings. By the early 1990s, some workers were nostalgic for the EIGs. 'We used to meet at lunchtime and discuss all the problems, and supervision would come and you would talk things out', one worker recalled. 'They cut that out! It was great.' Another commented, 'Nine times out of ten we would walk away [from the EIG] and have nothing accomplished. But when something was accomplished it was a big deal, because it had to do with the people who were busting their ass, people on the line working. When we finally got something done, people were happy. And if you keep people happy on the line, you know, they produce a better job.'

Others were more cynical about the programme. 'So, once a week you have a meeting', one worker said. 'It's like psychiatry, you tell them your problems, you go home. That's the way I see it, personally.' One of his co-workers agreed: 'It's just to pacify you so you don't write up grievances. It's a half-hour's pay for sitting there and eating your lunch. It takes forever to get anything done. Like just to get a water fountain, it takes months of screaming and yelling and bringing it up. To get a fan, it's the same thing.' Sometimes workers were unwilling to voice their complaints in the first place. 'In my group, nobody would say anything', one worker reported. 'They'd eat their lunch. Because we had a pain-in-the-ass foreman, nobody would say anything against him, they didn't want him riding their back. You could get little things done, but it was only there for the company. Workers got nothing out of it but the half-hour pay.'

Although most workers were initially hopeful that the 'new Linden' would truly be different from the old, they quickly found that this was not the case. 'The "new Linden"', one worker intoned with disgust. 'It got lost in the wash.' As another recalled:

You still have the management that has the mentality of the top–down, like they're right, they don't listen to the exchange from the workers, like the old school. So that's why when you ask about the 'new Linden', people say it's a farce. Because you still do not feel mutual respect, you feel the big thing is to get the jobs out. This is a manufacturing plant, they do have to produce. But you can't just tell this worker, you know, take me upstairs [where the 80-hour training classes were held], give me this big hype, and then bring me downstairs and have the same old attitude.

Another worker was equally disillusioned:

It sounded good at the time, but it turned out to be a big joke. Management's attitude is still the same. It hasn't changed at all. Foremen who treated you like a fellow human being are still the same. No problems with them. The ones who are arrogant bastards are still the same, with the exception of a few who are a little bit scared, a little bit afraid that it might go to the top man and, you know, make some trouble. Everyone has pretty much the same attitude.

Many workers believed that the older foremen – the 'dinosaurs' – were particularly resistant to change. 'You talk to any foreman in there that had over twenty, twenty-five years and they'll tell you it [the "new Linden" idea] was garbage, a waste of time and money. Only a fool would expect them to change. It was only brainwashing to get you to do more work.' One older superintendent was especially notorious – some workers called him a 'Nazi'. A union committeeman who dealt with him regularly explained:

I see what management is trying to do. I know that the dinosaurs will be gone from here someday and the union and management will probably have a better relationship. But in my department, we have a superintendent that doesn't believe in that stuff. He doesn't believe in it. He's back in the 1940s when the union and company fought constantly. It just can't work that way any more. We have to learn to get along. But he's from the old school and doesn't believe in employee involvement and that kind of thing. He puts a fight up about it.

Some workers grudgingly acknowledged that the quality of their relationship with supervision had improved somewhat. Grievance rates did fall slightly, although this probably reflected a decline in the local union's power rather than increased satisfaction with conditions in the plant. In any case, whatever improvements did occur in labour–management relations fell so far short of what most production workers felt they had been promised, that they still were disappointed. Some suggested that the commitment to change was only present among upper management, with first-line supervisors going along with the programme only insofar as they feared reprisals from above. Most agreed with a committeeman who stated that 'with higher-up management you can see the change, but on the line it falls apart'. As a worker explained:

> They're [foremen] a little more worried because I guess they're under pressure from getting laid off themselves. Because they're supposed to cut 25 per cent, and they're hand picking them. So they're all nervous about every little thing that goes on. They're a lot nicer now because before they used to yell a lot, and scream and curse and threaten. They were warned – I think they were told that they're not allowed to do that anymore, you know, degrade a person really. Because it only ends up with sabotage or whatever afterwards. There's still a few that get hot-headed and start yelling and screaming, but then it never works out because there's a payback for it.

Many middle managers themselves agreed with this view. As one, a self-described convert from the 'hard-nosed old school' to the new gospel of employee participation, complained:

> Upper management is trying very hard to get involved with the local union people and the hourly people. But I think they missed a very important step in the process, and it's the first-line supervisor. I think they stepped over him completely. It's obvious that GM is trying to reduce 25 per cent of its white collars. Here's upper management, and here's the union, and we're going to skip this guy in the middle. I guess upper management thinks that because we're salaried that we're automatically involved. But see, I put my pants on the same way everyone else does, and I got questions and problems. I don't think we in management have the opportunity to speak openly to our people without the fear of recrimination. Don't say anything, because your boss will get mad, and if your boss gets mad at you then you're not going to get a raise. You're not going to get a raise anyway because they're not giving any, but there's always that threat.

On the whole, workers laid the blame for the failure of the 'new Linden' squarely on management's shoulders, and for good reason. They tended to be most critical of the GM representatives with whom they had daily contact, namely the first-line supervisors. But top-level corporate management's own commitment to transforming the industrial relations regime was at the root of the problem. First-line supervisors were offered no incentives to fundamentally change their own behaviour; on the contrary, their own ranks were constantly being reduced, even as they were placed under continual pressure from above to 'get production out'. Under conditions like these, where workplace reform is imposed in a mechanical fashion, without genuine commitment from management, and without winning the trust of the workforce, it is not likely to succeed.

Indeed, despite the diffusion of new technologies and participatory rhetoric, many workplaces have changed their internal organisational structures only marginally, if at all. As Appelbaum and Batt report in their exhaustive study of workplace reforms, 'Despite the reported gains in performance and the

apparent acceleration of experiments with innovative practices, the overwhelming majority of US workplaces are traditionally managed' (1994:148; see also Osterman, 1994). Although many companies have been spurred to adopt piecemeal reforms, these typically affect only a minority of employees and they often prove to be short-lived. Thus despite the impression of widespread change conveyed by both the business press and the academic literature on the subject, only a few firms have radically transformed their work systems, and many have not attempted even the most superficial reforms. The survey data reviewed by Appelbaum and Batt (including service sector firms as well as the better-studied manufacturing cases) suggest that between one-fourth and one-third of US firms have undertaken some significant workplace reforms. The proportion of US workers affected by such changes appears to be much smaller, however, and in most cases reform has been limited in scope. Significantly, unionised firms have been among the most successful in achieving thorough and enduring work reorganisation – contradicting the view in much of the literature that organised labour is a major obstacle to change.

Another recent assessment of the extent of workplace reform by Ichniowski and his colleagues came to a similar conclusion:

> A majority of contemporary US businesses now have adopted some forms of innovative work practices aimed at enhancing employee participation such as work teams, contingent pay-for-performance compensation, or flexible assignment of multiskilled employees. Only a small percentage of businesses, however, have adopted a full system of innovative work practices composed of an extensive set of these work practice innovations. (1996:325)

Among the reasons cited in this study as to why the diffusion of workplace reform has been so limited are 'system inertia' and 'a low level of trust between labour and management' (Ichniowski *et al.*, 1996:325–7). It seems that unlike organised labour, which (albeit from a position of weakness) has gone along with the workplace reform programme with only limited resistance, corporate management has remained committed to the traditional, authoritarian system – except for a few showcases for the much-discussed 'high road'. Indeed, despite the pervasive celebration of 'reengineering', 'lean production', and all the varied participative techniques that have been explored over the past two decades, most US businesses continue to be 'fat and mean', as Gordon's (1996) recent book puts it. They remain dedicated to intensifying supervision; reducing wages, benefits, and job security; and combatting labour unions.

Conclusion

Managerial intransigence helps explain not only the surprisingly limited extent of workplace transformation, but also the many indicators of deterioration in the conditions of working people in the late twentieth-century US. For the first

time in the post-Second World War era, economic inequality among households increased sharply in the 1970s and 1980s, as the very richest Americans' share of both income and wealth grew dramatically. In the same period, real wages have fallen precipitously, especially for non-college-educated males; fringe benefits have become more difficult to obtain; job security has been increasingly elusive; and as noted above, labour unions have lost both membership and influence (see Levy, 1995). The much-lamented slowdown in productivity growth is at best a partial explanation for these developments.

Moreover, as Gordon points out, despite the widely discussed phenomenon of 'downsizing', the ranks of managers and supervisors in the corporate sector have not shrunk but, on the contrary, actually burgeoned in the 1990s. This in turn is largely due to the fact that while a few US corporations have embraced the 'high-performance workplace', the vast majority instead have continued to rely on the authoritarian 'Stick Strategy' in their approach to managing lower-level employees. While piecemeal adoption of workplace reform is widespread, the more thoroughgoing 'high trust' approach remains a rarity in the US. As Gordon (1996:91, 94) notes:

> The extent of adoption of truly 'high performance workplaces' is narrower and more superficial than often advertised; we have not yet witnessed a 'revolution' in US labor relations. And, at the same time that some employers are abandoning the Stick Strategy, at least as many, probably more, are adopting, consolidating and deepening it ...
>
> So much emphasis has been placed on 'high-performance' innovators that we've learned much more about them in recent years than about those who carry on as before. Wages have been falling. Job security has been eroding. Companies haul out the tanks to avoid and even to break their unions. Firms have been relying more and more on contingent and temporary workers, relieving themselves of the obligation to pay benefits ... Some firms are seeking to reward and involve their workers. Many more firms appear to fatten the bottom line by cheapening their workers' labor power.

In short, the low-wage, low-trust, low-skill 'low road' is the path most US firms are following, despite overwhelming evidence that the 'high road' a few of them (and many more firms in other nations) have forged would serve the long-term interests of both corporations and workers far better. The already-weakened organised labour movement has long since recognised the desirability of the alternative path, but is powerless to make it the dominant one. The prospect of public policy initiatives to provide businesses incentives to shift their course – or for that matter to redress the power imbalance between labour and management which makes the 'low road' so easy to follow – seems extremely remote. Thus the critical obstacle to large-scale workplace transformation and the potential prosperity it could foster is the virtually unchallenged power of intransigent corporate managements who are loath to abandon their authoritarian ways.

References

Appelbaum, E. and Batt, R. (1994) *The New American Workplace: Transforming Work Systems in the United States*, Ithaca, NY: ILR Press.

Babson, S. (ed.) (1995) *Lean Work: Empowerment and Exploitation in the Global Auto Industry*, Detroit: Wayne State University Press.

Block, F. (1990) *Postindustrial Possibilities: A Critique of Economic Discourse*, Berkeley: University of California Press.

Bluestone, B. and Bluestone, I. (1992) *Negotiating the Future: A Labor Perspective on American Business*, New York: Basic Books.

Eaton, A.E. and Voos, P.B. (1992) 'Unions and Contemporary Innovations in Work Organisation, Compensation, and Employee Participation' in Lawrence, M. and Voos, P.B. (eds) *Unions and Economic Competitiveness*, Armonk, NY: M.E. Sharpe.

Garrahan, P. and Stewart, P. (1992) *The Nissan Enigma: Flexibility at Work in a Local Economy*, New York: Mansell Publishing.

Gordon, D. (1996) *Fat and Mean: The Corporate Squeeze of Working Americans and the Myth of Managerial 'Downsizing'*, New York: Free Press.

Graham, L. (1995) *On the Line at Subaru-Isuzu*, Ithaca, NY: Cornell University Press.

Hammer, M. and Champy, J. (1993) *Reengineering the Corporation*, New York: Harper Business.

Heckscher, C.C. (1988) *The New Unionism: Employee Involvement in the Changing Corporation*, New York: Basic Books.

Hirschhorn, L. (1984) *Beyond Mechanisation: Work and Technology in a Post-Industrial Age*, Cambridge, Mass.: MIT Press.

Inchniowski, C., Kochan, T.A., Levine, D., Olson, C. and Strauss, G. (1996) 'What Works at Work: Overview and Assessment,' *Industrial Relations*, 35, 299–333.

Kochan, T.A., Katz, H.C. and McKersie, R.B. (1986) *The Transformation of American Industrial Relations*, New York: Basic Books.

Levy, F. (1995) 'Incomes and Income Inequality' in Reynolds Farley (ed.) *State of the Union: America in the 1990s*, vol. 1, New York: Russell Sage Foundation.

Milkman, R. (1997) *Farewell to the Factory: Auto Workers in the Late Twentieth Century*, Berkeley: University of California Press.

Monden, Y. (1983) *Toyota Production System: Practical Approach to Production Management*, Norcross, Georgia: Industrial Engineering and Management Press.

Osterman, P. (1994) 'How Common is Workplace Transformation and Who Adopts It?', *Industrial and Labor Relations Review*, 47, 173–88.

Parker, M. and Slaughter, J. (1988) *Choosing Sides: Unions and the Team Concept*, Boston: South End Press.

Parker, M. and Slaughter, J. (1994) *Working Smart: A Union Guide to Participation Programs and Reengineering*, Detroit: Labour Notes.

Piore, M.J. and Sabel, C.F. (1984) *The Second Industrial Divide: Possibilities for Prosperity*, New York: Basic Books.

Shaiken, H., Lopez, S. and Mankita, I. (1997) 'Two Routes to Team Production: Saturn and Chrysler Compared', *Industrial Relations*, 36, 17–45.

Thomas, R.J. (1994) *What Machines Can't Do: Politics and Technology in the Industrial Enterprise*, Berkeley: University of California Press.

US Department of Labor, Bureau of Labor Statistics, 1996. *Employment and Earnings*, vol. 43.

Womack, J.P., Jones, D.T. and Roos, D. (1990) *The Machine That Changed the World*, New York: Rawson Associates.

Zuboff, S. (1988) *In the Age of the Smart Machine: The Future of Work and Power*, New York: Basic Books.

3 Work Organisation Inside Japanese Firms in South Wales: A Break from Taylorism?

Andy Danford

Introduction

A number of influential analyses of Japanese lean production have presented its mode of organisation as both a distinctive and laudable alternative to conventional Taylorised systems of mass commodity production. For example, Womack *et al.* (1990:101) argue that as well as removing all human and material waste from the manufacturing operation, the Japanese 'model' places the 'dynamic work team' at the heart of the lean factory. Shop-floor work in this highly stressed system somehow becomes 'enriched' and 'de-Taylorised' by incorporating new conceptual tasks and responsibilities. In a similar and in some respects more evangelical vein, Kenney and Florida (1993) attempt to locate the advantages of lean production in the shifting social relations between intellectual and manual labour which underlie their conceptualisation of Japanese technological and organisational efficiency. They place Japanese manufacturing practice within a framework of 'innovation-mediated production' characterised essentially by the integration and harnessing of the intelligence and knowledge of R&D staff, design engineers and shop-floor workers.

More critical appraisals of Japanese management and its application in the West focus upon the ideological and material impact on workers of such practices as labour flexibility, teamworking and kaizen. Whilst their analyses of transplant operators' particular labour processes sometimes tend towards ambiguity on whether these can be characterised as Taylorist, neo-Taylorist or post-Taylorist, many such writers are more forthright in arguing that taken as a whole, Japanese management innovations constitute notably sophisticated systems of management which border on total control (see, for example, Delbridge *et al.*, 1992; Garrahan and Stewart, 1992; Graham, 1995; and Sewell and Wilkinson, 1992).

Despite such a contrast in approach, these different perspectives nevertheless share similarities in their implicit acceptance of the existence of some distinctive Japanese work organisational paradigm. Moreover, what then becomes of prime importance for analyses of shifts in the nature of work organisation and the labour process in UK-based mass production is the extent to which British firms have emulated the 'Japanese model' and following this, the extent to which British workers have become empowered by, or subordinated to, the new system of production.

However, can we really conceive of Japanese production practice in terms of some novel, post-Taylorist, post-Fordist work organisational paradigm? In reality, as Elger and Smith (1994:38) note, Japanese transnational corporations may be no different in intent from their Western counterparts, seeking advantage in different regions of the globe for market and cost reasons, and selectively adjusting their factory regimes to fit into local market requirements, particular industrial sector logics and particular labour relations conditions.

This chapter casts further light on these questions by providing quantitative and qualitative survey data analysis of the organisation of work within different Japanese manufacturing transplants in South Wales. It challenges managerialist assumptions that a notable characteristic of Japanese transplant labour processes is one of a rupture with conventional Taylorised mass production techniques. In so doing, it provides further evidence to question the existence of a 'Japanese production model' comprising a consistent ensemble of new management practices. Although some of the transplants in different manufacturing sectors did operate particular 'Japanese-style' production innovations, rarely did these constitute a coherent totality of practices.

Does this mean then that there is nothing sufficiently distinctive about Japanese transplant management to warrant investigation in its own right, or indeed, analysis of the diffusion of ideas and practice into indigenous firms? Not quite. Whilst rejecting the standard managerial approach, the chapter argues that from the particular standpoint of the factory worker, Japanese management practice is conspicuous for its generally meticulous approach to labour regulation, which in turn, is aimed at securing enhanced leverage over effort and worker compliance to boot.

The Survey

The survey data are drawn from the author's research on the impact of Japanese management practices on British-owned firms in South Wales. The survey was carried out between January and June 1994. During this period there were seventeen fully Japanese-owned manufacturing transplants based in the South Wales region of which fifteen agreed to participate in the survey.[1] Most of these were assembly and component manufacture transplants concentrated in the consumer electronics and electronics components sectors although firms operating in the autocomponents and chemicals/plastics sectors were also present. This paper focuses upon the eleven participating firms in the electronics and autocomponents sectors (see Table 3.1).[2]

The survey utilised both quantitative and qualitative methods. Questionnaires and interview schedules were used to establish the incidence of different production control systems, working practices and Total Quality Management (TQM) practices whilst interviews with managers and, in most factories, shop-floor observations allowed a more in-depth analysis of these. In addition, interviews were carried out with a number of shop stewards, trade union officials and employer organisation representatives in the region.

Table 3.1   Participating firms by sector and size

Company	Manufacturing sector	Total employees
Calsonic	Autocomponents	701
Aiwa	Consumer Electronics	980
Matsushita Electric	Consumer Electronics	1650
Sony	Consumer Electronics	2750
Hitachi	Consumer Electronics	800
Star Micronics	Consumer Electronics	206
Gooding Sanken	Electronic Components	233
Electronic Harnesses	Electronic Components	150
Yuasa Batteries	Electronic Components	640
Matsushita Electronic Components	Electronic Components	251
Matsushita Electronic Magnetrons	Electronic Components	40

Work Organisation and the Labour Process

Most of the transplants organised their production on the principle of continuous flow assembly lines involving repetitive and monotonous task routines. These lines would be automated where batch size or standardised components made this feasible, otherwise, production relied principally upon labour-intensive manual work. The nature of the labour processes in the different transplants will now be examined, sector by sector.

Autocomponents

Calsonic is the only wholly Japanese-owned subsidiary operating in the auto sector in South Wales. The factory manufactures different types of heat exchanger units with a customer base spread across the European vehicle assembly industry. Unlike the other transplants in the survey, Calsonic is not a classic Japanese greenfield operation. Its Llanelli factory was formerly an old British Leyland/Rover plant which underwent a management–employee buy-out in advance of the Rover privatisation in 1988. The Calsonic Group subsequently purchased the plant in 1989. However, despite this brownfield status – and the legacy of shop-floor control over the labour process which accompanied it – the combination of competitive market pressures and the emergence of a more compliant trade union organisation[3] weakened by almost continual threats of redundancy since 1988, facilitated a significant restructuring of work organisation involving the implementation of just-in-time production control techniques and teamworking.

Looked at purely in technological terms of 'efficiency' and 'flexibility', this restructuring could be described as the substitution of continuous flow, cellular production for the more inflexible, dedicated machine layouts associated with conventional Fordist techniques. The Calsonic management inherited an orthodox form of work organisation based on the separation of machines and work stations into discrete functional areas or 'clusters' (Schonberger, 1986). Gradually, cell-based teamworking replaced this arrangement allowing different machines and tasks to be grouped together by product family rather than single function. The different teamworkers also became more personally responsible for the quality of their work and more responsive to the just-in-time supply requirements of the customer.

However, these changes also had a major political dimension. Rather than introduce quixotic notions of 'ownership', 'self-management', or, as one writer has put it, 'the creation of little factories within a factory' (Turnbull, 1986:203), the reorganisation was aimed primarily at intensifying work rates and reimposing managerial prerogatives. In particular, it resulted in the rationalisation of jobs, the removal of both formal and informal job demarcations and the dismantling of those production buffers which gave operators occasional breaks from the incessant intensity of production. Using classic work measurement techniques, teams of industrial engineers set about reorganising work stations, reducing the number of non-profitable process tasks, removing waiting times in stores and transit, removing factory floor pallet areas for temporary work-station storage and removing the stores themselves. What appears, ostensibly, as a series of quite mundane organisational changes had more profound implications for shop-floor operators. One shop-floor manager commented:

> Our style of working on the shop floor has undergone quite a radical change as a result of all this. We've virtually got rid of all the old buffers which literally used to pile up shoulder high at every work station. No longer do our operators work stop–go, stop–go, sometimes going flat out, sometimes taking a rest. It's now bell-to-bell, steady, continuous working – with the machines and technology driving the men rather than the other way around. It might not sound like much of a change but it's a big change for us I can assure you.

The introduction of teamworking did little to enrich the operators' work. During the processes of assembling, clinching and brazing the different metal rods, tubes and gills that comprise a radiator assembly, operators in the labour-intensive manual areas might rotate from one narrow task to another. But their work remained essentially fragmented and low-skilled.

The factory also contained high volume automated areas, where assembly and brazing operations were performed by dedicated robotic-based technology. In these areas, although the different teams of operators enjoyed higher status because they were employed on 'state of the art' technology, they also suffered deskilling. In effect, they were converted into unskilled 'line feeders' (Jurgens *et al.*, 1993) with the sole responsibility of loading materials and parts into machine silos, magazines and fixtures.

This segmentation of production tasks had a significant gender dimension. A rationalisation of jobs in the labour-intensive production teams resulted in many women leaving the factory over recent years. At the same time, operators working in the automated areas enjoyed relative job security. The fact that the latter were all men was no coincidence. Stereotypical assumptions concerning 'natural' men's and women's skills contributed to a gradual gendering of the work process (Cockburn, 1985). The management at this plant, like many interviewed elsewhere, believed unquestioningly that women in manufacturing were only suitable for light, repetitive assembly work. Anything beyond this constituted entryism into traditional male territory.

Consumer electronics

A similar dichotomy between capital intensive, automated component insertion and labour intensive manual assembly characterised the organisation of production in the large electronic assembly transplants. The technological logic of this has been described in some detail by Taylor *et al.* (1991 & 1994) and Delbridge (1995). Without exception, predominantly male operators were deployed in the automated areas, feeding and monitoring computerised component insert equipment used for mounting standardised electronic components into printed circuit boards. Female operators were then employed along conventional assembly lines for the more numerous and complex manual assembly operations which go into the manufacture of domestic videos, TVs and the like.

Whilst patriarchal assumptions governing distinctions between 'men's work' and 'women's work' informed the division of labour, this was not the only factor. The mass exploitation of large pools of low-waged female labour from the ex-mining communities of South Wales provided major advantages to these different capitals in terms of minimising wage costs and enlarging surplus value.[4] Matsushita Electric apart, where union organisation was relatively strong and occasionally militant, most of the electronics plants in the survey participated in informal wage-setting arrangements.[5] As a result, most women employed as bottom grade assembly line workers earned a 'going rate' of around £140 per week gross compared to the £155–£170 plus shift premia received by their higher graded male colleagues.

In the automated areas, although the technology itself was complex, the male operators were again effectively reduced to little more than line feeders. Their daily tasks comprised loading basic printed circuit boards, component ribbons and cassettes to machines; multi-machine minding; picking up and reloading dropped components; and feeding off finished work. Equipment breakdowns were the responsibility of skilled maintenance teams or local contractors. The work was both monotonous and degrading.

The same adjectives can be used to describe work in the main manual areas except that this was also marked by its exceptional speed and intensity. The basic labour processes were no different from those encountered in Cavendish's (1982) ethnography of life on an assembly line. Operators sitting at discrete positions along a conventional production line carried out a small number of repetitive manual operations at rapid speed. Whether the task was component insertion, dry joint probing, mechanical assembly, final packaging, or whatever, the basic skills were the same: rapid component handling and perfect hand co-ordination.

Many operators appeared to the observer as highly charged automatons. At Matsushita Electric in Cardiff for example, experienced component inserters were expected to complete their operations on ten boards per minute. Most cycles comprised fitting eight components to a board. Thus, most of these operators were fitting eighty components per minute, more than one per second. The key difference between the labour process in these plants and traditional British practice – as outlined by Cavendish for example – is that bell-to-bell working means what it implies. The process allows no potential for creating individual buffers and informal breaks; talking on the line is a disciplinary issue; all tasks are value-added only so that extras, such as stopping work in order to change a component box, are allocated to line side feeders; and operators enjoy no short breaks during machine downtime – they immediately move on to alternative lines. Workers are expected to squeeze sixty minutes' labour power into every hour. As a shop steward complained:

> ... if the targets are constantly missed then the operative is taken to the desk. You get warnings from your supervisor and you're told that, 'you're too busy talking' or 'you're looking around you too much and not concentrating'. But sackings are rare. Ninety-five per cent of the poor performers are transferred to an easier department if there is such a bloody thing. So, the system is if you're caught talking and dreaming you're generally given a first formal warning and then you're moved. It's harsh isn't it? Some of the departments on the shop floor work under tremendous pressure. On the insertion lines and the control block lines you just haven't got time to blink.

Electronic components

The organisation of work in this sector followed no set pattern, although, like all other transplants in the survey, these Japanese electronic component suppliers displayed an invariable work intensity and sense of discipline on the shop floor.

The diversity of job design and manufacturing technique was a function of quite different product and process technologies and specific market characteristics and traditions. At Gooding Sanken's new Welsh Development Agency greenfield site, for example, the shop floor was again divided into automated component insertion and manual assembly areas. Here, however, fixed workbenches arranged as long assembly lines but without expensive conveyor-belt technology, sufficed for the plant's low volume market requirements. The operators' labour processes again comprised repetitive manual assembly tasks whilst the intensity of work was dictated by fixed cycle times and tightly policed by shop-floor supervisors. Distractions from the task in hand, such as talking to workmates on the line, were a common occasion for reprimand and disciplinary threat.

By comparison, both Yuasa Batteries and Matsushita Electronic Magnetrons exploited more capital-intensive work processes. Since it was established in 1982, successive investments in automated process technology enabled Yuasa Batteries to manufacture around five million sealed lead acid batteries of different designs each year. Although this technology furnished the plant's thirty in-house maintenance staff with a number of new skills, the 450 process operators employed on the shop floor were again reduced to mere machine feeders and minders. Indeed, the minimal skills required here allowed the company to recruit most of its workforce straight from local secondary schools.

Similarly, Matsushita's Electronic Magnetrons Cwmbran plant presented itself as a hi-tech 'factory of the future' on the basis of its total automation and integration of the manufacturing process. The factory employed just nineteen direct operators who each day produced 7500 magnetrons for the domestic microwave industry. The operators' labour processes were organised around five robotic work stations located along one line and each linked by a sophisticated enclosed conveyor system. Put crudely, operators fed the required materials and components onto conveyors at each work station; robotic equipment performed different press, clench and assembly operations; and on this cumulative assembly basis, every minute, twenty completed magnetrons appeared at the other end of the factory, ready for despatch.

Maintaining the same inverse relationship between automated production technology and operator skill observed elsewhere, the work was rudimentary, sometimes intense, but always demanding in the sense that workers had to survive a monotonous and lifeless working day, week in, week out. Japanese managerial efficiency, combined with the exploitation of sophisticated new technology of a type that would enthral our contemporary business writers, had created a degrading, no-skill labour process. As one manager put it when questioned on labour flexibility:

In fact, we rotate our operatives every one to two hours. This is not a requirement of the production process, it's purely for 'job enrichment'. The problem here is that the work is very boring on the line and if we leave an operative at a single work station for more than a couple of hours then the work becomes so monotonous that mistakes can be made. In truth, without being disrespectful, we could train monkeys to do these jobs. The only skill involved is the use of a bit of aptitude when things go wrong.

The chapter's remaining sections investigate particular management practices which govern the intensity of production, the deployment of labour and worker participation. However, the significant preliminary point to emerge from the analysis thus far is that the basic shop-floor labour processes in these South Wales manufacturing transplants were not 'enriched' by the implementation of some novel Japanese work organisational paradigm. Without exception, production operators were employed on a variety of low-skill, monotonous and repetitive tasks in the interests of efficient capital accumulation.[6]

Lean Production Control

Although the processes of just-in-time production control (JIT) are rarely researched in any empirical depth, the concept remains central to managerialist presentations of efficient, waste-free Japanese production practice. Schonberger (1982) places JIT at the heart of Japanese production management and defines it idealistically as an inventory control system where work and materials are constantly on the move, 'a sort of hand to mouth mode of operation characterised by stockless production'. Oliver and Wilkinson (1992) expand upon this by describing JIT as a waste minimising system which seeks to match production exactly to market demand. They go on to denote three conditions necessary for its operation: swift machine set-up times; simple unidirectional material flow; and the implementation of TQM practices. On the basis of their quantitative analysis of recent developments in the UK, these authors argue that JIT is now becoming common practice in manufacturing firms.

To what extent is JIT established in the Japanese transplants of South Wales? The real picture is more complex than the above analyses would suggest. Only four out of the fifteen firms surveyed claimed to use a JIT system. And surprisingly, this small number did not seem to be a function of any constraint in specific industrial sectors. Of the four, one JIT company operated in the autocomponents sector, two were in consumer electronics and one in plastics.

However, this does not mean that the remaining companies conformed to the opposing – and sometimes inaccurate – 'Fordist', 'just in case', high buffer, ideal type. Many fell somewhere in between, following lean production strategies based on strict manning levels and a constant scrutiny of both work in progress and stock.

Looking firstly at the JIT companies, both Sony and AIWA claimed to operate pure JIT systems, an unusual achievement for UK-based consumer electronics assemblers since a large proportion of the high value-added electronic components are imported from the Far East. Over a period of twenty years Sony developed its 'global localisation' strategy resulting in a fully integrated TV production plant at Bridgend. Key assemblies such as cathode ray tubes were manufactured in-house whilst, reportedly, 90 per cent of other components were supplied 'locally', that is, from the UK and other EU countries. This complex network of suppliers delivered materials and components to the factory every two hours on average, some direct, some via local warehouses. The AIWA plant at Newport operated a more imperfect form of JIT since many of its electronic components were imported from the Far East. However, the company claimed to maintain close control over order schedules from its foreign suppliers – including detailed procedures for monitoring all supplier transport containers – to the extent that weekly shipments were possible, with daily supplies received just-in-time via port-based warehouses.

Calsonic's production control system was designed to supply the JIT requirements of Rover-Honda, Nissan and other prominent vehicle assemblers. The management at this ex-Rover plant described their system as far more stressed and tightly controlled than previous practice. In earlier times, the plant would receive a weekly order for a supply of radiator assemblies which was rarely subsequently refined in terms of daily despatch requirements. Orders were received over the phone and casually adjusted by the same method if necessary. This loose form of control, along with large-batch production and the prevalence of buffers on the shop floor, created a relatively relaxed system of co-ordinating supply with customer demand.

Under the new regime, the systematic reduction of buffers and machine set-up times facilitated smaller batch sizes and a more precise JIT supply and delivery system. Calsonic's main customers provided fairly accurate monthly estimates of supply requirements and from these, bi-weekly and weekly forecasts were generated. Through interaction with the customer on Electronic Data Interchange, production planners were able to use these forecasts to issue daily shift production plans which incorporated any final day-to-day adjustments. From these, the planners established tightly controlled product despatch timetables, involving normally three despatches per day to each customer at different fixed times.

These critical despatch schedules intensified the stress of mass production on the Calsonic shop floor. The system exerted a continual disciplinary pressure on the teams and shifts responsible for meeting the customer's quality and quantity requirements on time. Any team of operators failing to meet these requirements was expected to work on until such problems were resolved. If the deadline was still missed then Calsonic was forced to deliver free of charge to the affected customer. Consistent failures placed contracts and jobs in jeopardy. And we are not talking about one deadline but a whole series of routine deadlines for each customer, each day.

Although the majority of firms surveyed did not operate such closely controlled JIT systems, they did attempt to tighten their production schedules and reduce work in progress and stock levels. For those transplants locked into long-term, 'co-operative' supply relationships with the JIT assemblers, these objectives could be undermined by the ability of the latter to pass their costs down the supply chain. A number of managers spoke bitterly of this. One said:

> No, this company does not operate JIT. And exactly what is JIT may I ask? Who can define it, can you? I certainly can't. I believe the concept of JIT is an idea that has been blown up out of all proportion by the media and you academics. And it's all very well for the big final assemblers such as those in the auto industry to claim to work a JIT system, which they might well do, I don't know. But in fact, all they are doing is pushing their stock holdings down the supplier chain. And it's logistically impossible for all these suppliers to themselves run a JIT system. So at some early stage, one level of suppliers will have to pick up the bill by holding excessive levels of stocks.

This point certainly resonates with the experience of one supplier to Sony:

> I don't know what system Sony operates. All I know is that their order schedules are unplanned and chaotic. We can't do anything else other than keep good stock levels with which to supply them.

Notwithstanding these countervailing pressures, most of the Japanese transplants still attempted to regulate their production costs by maintaining leaner production control measures. Every firm operated a system for generating monthly, weekly, sometimes daily estimates of likely sales demand. This was often accompanied by procedures which secured management accountability for work in progress and stock levels.

The ramifications of these control measures can be profound on the shop floor. For the production operator, 'minimal human and material waste' in the form of low stock and low buffers, translates into no break or respite from the continuous grind of mass production. Indeed, lean production control, whether in the form of JIT or more prosaic forms of reducing inventory costs, constitutes a critical component in management's repertoire of measures which aim to close up the pores of the working day. This is one of the more 'mundane' factors which characterise labour regulation within Japanese transplants. One example is the simple practice of bell-to-bell working. One ex-British Steel shop steward remarked on this: 'I must admit, coming from British Steel I was astounded by it at first. What it boils down to is that in a Japanese plant your life is controlled by a buzzer.'

Few analyses of Japanese working practices dwell to any extent on the discipline of bell-to-bell working. Yet the manner in which this is imposed on transplant workforces makes it one of the more obvious manifestations of the Japanese obsession with reducing idle time and squeezing out sixty minutes of useful work from every worker in every hour.

Every one of the firms in the survey practised this down to the letter, using bells or sirens to announce the beginning and end of each break. Typically, workers were granted two ten-minute tea breaks and one half-hour lunch break each day. Observations at a number of plants during break periods highlighted exactly how precious these few minutes were. If the Japanese managements wanted their sixty minutes of work every hour, then similarly, operators were forced to scramble around to ensure that ten minutes eating, smoking and resting time could be extracted from every break. A number of times, at the moment when the break bell rang, affected groups of operators would immediately drop tools and race each other to the canteen, as if in a 100-metres Olympic final. This appeared to the observer as a kind of 'McDonaldised' break system taken to extremes (Ritzer, 1993).

Operators who did not report back to their work stations at the end-of-break bell, or who did not seek permission to visit the toilet during work periods, would be immediately subject to the disciplinary procedure. But some managers were not even satisfied with this. At Matsushita Electric, for example, until 1990, two sirens would be sounded for starting work. The first came three minutes early as a warning. Workers were supposed to return to their work stations in preparation for the second siren. But more often than not, they would cram a final coffee or cigarette into the last three minutes and race to their work stations thirty seconds before the second siren – much to the resentment of Matsushita. During the Cardiff plant's 1990 pay negotiations, management refused to offer its shop floor a pay rise unless operators agreed to report to work stations, and be ready to commence work with tools in hand, immediately upon hearing the first siren. With bitterness, the workforce was forced to donate to the company three minutes break time, that is, nine minutes a day, forty-five minutes a week, in order to receive a cost of living wage increase. It is this order of 'attention to detail' which tends to separate the Japanese from many British manufacturers.

Labour Utilisation and the New Working Practices

The survey investigated the transplants' use of those new working practices which seek a more efficient utilization of labour on the shop floor; practices such as teamworking and other labour flexibility measures. The survey results are summarised in Table 3.2.

Teamworking and labour flexibility

The concept of Japanese-style teamworking suffers from a distinct lack of clarity in definition. One of its pioneers has described the practice as the cellular organisation of labour and machinery in accordance with continuous flow principles. Here, machines are grouped by product family rather than function and each team member is required to operate the different machines in turn, moving items through a processing sequence, one piece at a time (Toyota Motor Corporation, 1992). Some writers have taken a more prosaic view, reducing this idealised craft-based version to one of mere multi-machine minding (Monden, 1983) whilst others have complicated things further by arguing that single process-based cells are also operable and may be used where large machines dedicated to particular functions are common, such as in a press shop (Alford, 1994).

Table 3.2   Use of new working practices (N = 11)

Practice	Number of companies where used (N)	Percentage of companies where used (%)
Teamworking	5	45
Customer philosophy	9	82
Flexible working, in principle	8	73
Job rotation	6	55
Use of floats	9	82
Operators' involvement in job design	0	0
Operators responsible for SPC	1	9

If the precise format of the typical team organisation is unclear, at least most managerialist writers agree on its purpose. That is, teamworking simplifies factory material flow and minimises manning levels; and, on an ideological level, it mobilises a sense of 'ownership', autonomy and business orientation amongst team members (Oliver and Wilkinson, 1992). Moreover, on the basis of primarily quantitative data analysis, many such writers also agree that teamworking has become a prevalent facet of work organisation within both Japanese and British firms in the UK (for example, IRS, 1990; Oliver and Wilkinson, 1992).

Unfortunately, what is missing from this type of discussion is a sense of shop-floor politics. Teamworking is constructed as a mechanism of workplace efficiency or as a mode of work organisation which may be of mere 'technical interest'. The idea that it could represent a significant managerial instrument of labour regulation which critically undermines traditional shop-floor controls over the labour process tends to get glossed over.

How have the Japanese exploited teamworking in their South Wales transplants? In fact, as Table 3.2 shows, less than half of the firms surveyed operated teamworking as a distinctive form of work organisation. Furthermore, only Calsonic, in the auto sector, organised production into ideal typical cells.

At this factory, small teams consisting of between six and twelve operators were given the responsibility of producing families of car radiator assemblies for specific customers. Each team had its own leader, an elite operator who represented the 'totally flexible worker'. The team leader was responsible for such matters as the multi-task development of all team members, labour deployment and team performance. The latter was also monitored openly by the use of a combination of digital and manual display boards showing production targets; production performance; defect levels; individual operator's task proficiencies; and, under the heading of 'team morale', individual absenteeism records.

Case study analysis would be needed to establish the extent to which teamworking in this plant changed worker attitudes. But on the basis of the survey investigations there was little evidence of self-management or 'worker empowerment'. The company maintained strict lines of accountability from teamworker to teamleader to foreman to production manager; orders were received from supervision and expected to be strictly obeyed.

Nevertheless, it is ironical that this pre-war, multi-union site managed to organise a more fundamental restructuring of work organisation than most of the greenfield Japanese plants in the survey. In fact, the crucial difference here is that much modular assembly work in the auto industry actually lends itself to a team-based organisation rather than a conventional assembly line; and more importantly, competitive pressures within this sector are ensuring that established companies introduce the practice as a low-manning, labour-intensifying measure by purging the shop floor of its traditional labour demarcations and controls.

In contrast, the greenfield transplants in the electronics sector had no legacies of shop floor control to contend with. These companies continued to exploit rigidly fragmented labour processes organised along single, straight assembly lines in accordance with the traditions of this sector. Their teams merely constituted the total number of operators on the line, which could sometimes extend to above fifty workers. Again, their purpose was not to facilitate 'total flexibility' or 'self-management'. 'Teamworking' was a euphemism for the creation of organised units that could be held accountable for line output and defect performance. As a manager in one of the larger plants explained:

> We operate an informal team structure which might change even on a daily basis, but these teams are not organised for the purpose of teamworking, more for ease of communications and to provide a line of accountability to the team or line leader. The team might consist of around ten operatives and each will be co-ordinated by line leaders who really take up the role of the traditional charge hands.

A majority of the firms surveyed, whether using team organisation or not, were attempting to enlist their employees into a 'customer ethos' to ensure that individual operators meet the needs of downstream 'customers' (Delbridge *et al.*, 1992). For example, a personnel manager at one company stated:

> Every one of our operatives is supposed to regard other operatives upstream or downstream of the line as customers. And his downstream customers are expected

to, and will, create a fuss if the work they receive is not up to scratch. We've always supported this explicit customer philosophy promoting the 'individual as customer' idea. Not only will operatives complain to each other about any colleague's poor work but they also register complaints, sometimes bitter complaints, with the Company Advisory Board.

This, of course, was a new workplace individualism presented from management's standpoint. In fact, the needs of the external customer *were* consistently brought to the attention of shop-floor operators through continual quality campaigns, communications meetings and kaizen. It is likely that workers did have a greater sense of responsibility to the customer and the market. But this customer awareness did not necessarily extend to social relations between workmates. For example, when quizzed about the 'block assurance' customer/supplier system supposedly operating at their plant, two stewards at Matsushita Electric commented:

> No way! How can we check our own work let alone other people's work? We haven't got any time. And the idea that you could give your own people a telling off for bad quality! You're joking! We're all on the same grade on the shop floor, we're all the same. If I were to turn round and give my mate a bollocking he'll just look at me and say 'fuck off, who do you think you are?'

And on the idea of 'ownership'?:

> Ownership of work? You've got to challenge this terminology strongly. What's it supposed to mean? You only have the bloody unit in front of you for two seconds. So how are you supposed to own it?

There was no evidence, then, that the organisation of workers into teams, in whatever form, acted to enrich the labour process. Even the practice of multi-tasking was confined to narrow limits. In line with many other inward investors in the UK, the Japanese transplants were more concerned to incorporate total labour flexibility into their employment contracts than to put this principle into practice (Peck and Stone, 1992; Morris *et al.*, 1994). Although three-quarters of the firms had full flexibility agreements with their trade unions, only half operated any form of job rotation and in most of these firms this practice was used solely to cover for absenteeism. For many operators, life on the line meant staying at the same position day-in day-out performing similar task routines.

When quizzed about the enriching potential of job flexibility and rotation, many managers expressed a candid cynicism. One commented:

> I believe that this idea of continual movement between tasks to enrich the work process is frankly a lot of bullshit. Most workers prefer to stay in the same spot most of the time. They prefer one continuous boring routine to a number of continuous boring routines. And most of all they prefer working with the same people.

Indeed, a similar view was expressed by a GMB shop steward:

> The GMB agreement is that there's no demarcation whatsoever on the shop floor.
> But in practice operatives do tend to stay on the spot doing the same job. The most
> common reason for moving around is when you're covering for absenteeism. It's not
> done for flexibility's sake. If you've got people absent from a busy line then the
> supervisors will throw other operatives on. Many of our people don't like it mind,
> especially the older ones. When people have been doing the same job all their lives
> they get used to it. They regard the job as their job, it sort of belongs to them. So they
> hate being moved off it.

For most of these transplants, full functional flexibility and productive
efficiency did not go hand in hand. Although many of the firms did employ
'floats' – elite operators who performed any task upon request in order to cover
for sudden surges in demand for particular product lines, line balancing
problems and absenteeism – in most cases these constituted less than 10 per
cent of the shop-floor workforce. Maximising output and minimising waste
formed the driving logic behind continuous, lean production. Concepts such
as 'enrichment' and 'empowerment' just did not come into the equation.
Production supervisors were held accountable for line performance and they
knew from experience that they could extract more output from groups of
operators performing the same daily tasks than from others who were
continually switching lines.

Placing full flexibility into labour contracts therefore served two purposes.
Firstly, it provided management sufficient flexibility in labour deployment to
allow for absenteeism and fluctuations in product demand. Secondly, it
legitimised the imposition of managerial prerogatives; and it suppressed the
emergence of rank and file controls over the labour process in the form of skill
and job demarcations, regulation of effort rates, and so on. And these principles
of management-controlled flexibility were not negotiable. One shop steward
reflected on the activities of an unsuspecting young manager recently recruited
at Matsushita Electric:

> He's an unusual character for this place. He actually went around the lines talking
> to the girls about their work and discovered that they were all bored stiff. He even
> asked me my opinion. And I told him that there's a large number of youngsters here
> who get bored easily and some of them might appreciate flexibility more than the
> older ones. But the supervisors are all completely anti-flexibility. They've got their
> efficient lines and they want to keep them. So this manager drew up a plan. But the
> management aren't going to allow it to happen. Rotation will affect efficiency and
> rejects. This guy's new so he's got a lot to learn. But the best of luck to him. He'll
> need it in this place.

Job design

The Japanese work organisational paradigm is supposed to provide some
space for direct production workers to participate in job design through such

activities as statistical process control (SPC) and kaizen. However, not much evidence of this could be detected amongst the Japanese transplants in South Wales. The limited worker involvement in kaizen is discussed in the next section. As far as monitoring and adjusting production line work through SPC is concerned, only two companies in the survey ever involved their operators in this. And one of these, Calsonic, was recently forced to cancel its SPC programmes due to worker apathy.

The role of the industrial engineer in these factories provides a more constructive indicator of real worker involvement in job design. To what extent had the work of these engineers altered or even become redundant in the supposedly 'democratic', 'post-Taylorist' Japanese transplants? The answer was very little at all. At all of the larger plants, teams of industrial engineers were employed to carry out routine work measurement utilising traditional time and motion studies. These were used in customary fashion for setting targets, for line balancing and for cost and benefit analysis. At AIWA for example, one engineer was employed for every thirty operatives.

In fact, for most of these firms, it takes some imagination to envisage how matters could be any different once production tasks had become so fragmented and shaped by the exigencies of the continuous flow production lines. However, the irony here was the extent to which some of these Japanese managements resolutely rejected *any* worker input into job design. For example, one personnel manager stated firmly that:

> Company procedures govern the way we organise work. Indeed, the company highly disapproves of the idea of allowing workers to change methods by themselves, this practice is just not accepted. All operatives must comply with the company procedures.

And another:

> The idea of workers designing their own jobs is frowned upon. Individual innovation with regard to work design is most certainly not the company philosophy here. It's our Japanese managers who are responsible for establishing all work procedures.

At Calsonic, teams of industrial engineers formed key personnel in the firm's 'management-led kaizens' in which managers and engineers, rather than operators, designed and implemented major adjustments to work organisation. Conventional time and motion techniques were applied here. In a recent and typical exercise examined in some detail by the author, the engineers attacked production line buffers in one area by reducing non value-added process steps from sixty six to thirty-seven operations; manning levels decreased from eighty to seventy-four operatives; and 'drumbeat' production throughput increased from 2.35 units to 2.8 units per man hour.

Such productivity improvements were clearly a function of both improved capital and labour utilisation and labour intensification. And as practical exercises in the systematic increase in the rate of extraction of relative surplus value, they will always run counter to the interests of shop-floor operators. However, the fundamental difference between this industrial engineering process and traditional British practice is that the former is not subject to trade union control or influence. Not one transplant sanctioned any trade union input over the setting of standards or work reorganisation. One shop steward stated:

> They stand over the operative for half an hour, or an hour maybe, timing the job and then they make a calculation for the whole eight hours. But it's a different ball game when you're knackering yourself trying to keep to these standards for eight hours a day.
>
> I just find it all extraordinary here. I mean, it's impractical. You go flat out for one hour, you can't help it when you're being watched, when there's someone looking at you, right over your shoulder all the time. And then they expect you to keep this up for eight hours a day. They're impossible targets most of them.

And trade union influence?

> At British Steel, when we had the big time and motion studies, the shop stewards always participated to make sure the whole thing was fair and above board. And the management would always ask our permission first! But here the whole thing is indiscriminate. Ask our permission my arse! The time and motion people just suddenly appear and we're not even allowed to watch them. Okay, we might complain about a target here and there but you never get anywhere. The company never allows us to see the records and measurements.

The targets established by these studies were rarely employed in conjunction with individual bonus systems. They were used to establish line performance targets and to facilitate line balancing. But they offered more than this. The untrammelled process of industrial engineering could sometimes be effectively exploited to assert management control in both a highly symbolic and absolute fashion. The same steward again:

> But it's strange, weird really. They know full well we can't reach some of these targets. It's just stupid. They seem to take more satisfaction in the work study findings, in the actual work measuring than they do in us reaching their impossible targets. They just like the watching. There's nothing worse than having someone standing over your shoulders all the time knowing they're watching your every move.

Total Quality Management Practices

The principles of Total Quality Management (TQM) place considerable emphasis on enlarging employees' responsibilities, reorganising work and increasing employees' involvement in problem-solving activities (Geary, 1994:643). The management literature stresses that the central TQM objective here is meeting the customer's needs through the continuous improvement of both product and process quality.

The extent of the use of TQM practices in the transplants is summarised in Tables 3.3 and 3.4. This section will focus upon kaizens and quality circles.

Table 3.3   Use of different quality improvement practices (N = 11)

Quality improvement practice	Number of firms where used	Percentage of firms where used
Kaizen	4	36
Quality Circles	3	27
Kaizen/QC Conferences	2	18
Suggestion Schemes	3	27

Table 3.4   Companies using kaizens and quality circles: organised times and participation rates

Company	Kaizen/QCs held in company time	Kaizen/QCs held in workers' time	Participation rates
Calsonic	Yes	Yes	40%
AIWA	No	Yes	Majority
Matsushita Electric	Yes	No	Supervision only
Sony	No	Yes	Majority
Hitachi	Yes	No	Figs unavailable
Electronic Harnesses	Yes	No	Supervision only
Matsushita EC	Yes	No	Supervision only

The terms kaizen and quality circle were often used interchangeably by the different management interviewees. Kaizen is both a philosophy and a specific concrete practice for involving workers in quality matters. As a philosophy, it stresses a new pro-enterprise attitude based on a management–labour consensus of general support for continuous improvement at the workplace and, in particular, for the development of a consistent process-oriented way of thinking (Imai, 1986). In practical terms, this may mean involving the whole workforce in small-group activity which seeks gradual improvements to the efficient operation of different production processes. Similarly, quality circles also involve small groups of employees, normally led by a team leader or supervisor, in discussions on how to resolve work-related problems (Geary, 1994). Thus, as far as the institutional mechanisms of continuous improvement are concerned, the kaizen group is little different from the quality circle.

Kaizen and quality circles are also mechanisms of labour exploitation. Under the cloak of a benign 'one team' ideology, workers become involved in securing for their employer higher levels of capital and labour utilisation, reductions in idle time, an intensification of their labour and a more sophisticated form of worker subordination. They do this by apparently offering to management knowledge of those facets of individual tacit skills and customary practice which provide workers with the means to exert some control over the labour process. Therefore, kaizen and quality circles act to convert rank and file control into management control: 'the company has an ambiguous, but inescapable, relation to worker know-how; it is at once a threat to the company, for it can lead to worker-control-in-work, but when rendered generalisable through the imperative that everything belongs to the company, it becomes a boost to the enterprise' (Garrahan and Stewart, 1992:76).

Although the outcome of such a system might still reproduce a classic separation of conception and execution of tasks – since 'kaizened' production work remains highly fragmented and repetitive – the process of worker participation may, nevertheless, represent a marked shift from Taylorism, since workers themselves are acting as 'little industrial engineers'. To what extent then, did the workers in the Japanese transplants in South Wales participate in their own exploitation in post-Taylorist fashion?

As Table 3.3 shows, nearly two-thirds of the Japanese firms ran some form of continuous improvement group although only two of these operated the full structure of local groups reporting to factory level conventions. Most just met at the shop level, regularly reporting their deliberations to lower management. However, Table 3.4 indicates a less impressive picture. Participation rates were variable to say the least, with nearly half of these firms restricting kaizen activity to supervision only. Two firms, Matsushita Electric and Yuasa Batteries, originally organised plant-wide groups but these were eventually disbanded due to a lack of interest on the shop floor. A third, Electronic Harnesses, put a stop to full participation because of management fears that employees were straying beyond their self-exploitative remit. One manager stated:

> Our Japanese management felt that too much of the group discussion was directed towards wider issues such as production engineering and working practices, and wider corporate issues such as pay or management. Insufficient time was spent on quality issues, improving product quality, in other words real continuous improvement. The management felt that these groups should be discussing quality and nothing else.

Nevertheless, full kaizen activity was operational in at least some of the larger manufacturers. Calsonic, in the auto sector, was one of the more dynamic of these.

Calsonic operated kaizens at two levels. Management-led kaizens dominated by senior managers and engineers were responsible for all substantial work reorganisation. An example of this activity was outlined in the 'job design' section above. At a lower level, the company organised forty kaizen groups, each comprising between four and eight members, to discuss small-scale continuous improvements. These worker kaizens were controlled by management-appointed facilitators. They were responsible for monitoring and shaping the three key stages of the kaizen process: brainstorming, data analysis and adoption.

Brainstorming is consultancy-speak for problem identifying which was described as the freewheeling of ideas, 'encouraging people to come up with ideas from the top of their heads whilst under a state of enlightenment'.[7] But for some, this state of enlightenment too often drifted into disenchantment. As one manager stated: 'The operatives have taken to brainstorming of sorts but most kaizens I've attended, and that's quite a few, have tended to generate into slanging matches which tend to put people under pressure.'

Once ideas were 'thrown up into the air' and recorded, each group went through a 'democratic' voting process to prioritise the most practical suggestions. The groups met in company time but once suggested improvements were prioritised members were expected to work in their own time to collect and analyse data and to formulate counter-measures to each problem. The maintenance of strict documentary procedures allowed management to monitor the process at all times. The end results of this kaizen activity would be presented to senior management and if approved, implemented and proceduralised.

Does such worker behaviour represent a break from Taylorism? None of the kaizen groups in any firm in the survey was involved in fundamental aspects of work design. At Calsonic for example, the worker kaizens produced incremental improvements in matters such as component rejects and small process hold ups, but this did not represent essential industrial engineering work. And although Graham (1994) describes a process by which American operators working in a Japanese auto transplant come to perform time and motion studies on their fellow workers after being trained in the techniques of industrial engineering, there was little evidence of such activity in South Wales. In one instance, where an enterprising worker attempted this at Calsonic, his colleagues reacted with a predictable sense of shop-floor solidarity. A shop-floor manager:

> Sometimes there's been more opposition from the shop floor. It's still the case that only 40 per cent participate in the groups but we've also had more specific problems. For example, during one kaizen exercise an operative got out a stop watch and timed the activities of his colleagues. If an industrial engineer had done this there would not have been a problem but because he was an operative it caused an outrage. He was sent to Coventry by the whole of the shop floor and as far as I'm aware he still is. However, he's a big lad. He can handle it.

Overall then, the evidence from South Wales suggests that this 'partially autonomous form of worker participation' represents less the reversal of the Taylorist emphasis upon the specialist engineer (Wood, 1989) and more, as Wood himself also admits, strict management supervision of limited worker involvement in perfecting task routines after which workers are 'returned to Taylorised jobs' (457). The Japanese manufacturers in the region sometimes differed in their approach to reaching this latter objective. Calsonic, AIWA, Sony and others allowed their workforces a hint of autonomy in the process of proceduralising work routines whilst other firms would sanction no worker input at all. But in all cases, the outcome was the same: fragmented tasks, tightly supervised work routines, minimum waste, and maximum levels of output from a minimum number of low-paid workers. Therefore, as Thompson (1989) observes, such mechanisms of employee participation hardly constitute meaningful forms of workplace democracy or job enrichment. Neither do they undermine the processes of direct management control: 'certainly, the delegation to workgroups of some immediate and localised production decisions, such as those on the monitoring of product quality, can happily coexist within managerial structures of directive control' (226).

Conclusion

Two conclusions can be drawn from the foregoing analysis. Firstly, the survey data demonstrate that the Japanese transplants have not installed a distinctive, 'post-Taylorist' work organisational paradigm along the South Wales valleys. Although a number of plants displayed some of the salient features commonly associated with Japanese management practice, not one conformed with the idealised 'Japanese model' which stresses multi-skilled labour processes, just-in-time production, teamworking and employee participation in TQM.

The transplants did not display fundamentally different characteristics from their market competitors because even if their managements were disposed to experiment with different work organisational forms in unfamiliar environmental conditions, intense global market pressures do not provide the necessary space for such innovation. Moreover, the presence of the Japanese in South Wales and elsewhere in the EU is primarily a function of the rising value of the yen, EU market protectionism and advantageous local labour market conditions. The logic of their capital accumulation strategies in these circumstances will always be to efficiently exploit these markets to the full rather than venture into new 'empowering' labour processes and employment relations.

Thus, for many firms involved in mass production, quixotic management innovations are just not appropriate in an environment of intense global competition and cost cutting. In any case, the particular characteristics of different product markets, labour markets and process technologies – and different sectoral market pressures and traditions – will inevitably militate against convergence towards any single management paradigm. For example, global competitive pressures for labour-saving efficiencies in modular assembly production have provided the spur for the introduction of teamworking in many UK auto plants. But the same pressures have not prompted similar work organisational changes in the consumer electronics industry where the high volume manufacture of a relatively narrow range of interrelated equipment designs continues to require simple, labour intensive assembly operations organised along conventional production lines.

However, I am not arguing that the predominantly young workers in these Japanese transplants experience exactly the same employment conditions as previous generations of British manufacturing workers. Some things have changed. In the economic and political environment of footloose capital, de-industrialisation, mass unemployment, weakened trade unions and a pusillanimous left politics, many Japanese inward investors have succeeded in exploiting their greenfield site conditions by suppressing the emergence of rank and file controls over the labour process. Indeed, as Tomaney (1990) has argued, such firms have merely extended and redeveloped existing forms of labour control and efficiency maximisation. And although these changes might constitute 'rather more mundane management priorities than is generally applied by references to Japanisation' (Elger and Smith, 1994:48), the workers on the receiving end of this less fundamental 'management of change' might nevertheless be forgiven for viewing such developments with some trepidation.

This leads to the second conclusion. Labouring under the different types of lean production control practised by the transplants, these workers have become more completely subordinated to the supervisor, to the machine and to the intensified pace of production. Their time spent productively at work stations has been maximised by reducing production line buffers; by reducing stocks and work in progress; by more accurately synchronizing their output with customer demand; and by the strict policing of disciplined bell-to-bell working. Similarly, the strict managerial regulation of labour deployment ensures that shop-floor labour power is more efficiently consumed. The transplant labour processes most certainly varied in accordance with the diverse technical requirements of different production technologies, products and product markets but management's exploitation of labour and skills was more homogeneous. That is, there was no variation in the prohibition of traditional union-controlled job demarcations; or in the maintenance of task fragmentation; or in the narrow enlargement of certain jobs by task accretion – whether through team organisation or management-controlled flexibility on conventional assembly lines.

Moreover, for most transplant workers meaningful personal involvement in the processes of job design and continuous improvement was at best highly restricted. The different transplant managements emphatically denied the possibility of trade union influence over work measurement whilst the limited kaizen-style activities were strictly management-controlled to ensure their focus on raising labour productivity and effort intensification.

Japanese management practice in South Wales was therefore marked by a greater cohesion in its approach to labour regulation and control. To further the efficient extraction of relative surplus value and capital accumulation, the Japanese transplants, as employers of shop-floor operators above all else, are collectively driven by a characteristic ethos of 'management by detail'; that is, a more exact management of such little details as labour utilisation, labour discipline, labour control and labour cost.

References

Alford, H. (1994) 'Cellular Manufacturing: The Development of the Idea and its Application', *New Technology, Work and Employment*, 9:1, 3–18.

Cavendish, R. (1982) *Women on the Line*, London: Routledge and Kegan Paul.

Cockburn, C. (1985) *Machinery of Dominance: Women, Men and Technical Know-How*, London: Pluto Press.

Delbridge, R. (1995) 'Surviving JIT: Control and Resistance in a Japanese Transplant', *Journal of Management Studies*, 32:6, 803–17.

Delbridge, R., Turnbull, P. and Wilkinson, B. (1992) 'Pushing Back the Frontiers: Management Control and Work Intensification under JIT / TQM Factory Regimes', *New Technology, Work and Employment*, 17:2, 97–106.

Elger, T. and Smith, C. (1994) 'Global Japanisation? Convergence and Competition in the Organisation of the Labour Process' in Elger, T. and Smith, C. (eds) *Global Japanisation? The Transnational Transformation of the Labour Process*, London: Routledge.

Garrahan, P. and Stewart, P. (1992) *The Nissan Enigma: Flexibility at Work in a Local Economy*, London: Mansell.

Geary, J. (1994) 'Task Participation: Employees' Participation Enabled or Constrained', in Sisson, K. (ed.) *Personnel Management*, Oxford: Blackwell.

Graham, L. (1994) 'How Does the Japanese Model Transfer to the United States? A View from the Line' in Elger, T. and Smith, C. (eds) *Global Japanisation? The Transnational Transformation of the Labour Process*, London: Routledge.

Graham, L. (1995) *On the Line at Subaru-Isuzu: The Japanese Model and the American Worker*, Ithaca, New York: ILR Press.

Hetherington, P. (1994) 'Earnings of 32pc below poverty line', *Guardian*, 22 November.

Imai, M. (1986) *Kaizen*, New York: Random House.

IRS (1990) 'The Japanese in Britain: Employment Policies and Practice', *Industrial Relations Review Report 470*.

Jurgens, U., Malsch, M. and Dohse, K. (1993) *Breaking From Taylorism: Changing Forms of Work in the Automobile Industry*, Cambridge: Cambridge University Press.

Keep, E. (1991) 'Corporate Training Strategies: The Vital Component?', in Storey, J. (ed.) *New Perspectives on Human Resource Management*, London: Routledge.

Kenney, M. and Florida, R. (1993) *Beyond Mass Production: The Japanese System and its Transfer to the US*, Oxford: Oxford University Press.

Lincoln, J. and Kalleberg, A. (1990) *Culture, Control and Commitment: A study of work organisation and work attitudes in the United States and Japan*, Cambridge: Cambridge University Press.

Monden, Y. (1983) *Toyota Production System*, Georgia: Industrial Engineering and Management Press.

Morris, J., Munday, M. and Wilkinson, B. (1994) *Working for the Japanese: The Economic and Social Consequences of Japanese Investment in Wales*, London: Athlone Press.

Oliver, N. and Wilkinson, B. (1992) *The Japanisation of British Industry*, Oxford: Blackwell.

Pang, K. and Oliver, N. (1988) 'Personnel Strategy in Eleven Japanese Manufacturing Companies in the UK', *Personnel Review*, 17:3, 16–21.

Peck, F. and Stone, I. (1992) *New Inward Investment and the Northern Region Labour Market, Employment Department*, Research Series No.6 (October).

Ritzer, G. (1993) *The McDonaldisation of Society*, California: Pine Forge Press.

Schonberger, R. (1982) *Japanese Manufacturing Techniques*, New York: The Free Press.

Schonberger, R. (1986) *World Class Manufacturing*, New York: The Free Press.

Sewell, G. and Wilkinson, B. (1992) '"Someone to watch over me": Surveillance, Discipline, and the Just-In-Time Labour Process', *Sociology*, 26:2, 271–89.

Taylor, W., Elger, T. and Fairbrother, P. (1991) 'Work Relations in Electronics: What has become of Japanisation in Britain?', paper to the *9th Annual International Labour Process Conference*, UMIST, Manchester.

Taylor, W., Elger, T. and Fairbrother, P. (1994) 'Transplants and Emulators: The Fate of the Japanese Model in British Electronics' in Elger, T. and Smith, C. (eds) *Global Japanisation? The Transnational Transformation of the Labour Process*, London: Routledge.

Thompson, P. (1989) *The Nature of Work, An Introduction to Debates on the Labour Process*, Basingstoke: Macmillan.

Tomaney, J. (1990) 'The Reality of Workplace Flexibility', *Capital and Class*, 40, 31–55.

Toyota Motor Corporation (1992) *The Toyota Production System*, Operations Management Consulting Division: Toyota City.

Turnbull, P. (1986) 'The "Japanisation" of Production and Industrial Relations at Lucas Electrical', *Industrial Relations Journal*, 17:3, 193–206.

Wood, S. (1989) 'The Japanese Management Model – Tacit Skills in Shop Floor Participation', *Work and Occupations*, 16:4, 446–60.

Womack, J.P., Jones, D.T. and Roos, D. (1990) *The Machine that Changed the World: The Triumph of Lean Production*, New York: Rawson Macmillan.

Notes

1   This figure excludes the small number of Japanese firms employing fewer than twenty-five workers.

2   With the partial exception of Sony, these Japanese transplants were primarily manufacturing enterprises producing different consumer goods, components and materials for British and European markets. Perhaps the most striking aspect of their workforce composition was that although the firms employed few design staff – and some used subcontractors for plant maintenance – on average, the number of indirect staff still amounted to 30 per cent of the total workforce. Apart from management and administration, most of the latter comprised shop-floor supervision, industrial engineering and quality control personnel. Thus, just as Lincoln and Kalleberg (1990) noted in their survey of employers' practices in Japan and the US, despite dominant perceptions to the contrary, the 'flat hierarchy' and the principle of multi-skilled direct production workers taking on many of the tasks of redundant indirect employees are not characteristics of Japanese work organisation.

The transplants also employed a relatively high proportion of women employees. Overall, women constitute nearly 50 per cent of all transplant workers in the region although this figure obscures disparities across sectors and occupations. In particular, women are concentrated in the electronics sector where most are employed as bottom-grade production operators.

3   Of the fifteen firms surveyed, fourteen recognised trade unions. Calsonic maintained the multi-union tradition inherited from Rover (recognising the TGWU, TGWU-ACTSS, AEEU and MSF) although it had persuaded the site unions to merge into a single bargaining unit. The remaining thirteen unionised firms operated single union agreements: seven recognised the AEEU, four recognised the GMB and two recognised the TGWU.

4   Wales has the highest percentage of full-time workers earning below 68 per cent of average UK gross weekly earnings – the decency threshold set by the Council of Europe (Hetherington 1994).

5   Some management interviewees described how they compared shop-floor wage rates through participation in local wage surveys and more informal joint-consultation in local employers' associations.

6   The generally rudimentary, low-skill nature of these labour processes is further demonstrated by considering the extent and quality of training required for the operators to perform their work.

In keeping with the view that Japanese firms devote far more resources to training than their British competitors (Keep, 1991; Pang and Oliver, 1988), and assuming that this should represent something more substantial than 'on the job' or brief induction training, each transplant management was asked whether formal NVQ skills training was offered to shop-floor operators. Six of the fifteen firms did provide such training, but with the exception of a small minority of senior operators, this only extended to the most basic NVQ Level 1. Moreover, the absence of NVQ certification from the remaining nine plants was not the result of parsimonious attitudes towards employee training; it merely reflected a more candid appraisal by managers of both requisite operators' skill levels and the dishonest nature of contemporary state-funded youth training.

7   Kaizen Manual, Calsonic Group.

4 Renewal and Tradition in the New Politics of Production

Paul Stewart and Miguel Martinez Lucio

Introduction
Teamworking: Contextualising the New Participation

Organisational sociology and labour process debates on contemporary managerial changes to workplace institutions have tended to view teamworking as either work enhancing or work controlling (Babson, 1995; Waddington and Whitston, 1996). In the first instance we can distinguish approaches to teamworking which see it variously as: a new form of employee representation (Pils and Macduffie 1997); a novel way of organising the production and organisation process (Mueller, 1994); and as directly constituting a new form of employee autonomy (Adler, 1997 and 1998). Moreover, there are also concerns raised about the effects of teamwork and the way it presents us with a new logic of participation and control (Babson, 1995; Lewchuk and Robertson, 1996; Stephenson, 1996). However, there is also a school of thought which argues that we may be overstating developments with respect to discontinuities in this area (Frohlich and Pekruhl, 1995).

Yet it is possible to take another approach which, though drawing upon organisational sociology and labour process debates, focuses more on teamwork in terms of its impact upon structures of worker representation and industrial relations. One account within this framework sees teamwork as presenting workers with a set of opportunities and contradictions within the workplace via novel forms of trade union participation (Bacon and Storey, 1995). They argue that trade unions are inevitably drawn into a new set of workplace issues seen to be crucial in allowing for the development of new and managerialist points of collective representation although this occurs much more on management terms than has been the case in the past. By contrast to this optimistic perspective, Pollert (1996) has cautioned that participation in the guise of teamwork *can* lead to subordination where workers and their unions are incorporated into the managerial framework and marginalised because they are limited to alternative management agendas. However, once again there is evidence that trade unions find new roles within such ambiguous positions and new points of strength (Kelly, 1996; Martinez and Weston, 1992). We suggest that this process of union involvement needs to be located within a new politics of production, encapsulating more than Bacon and Storey's optimism yet less than Pollert's informed scepticism.

The new politics of production have arisen as a result of the advance of new conflicts around sites of struggle hitherto perceived as governed by the convention of separate spheres of interest between the control and regulation of labour relating to terms and conditions of employment on the one hand and labour process concerns on the other. As a consequence of the instability of this traditional bifurcation, issues such as health and safety, gender, ethnicity and age have become important as sites of mobilisation and contestation. The managerial epithet for the new production arrangements is 'lean production', and the immediate impact of this can be traced through its impact upon employee health and safety, changes to job routines and definitions of skill and the organisation of labour both in and away from production. The repercussions are that we are witnessing the objective erosion of the traditional meaning of industrial relations as conceived at plant level, though this is not to say either that erosion will continue or indeed, that there will be no retrenchment into the old management–union spheres of interest (Martinez Lucio and Stewart, 1997).

The significance for the argument we wish to make here is that it becomes important to delineate the ways in which labour modifies the development of central elements of new management practices, especially teamworking – the lynch pin in the social organisation of new production regimes (Adler, 1998; Danford, 1997). Teamworking can initiate a discussion of the *form* of worker representation in the labour process. In addition, it raises the question of labour involvement in matters regarding the *content* of production (tasks, rotation, temporal factors, and even on occasions the production process itself). Our aim is to shift the debate about teamworking away from traditional, Anglo-Saxon understandings of industrial relations and new management practices in such a way as to illustrate the social context of regulation and the political calculations that emerge within these.

There has been a tendency to overstate the role of formal industrial relations institutions as a mediating mechanism in the change process and to view questions of trade unionism and plant-based negotiations from within an overly institutionalist perspective (Ortiz, 1996 and 1998). Whilst recognising that the formal approach highlights the way in which differences at company level contribute to the distinctive configurations in workplace practice and politics, we nevertheless insist that the complexities of social, economic and political processes are rarely explained within this idiom. Our research suggests that the institutions and the historic corpus of worker rights that supposedly mediate management change have to be understood in the context of their mobilisation, development and location within antagonistic management–union discourses. Furthermore, they need to be evaluated in terms of the way social processes raise the question of control within the New Regimes of Subordination in the 'new' workplace.

In this chapter we will therefore outline the emergence of these new political and social issues with regards to a number of new production and employment issues in two General Motors plants (one in the UK and the other in Spain) and end by trying to draw out the implications of this analysis for our understanding of the new politics of the new workplace. Of course, this is not to infer the general from the particular. Rather, our contention is that the cases here illustrate how the process of organisational mediation of new management practices is the outcome of a complex political and antagonistic process which can indeed be seen to be occurring in other countries in the EU today. What is required is a new understanding of the notion of mobilisation and opposition within studies of the labour process in which the social institutions such as teamworking are recognised as central to its success (Carter, 1995; Nichols, 1991; Rowlinson and Hassard, 1994:6)

Contextualising the New Participation: In and Beyond the Workplace

Today, there is an increasing recognition of the broader factors within and beyond the automotive labour process and the sphere of joint regulation that contribute to its differentiated development (see Mueller, 1994). This recognition represents an important departure from the debates of the late 1980s indicating a desire to incorporate factors in the analysis of change and teamwork, the most significant being the role of labour. Jurgens *et al.* (1992) and GERPISA (1996) explicitly point to the impact of systems of worker representation, external regulatory processes, and the overall presence of the state as a key social actor within the areas of training and skill formation. The development of flexibility facilitated by team structures is in great part dependent upon these factors. Yet when we make reference to labour and its diverse strategies including the different forms of regulation in each country, how do we do this in such a way as to account for the diversity of its social and political character? The case of General Motors is important because throughout its European operations it represents a systematic attempt to introduce teamwork throughout a Multi-National Corporation (MNC) operating in very different social and economic environments (GERPISA 1996).[1]

Whilst there is variance in the national experiences of teamworking in terms of politics and industrial relations structures, broader employment patterns are emerging in respect of the form and content of worker representation which clearly counter the pessimism of some researchers. Whereas Ortiz's (1998) work emphasises the structure of institutional mediating mechanisms (for example, shop-floor representation in terms of legal and workplace union structures) in Spain and Britain with regards to workplace change, by contrast we argue that these institutional processes must be located within labour process structures. Whilst institutional mechanisms play a key mediating role (see Blyton and Martinez Lucio, 1995), developments within the new workplace are challenging the remit of workplace regulatory structures as a response to the emergence of wider political workplace issues. A central theme is the variegated nature of labour's response within a new politics of work.

The significance of new institutional arrangements and social organisation such as teamworking are to be located within but not reducible to the intentional strategies of MNCs. For Mueller, MNCs mobilise:

> varying doses of forcing and fostering guided by three central motives: first rationalisation by introducing competition into what were before hierarchical relations; second, coercing change in the established working regime; and third, building firm-specific corporate competencies including employee involvement and teamworking. (1996:363)

Whilst this helpfully delineates the general characteristics of the strategic imperatives of the MNC, it confuses intent with outcome. Corporations such as GM do indeed seek to 'rationalise', 'coerce' and increase employee 'dependencies'. But in practice the scope they have for achieving these is dependent upon both the limits of their product and labour market, state strategy and the intervening character of labour, normally in the shape of trade unions (Ruigrok and Van Tulder, 1995). It is for this reason that we argue the need for a more nuanced account which locates company strategy in the context of both national and locale-specific bargaining patterns and forms of labour intervention.

General Motors and the New Politics of Production in Spain

The General Motors-Opel car plant in Zaragoza in the region of Aragon is a greenfield site having been set up in 1981 with 8000 workers rigorously selected. The plant's production has been described as exceptional and in the early 1990s it was credited with the highest productivity ratios inside the GM Europe group. In other words it is a flagship plant within the Spanish automotive industry alongside the Ford plant in Valencia. The industrial relations of the plant are based on works council elections with the two main left confederations, the UGT (Union General de Trabajadores) and CCOO (the Comisiones Obreras), effectively dominating the plant.

In GM-Opel, an engagement with the development of teamworking has encouraged continual renegotiations and the reaffirmation of social difference. Management of GM-Opel's Zaragoza plant has historically found it difficult to find an agreement on the issue of teamwork and it has suffered from many setbacks as a result of the debate within labour – let alone the debate between labour and management. This is something which the plant's management has always tried to convey to European tiers of management but with less than resounding success. The problem is that 'new' teamworking requires a degree of employment stability and social cohesion within the workplace, together with a degree of internal labour market fixity, that is not always readily available. Until the recent round of changes in legislation governing job classifications and other relevant employment features, job categories have to a certain extent been externally delineated. These external regulations – the labour ordinances which provided very detailed work classification systems – were the point of reference for many trade unionists in large firms in Spain.

Plant management attempted to develop more flexible labour categories and new internal labour markets in the 1980s when the factory was set up in order to overcome what it interpreted as 'arcane' external state regulations (Martinez Lucio and Weston, 1994b). These new flexible measures in terms of broader job classifications and broader workplace sections with extensive internal rotation, were articulated in such a way that they became an obstacle to teamworking: workers felt that rights to internal mobility were seriously undermined by the prospect of such new developments (Blyton and Martinez Lucio, 1995 and Ortiz, 1998). This irony signalled the presence of significant tension between different constituencies of workers. Additionally, there is an argument that unions have historically been at their weakest in the workplace itself regardless of an assemblyist tradition in certain sectors, especially after the undermining of alternative forms of worker representation which had emerged in the 1970s in the form of the *consejos de trabajo*. This has created a tendency to prioritise activity at the level of the works council, collective bargaining and within the political-social sphere (Escobar, 1995). The problem for management here is that teamworking, and the whole question of elections and team leaders, opens up a degree of involvement in the workplace which necessarily expands the role of organised labour into the labour process itself. Moreover, the political nature of worker representation in Spain in terms of contested works council elections means that teamworking may literally politicise the point of production around politically challenged team leader elections between unions. The management of the Zaragoza plant has been very clear about this, as have the unions themselves and it was only when a closer understanding between the two union confederations emerged (the UGT and the CCOO) that discussions were more controlled, although this 'understanding' was not without its problems. What this illustrates is that the notion of worker rights in the context of the labour process and the structure of worker representation within it have both to be understood clearly for the mediation processes to be fully appreciated.

The plant is known as being innovative and unusual, which is one reason why the experience of teamworking is particularly compelling. Opel insisted that when the plant opened it be based on a more flexible manner of working unlike the supposed reality of other automotive plants in Spain. First, the plant operated without many of the labour ordinances that had been established by the Spanish state during the Francoist dictatorship. By contrast, Opel preferred broader labour classification systems which would allow a greater degree of tasks to be deployed amongst the unskilled and semi-skilled workforce on the assembly line. Secondly, the rotation of workers within sections ranging from thirty to sixty workers – and across the plant – was to be a common feature of the workplace. Third, whilst most workers came from other plants, some agricultural workers were initially employed on either temporary or permanent contracts. Many workers were attracted initially by the limits on weekend working which allowed them to engage in alternative employment.

The striking feature of this plant is that it was constructed in a way that minimised the effect of external regulations on production (Blyton and Martinez Lucio, 1995). The nature of functional flexibility, where rotation occurs within broad sections of between thirty and sixty individuals, was such that it became a dominant feature of the plant's identity. This rotation was perceived by some trade unionists as being central to dealing with the effects of a number of difficult tasks, and it was felt that this form of rotation provided for a broader experience of work. In many respects a larger part of the now broadly classified workforce became more widely involved – albeit at a lower skill threshold – in the range of tasks that constituted a section. However, one of the distinguishing features of the Zaragoza case is that, paradoxically, unions began to develop a supportive stance towards this form of functional flexibility. This facilitated the development of solidarity amongst workers within different sections in the face of the stresses of the lean labour process.

The temporal question has also been important because many workers continue to pursue external economic commitments in the agricultural sector, as was pointed out above. The consequence of this cross-sectoral participation has meant that a more intensive rate of work, when compared to other GM plants in Europe, was compensated by a regulated shift system whereby work was distributed across the week to take account of this labour market contingency. These developments were unique, in part because unions in Spain have rarely, until recently, developed an alternative view of functional and temporal flexibility in any exchange with management. Moreover, in terms of the plant's status as a greenfield site it was clear that bypassing external regulations did not mean avoiding internal negotiation with the unions over the regulation of employment relations.

Since 1991, through GM's European Quality Network programme, the plant management at Zaragoza has attempted to develop teamwork as a central part of its operations and much of this has been tied to new waves of investment. However, they have on occasion been divided on the efficacy of the implementation of teamwork. Kaizen-type meetings on continuous improvement were not a resounding success in the early stages. There has been a realisation by some within management that the unions – in particular the CCOO – have been questioning the implementation of new management methods on the basis that these will lead to ideological incorporation. In addition, management also feared that the industrial relations system could politicise workplace relations through conflicts over teamworking. Indeed, attempts at introducing Saturday working in 1992 due to a new wave of investment in the press shop led to a dispute consisting of short but highly visible strategic stoppages that were similar to those witnessed in General Motors-Vauxhall in the UK (see Stewart, 1997 on the 1995–96 Vauxhall dispute and Martinez Lucio and Weston 1994b on the nature of the 1992 GM dispute and its evolution in Spain). This dispute was tied to issues of teamwork, numerical flexibility and the right to permanent work and one of the outcomes was that an agreement was reached on voluntary Saturday working.

This key period gave rise to an increasingly complex debate between the unions and management (and within and between the unions) regarding the issue of flexibility and work organisation. For most of the 1990s no written agreement between management and unions on functional flexibility and teamwork has been ratified by a ballot of the workforce. The development of lean production has opened a debate on health and safety issues (particularly on stress) and temporal rights as a result of attempts to change the pattern of rotation. As a consequence of this concern amongst workers, the two main unions continue their ambivalence with respect to the impact of teamwork on previous rotation 'rights' and on health and safety practices. However, they have become locked into a process of searching for an agreement which would allow them to modify changes whilst at the same time accepting the location and development of team structures within the new 'wider' work sections. Interestingly, the smaller unions on the left seem to have been able to use the language of employment and health and safety in a very effective manner at key moments of change (Ortiz, 1996 and 1998). A range of counter-literature was circulated within the factory by specific groups that through detailed analysis and humour undermined the discourse of empowerment and partnership (see *La Cara Oculta del Trabajo en Equipo*, 1996 – a rank and file document on teamwork in General Motors).

Meanwhile, GM Europe has insisted on pushing local and front line management into developing these new production programmes regardless of internal management differences. These were displayed in an open conference with the CCOO nationally in 1993. The unions were unable to deliver an agreement on teamworking although a strong constituency believed that if properly regulated, teamworking would allow a broader role for unions in the area of production along with the possibility of checking the power of the supervisor – hence the CCOO's engagement with the union platforms and ideas of the IG Metall on teamwork. The lack of agreement led to a withdrawal from management of the notion of team leaders and instead a redevelopment and reinforcement of the supervisors and their authority. This had always been desired by the local Spanish management who feared the political and organisational consequences of 'opening up' the line management function and workplace arena through teamwork and team elections. In a small plant owned by Bosch near Madrid, the nature of supervisor resistance to teamwork in 1993 had startled many managers and trade unionists throughout the sector.

However, what is particularly important here is that a new set of dynamics has opened up which is explicitly tied to communication and training, together with the forms of worker representation necessary to regulate these issues. Teamwork has raised the problem that traditional rotation was being undermined as were the supportive social relations developed within these structures (Blyton and Martinez Lucio, 1995). In addition, health and safety issues were emerging from specific tasks and jobs and these were inevitably linked to the question of flexibility. This in turn led to new structures within the works council being developed to discuss health and safety and its regulation within the collective agreement. Specifically, the issue of job rotation, functional flexibility and health and safety have collided around the character of the collective agreement. Training has emerged as a possible vehicle for gaining trust and jointly regulating the introduction of new working techniques and this in turn has drawn key occupational groups into the debate. In other words, we need to go beyond the formal agreements on new management practices in order to understand how change is being mediated.

As already stated, much of this response to new management initiatives emerged at a time when there had been no ballot indicating the acceptance of teamworking by the workforce. Concurrently, a legal case decided in favour of the company's right to develop teamworking on the basis of the managerial prerogative inscribed by law and in the collective agreement when a minority leftist union took the company to court on the question of teamwork. Despite this legal victory, the company has still to develop forms of joint consultation and regulation regarding production processes and is currently operating in a climate in which the industrial relations debate has now broadened to include a range of previously undiscussed issues relating to health and safety questions. The misalignment between the 'new workplace' and the institutional structures of industrial relations has created a fascinating dilemma for management. In this respect worker representatives themselves are increasingly having problems coping with the linkages made by the different parties (management and unions) in the conflict over the nature and extent of what GM term 'lean mass production'.

In a wider sense, it is clear that the new contradictions and issues which are emerging in the workplace have not been elaborated within a clear institutional framework. The prevalent way to study the labour process is with very little reference to the labour market and economic context. The implications of contemporary management practices, however, are that they are breaking down the extant boundary between the forms of regulation governing internal and external labour market relations. Yet these external contextual factors may condition the development of a broader politicisation of the issues we have outlined above. For example, the dependent nature of the Aragonese economy allows for a direct political role for GM within the region which pressurises local state institutions to support more conciliatory industrial relations (Martinez Lucio and Weston, 1994a). Secondly, competitive relations appear to be emerging between the most organised points of worker representation within the car industry in Spain. Thirdly and of great importance, is the dependent nature of the car assembly process in key Spanish companies which are not at the centre of core production and decision making within MNCs. Fourth, the continuing tendency in Spanish management to opt for cost-based as opposed to value-added production and employment strategies (Pérez Díaz and Rodriguez, 1995) means that structural economic and social pressures seek to contain the evolution of the issues we have outlined above. However, regardless of these pressures, in the case of Zaragoza (from the point of view of the form and content of teamworking) the new workplace has not yet seen the clear emergence of a stable and politically consistent production regime distinctive from Fordist forms of regulation. So, regardless of the constraining effects of these external economic and political factors, management's new hegemony is limited by the way organised labour has been drawn into contestation over the traditional boundaries between spheres of interest. This contestation has arisen as a direct consequence of the 'new' production strategies at the centre of the labour process. We shall now assess the fate of GM-Vauxhall, the company's UK subsidiary, in respect of strategic commitments to 'lean mass production', set against a background of union intervention.

General Motors and the New Politics of Production in Britain

Whilst GM's European strategy (the European Quality Network Programme) is predicated upon an attempt to develop a fully integrated corporate strategy for the first time in the company's European operations, three mutually interdependent and reinforcing factors mitigate the possibility of this being realised in a non-conflictual manner. These consist of: firstly, the corporation's historical pattern of adaptation to regional peculiarities, including the character of the various national social settlements; secondly and in apparent contradiction to the latter, the systemic difficulties faced by GM as it attempts to develop a corporate plan to span national differences in pursuit of its so-called 'world car' strategy; and finally, the character of the response from organised labour, conditioned in part on the basis of these two contingent factors together with the scope for internal plant specific negotiations (Martinez Lucio and Weston, 1994a). This in turn results from the historical characteristics of the labour force and the impact which these have upon the organisation and politics of labour.

GM's Vauxhall plant with 4000 workers at Ellesmere Port is situated in an area of traditionally strong trade union organisation where the senior union in the plant, the Transport and General Workers' Union (TGWU) is a significant actor in the regional labour movement. Vauxhall-GM began production at Ellesmere Port in 1962 and the plant has experienced many vicissitudes since this time. Despite acute difficulties in the late 1970s and early 1980s, the plant is arguably now more secure than at any time in the last twenty years and some of this security can be attributed to the interventionist role of the TGWU. The compelling story for our purposes is how the TGWU's local intervention has not only seen the enhancement of key elements of the joint regulation process but has seen these extended into the labour process itself. Whilst the latter has been common across the sector now for some time, and indeed has very strong parallels with Vauxhall's Luton plant in the south of England, there are a number of features which make the Ellesmere Port plant distinct – specifically, the fact that the management–union agreement has allowed for quite detailed strictures on union prerogatives in respect of job rotation and flexibility, teamworking and employee representation.

Moreover, favourable conditions for the trade union agenda have developed around concerns over the consequences for health and safety which lie at the heart of the new politics of production. For example, in the paintshop so-called 'allowance time' has recently been introduced to take into account the increased efficiency of the new painting technologies. This is, in turn, tied to the question of job rotation which has seen the substitution of the previous pattern of worker-centred rotation by a management-initiated team system whereby job and task changes are derived from production schedules rather than the physical limitations of the worker. Such a rotation system was introduced on a fixed shift basis of twelve to twenty workers which has created certain inflexibilities for employees, with many reporting less job mobility and task flexibility than was experienced prior to the 1989 plant agreement which had paved the way for the introduction of new management practices. GM's intention had been to promote functional flexibility by increasing the skill base for each job. However, in practice, skill enhancement has been accomplished through an increase in job tasks per worker which in turn has paved the way for the intensification of effort across the plant. Nor has this increase in job loading led to any dramatic increase in mobility within the plant. As was the case prior to the agreement, plant-wide mobility is determined in accordance with the exigencies of production scheduling and workers rarely move outside their designated production area. Indeed in some areas the interchangeability of tasks is *less* than was common prior to the 1989 agreement.

The new politics of production can be traced to the 1989 industrial relations agreement, promising organisational change at Ellesmere Port. This agreement is known as the 'V6 Agreement' after a £400m investment programme targeted at a new automotive engine plant which was seen to be central to the continuance of passenger vehicle assembly operations at the site. In addition to the TGWU, there were three other signatory unions to the 'V6': the AEU, EEPTU (both have now combined to form the Amalgamated Engineering and Electrical Union) and the MSF (Manufacturing and Science Federation). More than 85 per cent of unionised employees are members of the TGWU. The 'V6' agreement was seen by Vauxhall's management as fundamental to the development of 'lean mass production'. In theory this consists of the introduction of technical and social changes to the labour process and workplace organisation, namely:

outsourcing, reduction of standard work cycle times, persistent stripping out of labour, extensive capital investment and reduced buffers. This, in turn, was allied to teamworking as the basis for the fragmentation of trade union and labour control of the labour process. Whilst Vauxhall has been less than successful with regards to the latter, on the technical side significant progress has been made, as indeed is the case with all manufacturers in the sector (Stewart and Garrahan, 1995). With respect to the former, management has been unable to win employees to the importance of teamworking and the other social paraphernalia of lean production such as team leader elections and team sponsored internal competition for developing production quotas and work standards.

These are geared towards luring employees into another form of employee participation and representation outside that offered by trade unions. The idea is that teams will displace trade unions as the magnet for employee demands for involvement, with team leaders replacing shop stewards as pivotal actors in the representation process. It is this which accounts for Vauxhall's persistent attempt to break the shop-floor prerogatives of the TGWU via a process of involvement through domestication. For example, health and safety issues are dealt with by joint union–management ergonomic committees, an important example of the North American phenomenon of 'Jointism'. The problem for management is that the internal institutional environment has not facilitated workplace reform in management's image (Fisher, 1995), Conservative Government industrial relations legislation and external labour market regulation notwithstanding.

The traditional nature of shop-floor politics in the UK assisted the trade unions and the TGWU in particular, as the senior union in the plant, to assert historic prerogatives. Unlike the experience of workplace organisation across the sector, the trade unions at Vauxhall survived successive phases of restructuring in reasonable organisational shape. Vauxhall has been steadily incorporating a version of GM's corporatist involvement strategy. Paradoxically, given what was happening throughout the rest of the sector and British industry as a whole, this provided a buffer for the unions from the exigencies of wider social and economic upheaval, even if significant redundancies have been made as a direct consequence of lean production (the plant saw staffing reductions in excess of 50 per cent during the 1980s).

The irony here is that GM's strategy of 'domestication' and incorporation (or 'Jointism', as referred to above) has served to heighten worker expectations about the virtues of the new production arrangements, and at Ellesmere Port two features of the change process have undermined management's plans for implementing change on its own terms. Whereas the Spanish trade unions were driven by concerns with changes in the production process together with their effects on labour regulation, in the case of the British plant, union responses have been conditioned by the persistence of already existing autonomous trade union strategies and policy initiatives. The unions' policies have become bound up with the development of two contradictions which are at the centre of management's core initiative – the implementation of 'lean mass production'.

At Ellesmere Port lean production standards have led to workers reporting increased levels of stress in work and in their home environments (Stewart and Wass, 1996). Trade unions are having to respond to this because the impact of the new politics of production on workers' health has widened the conventional remit of union involvement to include job loading, shift rotation and allowance time. It is now widely accepted that under the previous production regime in Britain known as Measured Day Work, mutual agreement on production norms allowed unions and management to jointly regulate production standards, which in turn ensured a bifurcation in spheres of interest. Trade union emphasis upon the general terms and conditions as set out in the employment contract worked so long as managerial intervention in the labour process desisted from upsetting this historically negotiated divergence of concerns. The crucial point here is that it is this division of spheres of interest which has been so thoroughly disrupted by the exigencies of lean production. It is in the light of this that we can assess the contradiction between a management agenda of involvement and the consequences of the *implementation of the involvement strategy*.

Management, by defining lean production in terms of a new industrial partnership, had little choice but to include union participation in the regulation of the institutional context in which production standards are realised – the team – after the 1989 negotiated settlement. This is of a piece with the company's international response to trade unions in the current period but this consequence has also opened up an opportunity for the unions, which is one reason why GM provides such compelling evidence for the operation of the new production politics. Moreover, the character of employee and union mobilisation against management's agenda is deeply ironic because mobilisation has in part been a response to the setting of an agenda which was supposed to lead the unions, and especially the TGWU, away from their perceived oppositional stance.

In fact, as is well documented, the unions from the start were significantly involved in determining the outcome of the agenda, whatever were management's intentions (Martinez and Weston, 1992; Fisher, 1995; Ortiz, 1996). More specifically, union and worker responses also need to be understood as a mobilisation against the *content* of new management practices, including HRM under the auspices of the plant-based union strategy known informally as 'Engage and Change'. It was this strategy which paved the way for the 1995–96 strike at Vauxhall UK on pay and productivity (at Ellesmere Port and Luton) which, though providing mixed outcomes for employees, was conducted against a background of general employee dissatisfaction with the nature of lean production (Stewart, 1997). Before the 1995–96 strike, under the auspices of 'Engage and Change' the TGWU were able to set specific limits:[2] to the character and role of teamworking and team leader prerogatives; the nature and scope of worker representation; aspects of recruitment procedures and lastly, the terms and conditions of workers in a number of targeted supplier companies. This is a key element of union control in relation to the new management practices and it is especially important given the less than critical account of the development of the latter by some in the UK.[3]

GM's commitment to Ellesmere Port will see the deployment of a new portfolio of products well into the millennium but it should be noted that each new product deployment in the automotive industry today is tied to management demands for a change in production and labour standards. Traditionally, changes to production standards and productivity rates saw the *quid pro quo* of wage increases. However, lean production, with low inventories, labour costs and maximum labour utilisation, has placed trade unions in assembler operations in an objectively powerful position, as witnessed by disputes at Ford-UK, and GM-Vauxhall in 1995 and 1996. Whilst in most companies trade unions balk at opportunities for reform, at GM things are different. The peculiarities of the company's international response to restructuring have seen trade unions in the UK develop their own agenda. Politically the implications of this, so far as traditional industrial relations are concerned, are that union policy and practice at plant level have seen the erosion of the old bifurcation of spheres of interest.

Contrasts and Continuities in the New Politics of Production at GM

In parallel to the plant management at Zaragoza, Vauxhall's leading personnel managers emphasised the centrality of teamworking in the introduction of new working practices. As at Zaragoza, team briefings and kaizen meetings have not as yet been implemented away from direct production. Whilst management made great efforts to control the organisation of labour via team meetings and kaizen briefings, the Vauxhall unions (within the remit of the 'V6' deal) have been able to undermine the purpose of these institutions where shop stewards have limited discussion of industrial and employment relations issues by enforcing the agreement on labour organisation and mobility. Such meetings, on the rare occasions when they take place, are confined to discussion of production issues rather than changes and reductions in employment. Because of this we argue that it is management's strategy, as against that of the unions (and notably the TGWU) which can be seen to have been partially obstructed, albeit temporarily.

The contrast with the development of 'lean mass production' at Zaragoza is significant because what has been emerging over the eight years since the signing of the 'V6 Agreement' is the introduction of a new and contested labour process constituted around a series of technical innovations in GM's assembly plants (involving body, paint, sub-assembly and trim shops). Whilst similar processes have taken place at Zaragoza, the contrast is focused more at the level of the social and organisational context within which technical change has occurred. Whilst it has been the externally / legally supported character of the industrial relations agenda in Spain together with alternative concerns about flexibility and team organisation, which have inhibited the development of management-driven teamworking strategies, at Ellesmere Port teamworking, kaizen and team leader prerogatives have been effectively mediated within the context of internal industrial relations agreements by eroding the time-honoured bifurcation of spheres of interest.

The logical technical limits to numerical and functional flexibility which teams are in part designed to compensate for, have now crept onto the agenda at Ellesmere Port where the organisation of workers' time has become another aspect of the union agenda, most notably in the paint shop. The paint shop case is an interesting example because it highlights how the unions have drawn an acknowledgement from management that lean production is about more than technical organisation and that the expansion of individual effort, employed to a maximum under lean production, must be adequately compensated. This example demonstrates, in other words, that the unions have begun to break the hegemony of the lean production school's simplistic linking of supposed technical and human efficiency and cost reduction. The unions have achieved this by drawing out the way in which lean production masks the substitution of human limits for technical limits by stock or buffer reduction programmes. As is by now well known, the propaganda *leitmotif* in such programmes is that waste becomes synonymous with non-value-adding human effort and of course waste also includes rest time. However, in contrast to trade unions' experiences at Zaragoza, current trade union interaction with the technical character of lean production at Ellesmere Port was not the initial motivating factor in challenging lean production.

In the case of Britain, the micro-politics of worker representation, due to the role of shop stewards for example (see Terry, 1994), have been central to the perception of and response to teamworking and no more so than at GM. The structure of worker representation within British industrial relations, and the anti-union governmental context, means that the emergence of teamworking was inevitably tied to the question of labour identity and action (Holloway, 1987). Teamworking has to be understood as a 'political' issue linked to broader questions of union politics. The precedent set by Japanese inward investors, mostly though not only in the automotive sector, who were constructing new, quasi enterprise forms of industrial relations that deny traditional voice mechanisms within labour, reinforced this reading of the political objectives of new management practices (Stewart, 1995; Stewart and Garrahan, 1995). The traditional nature of industrial relations structures in the form of collective bargaining has not in itself led to the modification of management strategies. The key point is that where there has been a strong union presence, then worker representation can envelop teamworking within the workplace, scrutinising its development and implementation.

It is clear that as a consequence of union voracity at the micro-level of production work organisation cannot easily be refocused by management around 'neo-collectivist' frameworks (see Storey and Bacon, 1993) in the form of teamworking. At GM-Vauxhall, this managerial problem has resulted from the prior organisation of worker involvement in changes to the labour process via the shop steward system. Herein lies the peculiarity of the radical debates on new management practices in Britain.

In the British context changes in management strategies are more explicitly political where they are tied into the nature of worker representation within the workplace. Furthermore, the voluntarist establishment of skill hierarchies and demarcations are in turn being mobilised by trade unionists so as to control management practices and frames of reference, although research on this has been less forthcoming. However, Stewart (1995) argues that the way shop stewards have interacted with previous forms of micro-level collective processes in the workplace means that the union has a legacy of labour process structures and social relations to mobilise in the face of change. Historically groups of individuals have worked in broader groups mutually supporting each other through informal support mechanisms that interfaced with shop stewards. Similarly, whilst the rotation within the broader sections of workers at Zaragoza was the product of new systems of production that attempted to supersede the traditional hierarchies of the labour ordinances, these very soon developed within mutually supportive rotation patterns and coverage and hence acted as a similar point of reference within worker struggles there.

In terms of teamworking the regulatory context and the form of work organisation is therefore a significant feature in the development of new sets of issues and conflicts within the workplace, but this can only be understood by locating developments within the labour process and economic context itself. Something some continuously fail to do.

Conclusion

Whither the new politics of production? If GM has been relatively successful at implementing key technical features of lean production, why is opposition to the social aspects of new management practices so important, especially where management will make concessions on some of the supposedly key social elements? In Spain and the UK the trade unions have achieved important gains in their struggle to contain the new production arrangements where teamworking and kaizen are crucially part of the battle for employees' 'hearts and minds'. Issues such as employee involvement in aspects of quality on the tracks have, for example, become a site of social antagonism. Teamworking and kaizen are designed to allow for internal (and external) balances to be struck around the contingencies of production operations. Whilst GM management is able to promote organisational and technical change, even to the point of scheduling team meetings, trade union controls over the content and function of these are vital because these restraints allow for the regulation of the labour process including; staffing levels, agreements on outsourcing and employment levels, job timings and schedules and the overall payment as part of the effort–reward bargain.

The aim of this chapter has been to draw an assessment of the social and political role of labour within the evolution of new production regimes and the 'new workplace' with particular reference to teamworking. Specifically, we have been concerned with the predilection to downplay the active role of labour and industrial relations regulation within these developments in a manner that ignores their social and political complexities. Given the limits of the managerialist literature, we welcome the referencing to the impact of 'social settlements' and 'industrial relations systems' in some of the more sensitive literature on the context of workplace change because it allows analysts to incorporate that which is 'beyond management' (Williams and Haslam, 1993). However, our primary reservation with the latter is that the concept of 'social settlement' tends to be limited to questions of wage settlement systems and utilised in such a way as to draw attention away from both the active and complex role of labour difference and conflict in conditioning management developments within and beyond the workplace (see Kelly, 1996). It is our contention that General Motor's facilities in Europe (notably in Spain and the UK) exemplify a new politics of production which is increasingly consolidated around four features of the workplace. This new workplace agenda addresses flexibility in the form of job rotation; teamworking, the social context within which the contradictions of the new agenda are being played out; health and safety and employee representation including the role of the trade unions.

Thus the new politics of production is constituted around a strategic imperative by trade unions to reconfigure and realign the production and technical goals and objectives of management with respect to labour control of the effort–reward process. Our cases emphasise how unsettled the various social settlements are and indeed how much these are a product of internal struggles, contested and uncertain though these may be. Management still has to contend with these regulatory processes and strategies 'from below'. These are not only a consequence of the regulatory processes in themselves for they also flow from the nature of the management strategies and the social and technical labour processes which result from them. Key questions of work that were once beyond regulation, or politically bound by them, are the source of new issues and interventions that are testing the institutional framework and the links within the domain of work and employment. This is why simply comparing different responses within competing industrial relations systems limits an awareness of the challenges management face. We need to ally the latter to the political context within which management strategies are implemented. In this respect, the 'crisis of industrial relations' is as much a challenge to management as it is to labour.

References

Adler, P. (1997) 'Hybridization of HRM: Two Toyota Transplants Compared', *Working Paper November*, University of South California.

Adler, P. (1998) 'Teamworking today – social implications' in Durand, J-P., Castillo, J. J. and Stewart, P. (eds) *Teamwork in the Auto Industry – New Horizon or Passing Fashion?*, La Decouverte, Paris.

Babson, S. (ed) (1995) *Lean Work*, Detroit: Wayne State University Press.

Bacon, N. and Storey, J. (1995) 'Individualism and Collectivism and the Changing Role of Trade Unionism' in Ackers, P., Smith, C. and Smith, P. (eds) *The New Workplace and Trade Unionism*, London: Routledge.

Blyton, P. and Martinez Lucio, M. (1995) 'Industrial Relations and the Management of Flexibility', *The International Journal of Human Resource Management*, 6:2.

Carter, B. (1995) 'A Growing Divide: Marxist Class Analysis and the Labour Process', *Capital and Class*, 55, 33–72.

CCOO (1994) *Cambio Tecnologico y Organizacion del Tabajo en la Industria del Automovil*, Madrid: CCOO.

Danford, A. (1997) 'The "New Industrial Relations" and Class Struggle in the 1990s', *Capital and Class*, 61, 107–41.

Escobar, M. (1995) 'Works Councils or Unions?' in Rogers, J. and Streeck, W. (eds) *Works Councils: Consultation, Representation and Corporatism in Industrial Relations*, Chicago: University of Chicago Press.

Fisher, J. (1995) 'The Trade Union Response to HRM in the UK: The Case of the TGWU', *Human Resource Management Journal*, 5:3, 7–23.

Frohlich, D. and Pekruhl, U. (1995) *Direct Participation and Organisational Change in Europe, Japan and the USA*, Dublin: European Foundation.

Garrahan, P. and Stewart, P. (1992) *The Nissan Enigma: Flexible Work in a Local Economy.* London: Mansell.

GERPISA (1996) *L'Industrie automobile mondial: entre homogénéisation et hiérarchisation*, Université d'Evry, Paris.

Holloway, J. (1987) 'The Red Rose of Nissan', *Capital and Class*, 32, 142–64.

Jurgens, U., Malsch, T. and Dohse, K. (1992) *Breaking From Taylorism: Changing Forms of Work in the Automobile Industry*, Cambridge: Cambridge University Press.

Kelly, J. (1996) 'Union Militancy and Social Partnership' in Ackers, P., Smith, C. and Smith, P. (eds) *The New Workplace and Trade Unionism*, London: Routledge.

Lewchuk, W. and Robertson, D. (1996) 'Working Conditions Under Lean Production: A Worker-Based Bench Marking Survey' in Stewart, P. (ed.) *Beyond Japanese Management: The End of Modern Times?*.

Martinez Lucio, M. and Weston, S. (1992) 'The Politics and Complexity of Trade Union Responses to New Management Practices', *Human Resource Management Journal*, June.

Martinez Lucio, M. and Weston, S. (1994a) 'New management practices in a multinational corporation: the restructuring of worker representation and rights?', *Industrial Relations Journal*, June.

Martinez Lucio, M. and Weston, S. (1994b) 'Las Politics de Empleo y las Nuevas Practicas de Direccion: Estudio de la Experencia de una Multinacional Europea', *Economia Industrial*, November–December.

Martinez Lucio, M. and Stewart, P. (1997) 'The Paradox of Contemporary Labour Process Theory: The Rediscovery of Labour and the Disappearance of Collectivism', *Capital and Class*, Summer.

Mueller, F. (1994) 'Teams between Hierarchy and Commitment: Change Strategies and the "Internal Environment"', *Journal of Management Studies*, May.

Mueller, F. (1996) 'National Stakeholders in the Global Contest for Corporate Investment', *European Journal of Industrial Relations*, 2:3.

Nichols, T. (1991) 'The Labour Process Before and After the Labour Process Debate' paper presented to the *9th Annual International Labour Process Conference*, University of Aston, Birmingham.

Ortiz, L. (1996) 'Unions' response to teamwork: the case of Opel Spain', paper to the *14th Annual International Labour Process Conference*, University of Aston, Birmingham.

Ortiz, L. (1998) 'Union resonse to teamworking: The case of Opel Spain', *Industrial Relations Journal*, forthcoming.

Pérez Díaz, V. and Rodriguez, J.C. (1995) 'Intertial choices: an overview of Spanish human resources, practices and policies' in Locke, R., Kochan, T. and Piore, M. (eds) *Employment Relations in a Changing World Economy*, Massachusetts: MIT.

Pils, F. and Macduffie, J.P. (1997) 'Japanese and Local Influences: Human Resource Practices and Policies of North American Transplants in North America' in P. Stewart (ed.) *Employee Relations: Continuity and Innovation*, Acts Du Gerpisa, 21.

Pollert, A. (1996) '"Teamwork" on the assembly line: contradictions and the dynamics of union resilience' in Ackers, P., Smith, C. and Smith, P. (eds) *The New Workplace and Trade Unionism*, London: Routledge.

Rowlinson, M. and Hassard, J. (1994) 'Economics, Politics and Labour Process Theory', *Capital and Class*, 53, 65–97.

Ruigrok, W. and Van Tulder, R. (1995) *The International Logic of Restructuring*, London: Routledge.

Stephenson. C. (1996) 'The Different Experiences of Trade Unionism in Two Japanese Plants' in Ackers, P., Smith, C. and Smith, P. (eds) *The New Workplace and Trade Unionism*, London: Routledge.

Stewart, P. (1995) 'A New Politics of Production? Trade Union Networks in the European Automotive Industry – The Case of GM' in Totsuka, H., Ehrke, M., Kammi, Y. and Demes, H. (eds) *International Trade Unionism at the Current Stage of Economic Globalisation and Regionalisation*, Tokyo: Friedrich Ebert Stiftung, H. Plambeck-Grossmann.

Stewart, P (1997) 'Striking Harder and Smarter at Vauxhall: the new industrial relations of lean production?', *Capital and Class*, 61, 1–7.

Stewart. P. and Garrahan, P. (1995) 'Employee Response to New Management Techniques in the Auto Industry', *Work, Employment and Society*, 9:3, 517–36.

Storey, J. and Bacon, N. (1993) 'Individualism and Collectivism: Into the 1990s', *International Journal of Human Resource Management*, 4:3, 665–84.

Terry, M. (1994) 'Workplace Unionism: Redefining Structures and Objectives' in Hyman, R. and Ferner, A. (eds) *New Frontiers in European Industrial Relations*, Oxford: Blackwell.

Thompson, P. and Ackroyd, S. (1995) 'All Quiet on the Workplace Front' A Critique of Recent Trends in British Industrial Sociology', *Sociology*, 29:4, 615–33.

Thompson, P. and Findlay, P. (1996) 'The Mystery of the Missing Subject', paper to the *14th Annual International Labour Process Conference*, University of Aston, Birmingham.

Waddington, J. and Whitston, C. (1996) 'Empowerment versus intensification: Union Perspectives of Change in the Workplace' in Ackers, P., Smith, C. and Smith, P. (eds) *The New Workplace and Trade Unionism*, London: Routledge.

Williams, K. and Haslam, C. (1993) 'Beyond Management: Problems of the Average Car Company', paper to the *Lean Production and Labor Conference*, Wayne State University.

Notes

1   Our argument draws upon our research begun in a number of projects since 1991 into new management practices in General Motors' car plants in two national contexts with distinct regulatory contexts and traditions (see Martinez Lucio and Weston 1994a and 1994b; Stewart and Garrahan, 1995). Both plants were visited since 1991 on various occasions during each year. We would like to thank, amongst a range of others, the following people who we interviewed on various occasions from 1991–1997: Juan Blanco and Lola Morillo, trade union researchers at the Comisiones Obreras; A. Carvajal and S. Organero of the union Comisiones Obreras in Zaragoza GM; L. Tejedor, J.M. Olivan and A. Pozo of the trade union Union General de Trabajadores at Zaragoza GM; Ramon Goriz trade unionist from Comisiones Obreras Zaragoza GM and now the National Metal Federation official for car manufacturing in that union; Adolfo Cuesta of the trade union Comisiones Obreras metal section; members of the personnel department of GM; Ken Murphy, John Featherstone, Michael Whitley, and the late Peter Titherington of the T&GWU Vauxhall Ellesmere Port, and Steve Craig. There were many other trade unionists and workers to whom we spoke and to whom we are grateful.
2   This is due to the referencing to productivity increases and alternative definitions of 'teamwork' such as welt work.
3   (See *inter alia*, Bacon and Storey, 1995 and for an incisive critique of the new managerialism in much of the literature on workplace management strategies, see Thompson and Ackroyd, 1995 and Thompson and Findlay, 1996.)

5 Emotional Labour and the New Workplace

Steve Taylor

Introduction

This chapter focuses upon 'emotional labour'. Following Hochschild (1983 & 1993), this term refers to the management of human feeling, during social interaction within the labour process, as shaped by the dictates of capital accumulation. Until recently, the phenomenon of emotional labour had been neglected by the British academy (James, 1989; Fuller and Smith, 1991; Filby, 1992; Fineman, 1993; Sturdy, 1994; Kerfoot, 1995; Newton, 1995; Bolton, 1997; Fineman and Sturdy, 1997). However, analyses of emotional labour are crucial to fully appreciate the emergence of 'the new workplace'. When restricting her attention to jobs where emotional labour was the *main* human capacity sold to an employer, Hochschild estimated in 1983 that one-third of all employment in the US and half of that performed by women could be classified as such. It can be safely argued that emotional labour has increased in significance since the early 1980s given the contraction of manufacturing, the expansion of the service sector and increased female participation in the labour force of western societies.

The significance of emotional labour is being increasingly recognised by service sector employers. Feeling management, as part of the valorisation process, is a predominant aspect of the new service sector workplace. Ogbanna and Wilkinson (1990), Fuller and Smith (1991), Filby (1992) and Fineman (1995) all provide evidence of increased employer emphasis upon selecting and training employees for the purposes of emotional labour alongside the development of mechanisms to supervise and evaluate its deployment. This chapter will specifically focus upon Total Quality Management (TQM) as one widespread form of service organisational restructuring where management attempts to control and regulate the feeling management of employees. Later, this chapter draws upon empirical research into the contemporary service sector of the north-eastern regional economy of Britain in order to indicate the nature of emotional labour within the new workplace.

It is claimed by some that the new service sector workplace, evidenced by the introduction of initiatives such as TQM, 'empowers' employees to deploy emotional autonomy during interaction with customers. In contrast, it will be argued here that the new workplace demands the deployment of emotional labour. Constraints upon feeling management are shaped by capitalist structures within the workplace which managerial initiatives such as TQM appear to be strengthening rather than fragmenting.

It will eventually be argued that the core propositions of 'labour process theory' (Thompson, 1989) provide a theoretical framework which can *inform* analysis of our empirical data. The 'structural properties' of the labour process shape the nature of emotional labour in important ways. However, the limitations of labour process theory must be recognised in terms of interrogating the *subjective experience* of such phenomena (Thompson and Findlay, 1996).

Emotional Labour: Definitions and Problems

Hochschild (1983) distinguishes between 'emotion work' and 'emotional labour'. In the former, feeling is managed in order to sustain an outward appearance and produce particular states of mind in other people for *private* purposes. The deployment of emotional *labour* – as defined above – is clearly different and can facilitate the 'transmutation of the private emotional system' (Hochschild, 1983). Whilst it is often difficult to distinguish between the performance of 'emotion *work*' and 'emotional labour' within the workplace, this chapter is solely concerned with emotional *labour*. The distinction therefore needs to be clarified. Emotional labour can be defined as, firstly, feeling management which is performed as part of paid work, serving the interests of an employer in maximising surplus value; secondly, being predominantly undertaken during social interaction within the workplace – the product of emotional labour is often the state of mind or feeling within another person (most often a customer or client) – however, we can also posit the possibility of emotional labour being directed at the self if it is demanded by an employer in order to serve the dictates of capital accumulation; thirdly, there must be some managerial attempt to prescribe, and / or supervise and measure employee performance of emotional labour.

Hochschild (1983) identifies two forms of emotional labour, wherein employees can induce or suppress feeling as part of the labour process: *surface acting* and *deep acting*. The former involves pretending 'to feel what we do not ... we deceive others about what we really feel, but we do not deceive ourselves' (33). It entails managing our outward appearance. 'Deep acting' means 'deceiving oneself as much as deceiving others ... we make feigning easy by making it unnecessary' (33). Hochschild goes on to identify two types of deep acting: the direct exhortation of feeling; and the use of a trained imagination. This chapter examines the deployment of both surface acting and deep acting in the service of valorisation and as shaped by the capital–labour relation.

Any attempt to empirically research emotional labour must begin by recognising some inherent problems with such an enterprise. How does one know if another is engaging in emotional labour? Often, the whole point of emotional labour is to *conceal* inner feeling. There is certainly no obvious reason why interviewees are likely to reveal such concealment to researchers when, as some authors argue, they may have difficulty in revealing some emotion work even to themselves. The distinctly gendered nature of emotional labour (Filby, 1992; Swan, 1994) also means that a male researcher will face inevitable problems when researching the emotional labour of female employees.

Elias (1987) argues that emotion is not totally socially constructed – it has physiological and behavioural components in addition to a 'feeling component'. It is through the feeling component that we learn to manage and control our biological, emotional impulses in accordance with the demands of social life. However, according to Elias, this is a largely unconscious and 'automatic' process. This clearly presents further problems with attempts to research emotional management and experience.

These problems were recognised throughout the empirical research upon which this chapter is based. An ethnographic approach was adopted as the best available means to observe and analyse emotional management within the workplace.

The New Workplace and TQM

We shall examine emotional labour within the service sector in the context of TQM implementation. It has been suggested that quality initiatives constitute the most far-reaching forms of organisational restructuring within the service sector (Kerfoot, 1995; McCabe and Knights, 1995; Walsh, 1995).

TQM is one of a number of managerial attempts to reconstruct work organisations in ways which are *customer focused*. Following du Gay and Salaman (1992), it can be suggested that this 'cult(ure) of the customer' is part of a wider 'discourse of enterprise' which is unquestioningly accepted by managements as 'rational' in terms of responding to the competitive environment in many sectors of contemporary western economies. It is alleged that the mass production of standardised goods and services will no longer satisfy consumer expectations and that we are witnessing the emergence of the quality-conscious consumer (du Gay and Salaman,1992). Radical organisational change has been charted as a response to this change. The discourse of enterprise, which includes managerialist literature prescribing the implementation of TQM, has been accepted as rational by those with work organisational power. Wilkinson and Willmott (1995) report that 'quality initiatives' are currently occurring in three-quarters of companies in the UK and the US and that such initiatives are supported enthusiastically by 90 per cent of chief executives who regard them as 'critical' for their organisations. The emergence of TQM programmes can certainly be identified within the service sector. Within financial services, for example, McCabe *et al.* (1994) found that 90 per cent of organisations have one or more quality initiative.

An essential element of TQM is the idea that senior management must actively manage the quality improvement process. The primary objective of this management is to 'enhance customer perceptions of quality of service actually received and thereby equate them with customer expectations' (Howcroft, 1991:13). Customer satisfaction is the overriding goal. Not only is it notoriously difficult for service organisations to compete in terms of substantive services offered but, as the quality competition increases, consumers become more sophisticated at discerning the difference between a 'genuine' quality service (deep acting) and a 'feigned' quality service (surface acting). Within service *delivery*, one can distinguish two types of 'quality' in terms of worker–customer interaction. 'Technical' (Groonroos, 1984; Lewis, 1988) or 'hard' (Hill, 1991) quality includes product knowledge and knowledge of operational systems. 'Functional' (Groonroos, 1984; Lewis, 1988) or 'soft' (Hill, 1991) quality comprises staff behaviour, attitude and appearance during interaction with customers. Clearly, the aim of TQM is to enhance both types of quality. For reasons of space alone, this chapter will solely discuss the impact of TQM upon the employee–customer relationship. Furthermore, it shall be especially concerned with managerial attempts to deliver *functional* quality through this relationship, as it is this that involves emotional labour.

The discourse of enterprise, and the prescriptive TQM literature which constitutes part of it, suggests that the delivery of functional quality can only be 'managed' by encouraging worker spontaneity, responsiveness and autonomy during interaction with customers. Functional quality is therefore constrained by bureaucratic control. Furthermore, for business success, the discourse of enterprise more generally encourages the 'empowerment' of all organisational members to add 'value' – to the company *and* themselves. Based upon an analysis of feeling management within one particular 'new' service sector workplace, this chapter explores the nature and effects of this process.[1]

The Research Site

Ethnographic research was conducted into a telephone sales operation within one regional centre (Newcastle upon Tyne) of a major British airline (Flightpath). This labour process had been shaped by the implementation of TQM prior to the research.

The research focuses upon the work of Telephone Sales Agents (TSAs). This work primarily involves agents receiving, and dealing with, calls from people who are interested in purchasing or reserving one (or a combination) of the vast array of travel-related services provided by Flightpath. TSAs work within a large 'open plan' office (a 'community'). They are equipped with a headset, a telephone system and a computer system. TSAs themselves push a button when they wish to receive a call. 'Dealing with' calls usually involves placing the caller on hold and accessing information from the computer system.

According to Flightpath Telephone Sales Worldwide management, the aim of the work is to transform as many calls as possible into actual bookings. It is a worldwide operation with international calls received. There are five regional centres throughout Britain and a centre in the US.

Within the centre studied, TSAs are divided into teams of nine. They are managed by one Sales Team Supervisor (STS). In turn, a team of eight supervisors is responsible to one Sales Team Leader (STL). These STLs are, as a team, responsible to the unit manager of the centre studied. S/he is then accountable to the head of Telephone Sales, UK. Everyone within the centre is on performance-related pay. Of all TSAs, 81 per cent are female. Fifty-two per cent of STSs are female. Above this level, only one STL is female.

'Emotional Empowerment' at Flightpath?

Flightpath as a whole has long recognised the importance of quality customer service. They have been running customer care campaigns since 1983. However, Telephone Sales Worldwide management argued that it was only during the 1990s, in response to intensified and internationalised competition within the airline industry, that they were able to implement quality management 'throughout and as part of their structures and processes' (Unit Manager, Newcastle).

Telephone sales is one unique part of Flightpath where employee/customer interaction and the generation of revenue occur instantaneously. TSAs are often the first contact a prospective customer will have with the company. Providing quality customer service entails responding to, and anticipating, customers' needs and expectations thus ensuring satisfaction and loyalty:

> Probably the most important goal that we have is that we have to establish a customer intimacy that goes beyond our competitors. Customer intimacy. That is, going beyond just reacting to what the customer is wanting. If we can take it that next step we are going to be ever so much better and if we do that the difference is our competition is going to be fighting after us and not after our customers and that is really what we want to see. (Head of Telephone Sales Worldwide)

Customer satisfaction through the provision of continually improving quality service, which it has been suggested can simultaneously involve new demands for emotional labour from service employees, is a clear differentiation strategy of Flightpath Telephone Sales. Interestingly, in accordance with the discourse of enterprise, telephone sales management argued that functional quality could only be delivered through employee autonomy and, by implication, the *non-performance of emotional labour:*

> We must respect that agents know what they are doing. That is the bottom line, we must never forget that. They do know, they know exactly what passengers want, what

they have been through, *exactly how they are feeling and what is going to work. We do encourage people to be themselves on the phone.* There is nothing worse than phoning up and listening to that awful spiel that you get with a lot of companies and I think that people [customers] do genuinely feel that they are speaking to another human being which is quite an advantage certainly in a selling context because they can identify with that person. We do give people room to build rapport ... some people do want to talk at length whilst they are making the booking. There is no harm in that ... we are quite happy with that. Our culture does support that. (STS)[2]

There were a number of elements to the Flightpath TQM programme which supposedly facilitated the deployment of TSA emotional autonomy. One which was identified by management as particularly important was the teamworking system. It is believed that a close working relationship between STS and TSA, which teamworking engenders, is the key to delivering quality customer service. Teamworking supposedly enables an STS to develop their staff and encourage the deployment of worker autonomy. Because of the close working relationship, it is felt that an STS is able to motivate, recognise and reward agent initiative in the delivery of functional quality:

It is a real skill to motivate people to use their own brains and abilities, by going up to people and saying 'I really like the way you did that or said that' and it does make people feel a lot more valued if they've got some say in what goes on. (STS)

Thus, given the small, manageable teams of nine and the close working relationship with a familiar supervisor, it is argued that supervisors can interact with their team members individually and as a whole in order to discuss ways in which their performance can be 'improved'. *Employee* decisions about how functional quality is to be delivered (often through their own techniques of emotion work) can be encouraged, recognised and rewarded through the supervisor–agent relationship. The enhanced motivation which this 'empowerment' supposedly facilitates is also seen as important in facilitating the delivery of functional quality through the personal management of feeling.

Central to any quality initiative are mechanisms for 'measuring' the quality improvement process. From a telephone sales managerial perspective, the mechanisms outlined below promoted rather than constrained TSA autonomy. They were beneficial to agents as well as the telephone sales operation. The major measurement mechanisms at Newcastle Telephone Sales consist of monthly targets which individual TSAs have to surpass. Management explicitly divided these into 'hard' and 'soft' dimensions.

'Hard' targets refer to quantitative measurement. Each TSA has a revenue target, relating to the value of Flightpath services which are directly sold to customers over the telephone. Each TSA is expected to surpass this each month. At the time of the research, this target was set at £8000 per month. STSs had a team target of 9 x £8000 which had to be surpassed each month. Further, STLs are targeted in terms of the monthly monetary performance of (eight) STSs within their community. The unit manager is ultimately responsible for ensuring that STLs deliver monthly returns to the value of 3 (STLs) x 8 (STSs) x 9 x £8000 per month. Other hard targets, labelled 'productivity evaluation', involve computerised measurement of the number of calls answered per agent per week, the amount of time spent by each agent in conversation with passengers per week and the amount of time spent by every individual each week within what is known as 'wrap up' – that between the termination of one call and the opening of a new one. The hard targets are devised by a core management centre. A forecast is made of the average number of calls which will be made during a particular period, based upon the number of calls received during the same period the previous year and various other factors such as particular promotions running at the time. This forecast is then divided up amongst the various units, the various communities and the various teams so that each individual employee has a particular revenue and productivity target.

The hard targets were seen by management as a benevolent system which encourages TSAs to deliver functional quality through their own (emotional) skills and abilities:

> I would say that the overriding aim of the targets is developmental. It's 'let's see how we can help these people' ... it helps us and them [agents] to recognise underperformance. In this case, we need to make them think about the targets and what they can get out of it. (Unit Manager)

The evaluation of the TSA labour process by 'soft' standards is inevitably more ambiguous. Management described them as referring to 'teamwork, commitment and ... call structure, their job skills if you like' (STS). It was stressed that evaluation of agents is a 50/50 split between hard and soft standards. This evaluation directly shapes performance-related pay. The assessment of TSAs according to 'soft' standards primarily takes place through 'remote' and 'known' monitoring. The telephone system within the unit enables any of the supervisory staff to 'listen in' to any agent/customer interaction at any time. This can be done with (known) or without (remote) the knowledge of the agent in question. STSs claimed that they randomly and frequently engaged in remote monitoring, and sometimes taping, as a form of 'quality assurance'. Furthermore, STSs routinely observe and tape the telephone performance of each team member with their full knowledge. Both are then used in weekly review and appraisal meetings between agent and supervisor. TSA performance-related pay is shaped by an STS monthly report which results from the weekly meetings.

Managerial Control and Emotional Exploitation

This section of the chapter will critically analyse the TSA emotional labour process, suggesting that the new service sector workplace, far from empowering employees to deploy emotional autonomy during interaction with customers, actually demands significant and increasing amounts of emotional labour.

There was some managerial attempt to prescribe the delivery of functional quality, and the techniques of emotional labour, through the training programme for TSAs. Agents are instructed to respond to the perceived feelings and expressions of customers in a manner which primarily upholds the commercial interests of Flightpath, rather than in a manner which expresses their own perception and feeling. These demands do not only encompass surface acting. Examples were also observed and reported of TSAs being taught how to 'deal with' customers that appeared 'insulting' or 'ignorant' through actively changing, shaping, 'working on' feeling:

> They train you to put the stress on yourself. If you have a rude or ignorant customer, you are supposed to pretend that something awful has just happened to them ... 'always feel sorry for the ignorant customer, do not hate him [sic]' ... this is what they tell you to do, 'put sympathy on to him and not yourself'. (TSA)

However, TSAs, telephone sales management and trainers stressed that the training programme acted only as a prescriptive framework for the delivery of functional quality, within which employees were expected to use their discretion. Many (for example Fox, 1974; Cressey and McInnes, 1980; Brown, 1992) have noted that *some* employee autonomy is inherent to all labour processes. Telephone sales management could not possibly prescribe the detailed nature of every possible worker/customer interaction through the training programme. Consequently, there was some evidence of TSA emotional discretion in the delivery of functional quality. TSAs argued that they frequently, with the encouragement of management, interact with customers in their own personal or 'natural' manner. This is known as 'building rapport':

> It's the type of job you'll never know what you are doing next ... when you are training, they've got this strategy how you've got to do everything but then you lose it and they just say 'do it your own way, do it as it comes naturally'. If they want to ring up and speak to a machine you can just get an answerphone to do it. You've just got to do everything as natural as you can. (TSA)

Furthermore, many agents suggested that their own 'natural' technique for interacting with customers is directly influenced by their own 'personality' and accompanying 'feeling rules':

> I'm naturally quite a chatty person and I'm chatty on the phone. I like to find a common link ... I've had feedback on my phone technique and they say 'keep that in, it's good, it establishes a rapport' which I don't mind doing because that is the sort of person I am anyway. (TSA)

These examples illustrate that TSAs exercise *positive discretion* within the labour process. Employees devise and implement their own individual ways of delivering functional quality which inherently involve forms of feeling management. The exercise of this discretion is deliberately encouraged and positively rewarded (in financial and symbolic terms) by management. This is what the 'emotional empowerment' intrinsic to the new service sector workplace consists of.

However, it can still be argued that managerial initiatives such as TQM, which are central to the emergence of the new service sector workplace, are the most sophisticated, thorough-going and effective managerial *attempts* yet developed to prescribe and control the (emotional) labour process (Sewell and Wilkinson, 1992). Of particular importance to the case being studied here are managerial mechanisms for 'measuring' the telephone sales labour process outlined above. These (electronic) techniques for individualised supervision and evaluation of the TSA labour process can be seen as a managerial control system which encourages 'positive' divergencies from managerial prescription but attempts to eliminate 'negative' discretion. Unless (or as well as) their own feeling management or emotion work is utilised simultaneously as positive discretion (that is, to deliver functional quality as defined by management) within the labour process, TSAs can be coerced into deploying emotional labour – surface acting and / or deep acting for purely commercial and corporate purposes – given the knowledge that they can be supervised at any time. It is important to remember that the results of this supervision shape the material remuneration which TSAs receive from the employment relationship. According to Hochschild (1983), such managerial prescription and control eventually facilitates consistent pressures for deep acting from employees, possibly resulting in the transmutation of the private emotional system and 'emotional alienation'.

There is clear evidence from this case study that the managerial control mechanisms at Flightpath do coerce some TSAs into performing both forms of emotional labour. Thus, in relation to how the individualised revenue targets can shape the nature of TSA / customer interaction:

> The things we are taught ... are to do with things that you should say and you shouldn't say and the way that you put things over ... it's not really the case that things are not allowed ... you say whatever you feel comfortable with, but at the end of it, we are all targeted each month for the money that we make, our individual revenue so if you want to make targets, earn more money and things then you are better off doing what we've been taught ... otherwise you'll not get your target. (TSA)[3]

Productivity statistics for every individual TSA are immediately available to management for, and at, any point in time. They are also visible to TSAs, STSs and STLs as they are being recorded. Should individuals fall below the 'norm' for one of the productivity measures 'one of their objectives ... will be to get back on target for whatever they have fallen behind on' (STS). The extent to which objectives are met also shapes individualised performance-related pay. There was considerable evidence that this form of managerial supervision can control the way in which employees interact with customers. They often adopt an 'emotional stance' as prescribed by management.

However, perhaps the most important mechanism for managerial control of the emotional labour process is direct supervision of employee/customer interactions through known and remote monitoring:

> You can do it [remote monitoring] from your desk ... you just tap their extension into your phone, Bob's your uncle. You can sit and listen to them ... What I say to them is 'if you have anything that you don't want us to hear, the doors are at the front of the office, see you later, what are you doing here?' If you think of it, why *would* you be saying something that isn't Flightpath, or isn't nice, isn't polite? (STS)[4]
>
> It [remote monitoring] does really have an effect on you because you know that if you don't do things by the book they could be listening and they could pull you up on it. You've got to be on your guard all the time ... I suppose in some ways you can't just be yourself. (TSA)

Known monitoring is also regularly used. Here, a supervisor sits behind an agent listening to calls and noting down comments. Agents are also forced to tape themselves and give the tape to the supervisor to analyse and then feedback during appraisal sessions:

> I really do use self-tape a lot because it's them at their best ... a lot of the time it isn't what they say, it's the tone in which they say it ... I will play something and I'll just stop it and go 'shall we listen to that again?', rewind it and then they'll go 'I didn't know I said it like that.' It makes them analyse themselves and really wake up to their *mistakes*. (STS)[5]

Thus, mechanisms for detailed managerial supervision and control of the telephone sales labour process explicitly support the exercise of positive emotional autonomy but appear to restrict negative emotional autonomy. Only particular forms of feeling management are required – those that support the commercial interests of Flightpath (at least as this is perceived by telephone sales management). This is precisely what Hochschild (1983) means by 'emotional labour'.

Moreover, there is evidence to indicate that, embedded within the aforementioned supervisory and control mechanisms, are managerial demands that TSAs increasingly deep act rather than surface act in their deployment of emotional labour. Thus, management argued that customers can increasingly perceive the difference between 'a front which is put on to serve the customer ... this can be so false ... and actual genuine customer service where our agents do want to serve people, they are genuinely friendly and pleasant ... I think this is what sets us apart, why we are so successful' (STL). Managerial demands for deep acting have in turn been shaped by the 'forces of competition' within the airline industry.

As a direct consequence of the thorough-going managerial supervision and control, indication exists of deep acting amongst some TSAs. When asked why, within the workplace, they did not react to what they perceived to be 'annoying', 'difficult' or 'strange' people in similar ways to the way they would in private life, many agents made an argument that:

> You can't *let yourself* be impolite towards a customer or feel angry with them. You have to always remember that they are a customer ... they pay our wages ... If I'm working on a Friday night, I often think 'what are you doing ringing up for *flight* information on a Friday night?' ... I mean, I ask you, you don't ring an *airline* on a Friday night ... But then I have to think to myself, that they must just be different people to me and the types that I know ... (TSA)[6]

The above agent narrates one way in which the feelings of exasperation and frustration, brought on by having to answer calls on a Friday night, are actively fought and willingly suppressed by reminding herself that customers are 'valuable' and often 'different' from her. From a managerial point of view, if this process did not take place, customers could be offended and lost to the company. There is a difference between this case and Hochschild's notion of surface acting. Within the latter, feelings of anger and irritation would remain despite contradictory outward dispositions displayed by TSAs. Such deep acting has been directly shaped by the individualised managerial control system which can even begin to change employees' very 'personality':

> They [management] make you think about the customer really ... it's all part of the job, appreciating the different types of person you get and how everyone is different with their own values and expectations ... you've got to try and learn not to get angry with people just because they might be different ... I suppose the targets are good in that way because they make you appreciate people more, have a different attitude. If you don't do it, you might not sell and hit target or you might get pulled up because of listening in, in your appraisal or whatever ... a lot of people keep telling me I've actually mellowed since I came here so it's done something for me. (TSA)

The Incomplete Transmutation

Notwithstanding the above examples of intensified emotional exploitation, as shaped by competitive pressures and the emergence of the new workplace within the service sector, this section argues that Flightpath managerial control of the telephone sales labour process is not 'total'. In particular, some TSAs are able to resist managerial demands that they engage in emotional labour.

It was suggested above that 'remote monitoring' was one of the major ways in which management attempt to facilitate employee emotional labour – and particularly deep acting – during TSA/customer interactions. However, many TSAs claimed that, with experience, they had learnt to ascertain when their interactions were being directly supervised. Being situated within an open-plan office, this was recognised by the actions of the supervisor and regular gazes in their particular direction:

When I know she [the supervisor] is not listening, I can't help but change my accent, what I actually say and the words I use. She would only pull me up for not talking the way I'm supposed to ... I had one really ignorant git on the phone once, I was seething, but I knew she was listening so I had to contain it. When she is not listening, I just prefer to be myself ... when I am positive she is not listening, I have been really short with bad customers, it's a great feeling. (TSA)

Such claims were certainly supported by observation within the research. This agent is suggesting that there is a distinct difference between his own personality, display and feeling and that which is demanded by the company. He does engage in surface acting but even this *display* is only performed when he is aware of managerial supervision. Clearly, both remote and known monitoring can shape TSAs' emotional *displays* during some employee/customer interactions. These managerial control mechanisms can also, for some (although a minority of) agents, shape the feeling behind the display. However, when other TSAs are able to interact 'naturally' with customers – utilising their own 'feeling rules' – they seize the opportunity. When questioned whether they are overtly rude or dismissive with certain callers, many agents responded in a similar way to the following interviewee: 'Oh God yeah! Of course we are. We're just like everyone else you know. That's when you turn round and make sure nobody's listening in, you *can* tell if there's anybody listening in.'[7]

Another agent stated:

I just prefer to talk to people naturally, I think they (customers) prefer it as well ... I don't care about building rapport, I don't even care whether I get pulled up ... I talk to people as I would talk to any friendly person outside of here ... it doesn't really get any more sales but it doesn't get any less ... if people are going to buy something, they are going to buy something. I hate laying it on thick. They [customers] don't like it either. (TSA)

Thus, in addition to 'learning through experience' in order to recognise signs of direct managerial supervision and therefore when to deploy the 'company personality' and when to deploy their 'own', some agents even suggested that they ignored managerial prescription of the agent/customer interaction whether they were being supervised or not. If challenged by management, some agents responded by directly attacking the contradiction within a managerial programme which claims to 'empower' employees while simultaneously prescribing, supervising and evaluating interactions:

I've had loads of battles with my supervisor 'cos she'll say 'change the way you say this', 'change the way you offer this' and I'll say 'but that's the way I do it', 'that's me, that's my personality, I can't change myself' and she says 'well you'll have to' but I don't. They either want us to be natural when interacting with customers or they don't, they can't have it both ways. (TSA)

There were numerous examples of overt TSA resistance to managerial prescription of the employee/customer interaction. Some agents were observed, and many stated that, they simply disconnect calls from customers that are particularly rude or ignorant. In some cases, calls are prematurely terminated because the agents take a dislike to the customer. Two-fingered salutes and the mouthing of obscenities to the telephone, or the rolling of eyes to colleagues when in conversation with passengers, were also very common. *Most* of these practices were undertaken when agents were convinced they were not being observed by management, either physically or electronically.

A very common TSA practice, often engaged in whether supervision was perceived or not and revealing TSA emotional discretion during interaction with customers, involves limiting the information given to an ignorant or offensive caller. Relevant and important information would be withheld from particular customers. A related practice involved talking to such passengers in a 'distant', 'disinterested' manner: 'If I don't like someone ... it's difficult to explain but I will be efficient with them, giving them what they want and no more, but I will not be really friendly ... I sometimes have a really monotone voice, sounding a bit cold' (TSA).

The above type of TSA response was often given to those callers who were clearly 'enquiring' rather than 'buying'. Many agents displayed an intuitive knowledge enabling them to distinguish between the two: 'It really annoys me when it's obvious people are just ringing up for information ... I love to fuck about with them. If it is someone from outside the area, I lay the accent on really thick. You can hear them getting embarrassed when they have to say pardon all the time.'

It will be remembered that the other mechanisms for managerial supervision of agent/customer interaction include the revenue and productivity targets. The majority of managerial staff interviewed assume there is a direct connection between individual agent performance in terms of the hard targets, and the nature of that agent's interaction with customers: 'If someone is underachieving in terms of what they sell then we know they are not talking to people in the correct way ... it's easy to sell in this business provided you do it in the correct way' (STS).

Through these mechanisms, TSA emotional labour is being supervised indirectly. If workers do not meet revenue and productivity targets, some managerial staff assume they are not inducing and suppressing feeling in the prescribed or expected fashion. Many TSAs disagree with the assumed link between volume of sales, productivity and emotional labour. The majority of agents argued that outstanding sales performance is more luck than management. However, there is also evidence that some managerial staff tolerated the exercise of negative discretion during employee/customer interactions provided that the agent concerned was a 'good performer'. Some supervisors admitted, and many agents revealed, that it was only agents who consistently underperformed in terms of *sales* figures whose interaction with customers was closely monitored and carefully appraised:

> As long as you always reach your monthly target and put about fifty per cent on top once in a while ... they don't really care how you talk to customers ... if you reach your targets, your appraisal session will last about five minutes ... if you don't, it can last two hours. (TSA)

This would explain some of the instances of employee resistance, even when directly supervised, which are reported above. All TSAs though were at pains to point out that the extent of managerial supervision beyond the revenue targets varied greatly between individual STSs and STLs.

Thus, it would seem that Flightpath managerial control of the telephone sales emotional labour process, and the transmutation of the private emotional systems of the TSAs concerned, is far from 'complete'.

Conclusions

It has been argued throughout this chapter that the emergence of the new workplace within the service sector – shaped by the implementation of managerial programmes such as TQM and widely informed by 'the discourse of enterprise' and 'the cult(ure) of the customer' – has facilitated detailed managerial attention to the delivery of 'functional quality'. In fact, it can be argued that the very emergence of 'the new workplace' within the service sector as a whole has entailed a shift of managerial focus away from the 'technical' aspects of service delivery and towards a concentration upon the *way* in which services are delivered. This functional quality is now the basis of competition within the service sector. This chapter has discussed the consequences of this for the emotional labour which is demanded from service employees during their direct interaction with external customers.

The inherent problems associated with an examination of emotional labour have already been noted. However, it can be argued that the ethnographic approach adopted within the research process at Flightpath, which included the verification of *reported* behaviour (in interviews) through detailed non-participant observation of the labour process, is the best available means to analyse such phenomena.[8] Thus, on the basis of the empirical research reported and analysed in this chapter, the often dominant and popular picture of an 'empowered' and 'autonomous' employee within the new service sector workplace must be rejected as a serious misrepresentation of reality. It has been argued that the new workplace, represented by Flightpath Telephone Sales, demands increasing amounts of emotional labour from service employees. Given greater managerial attention to the nature of employee/customer interactions, demands for service employees to 'surface act' and 'deep act' have become inscribed within selection and training processes, supervisory and evaluative systems. In fact, as the '(functional) quality competition' increases, service sector employers are increasingly demanding that employees deep act – actively work on and change their inner feeling to match the display required by the labour process – in order to meet the perceived expectations of external customers. As we have seen, the pressures to engage in deep acting can be immense – at Flightpath they were exerted by an individualised managerial surveillance system which is tied to an equally individualised remuneration system.

There is an issue about how representative the one case examined in this chapter is of *general* trends within the service sector. The widespread adoption of quality initiatives was noted earlier, but these initiatives can be immensely varied in their form and focus (Wilkinson and Willmott, 1995). Many recent studies do reveal an increased managerial concern with the delivery of functional quality through the employee/customer relationship and the manifestation of this concern within selection, training, supervisory and evaluative processes (Ogbanna and Wilkinson, 1990; Fuller and Smith, 1991; Howcroft, 1991; Cressey and Scott, 1992; Filby, 1992; Kerfoot and Knights, 1994; Knights and McCabe, 1994; Fineman, 1995; Kerfoot, 1995; du Gay 1996). Moreover the research at Flightpath was part of a wider project examining the impact of TQM within the service sector (Taylor, 1995). Here, it was found that while Flightpath telephone sales management were enagaged in the most far-reaching and detailed surveillance of employees' performance of emotional labour, management within the other service organisations studied suggested that the Flightpath 'model' was one they wished to adopt in the future. This assertion is backed up by the perception that Newcastle Telephone Sales was a 'centre of excellence' or 'paradise centre' in terms of its implementation of TQM. The unit was often visited by representatives of other Flightpath units and telephone sales operations from different service industries. The head of Telephone Sales, UK argued that the Newcastle unit was 'spearheading telephone sales UK'. These perceptions were clearly related to the huge commercial success of the unit studied. During the research period it became both the biggest, and the most profitable of all Flightpath telephone sales centres. Thus, the processes reported and analysed in this chapter may be currently developing within other areas of the service sector.

Despite the far-reaching and individualised managerial surveillance system in existence at Flightpath, it has been maintained that managerial control of TSAs emotional labour was not 'total'. There was evidence of employee resistance to, and negotiation with, managerial prescription. Much of this was facilitated by employee exploitation of a surveillance system which appears to be far from 'complete'. Thus, for example, demands that TSAs were to 'deep act' during interactions with customers were sometimes met with direct rejection – a refusal to even engage in surface acting – in the telephone sales labour process. More commonly, TSAs were able to engage in forms of 'surface acting' which appeared to satisfy managerial expectations. In some cases, it may have appeared as if employees were deep acting. However, on reflection, they were able to articulate a difference between 'the self' being presented at work and their 'personality' outside of the workplace. Thus, it can be posited that Hochschild's (1983) distinction between 'surface acting' and 'deep acting' is too stark and simplistic. Within telephone sales, there were employees who were able to engage in what can be labelled 'sophisticated surface acting' or 'deep acting for pragmatic purposes' (in order to earn an income, meet and surpass targets). As indicated above, those employees who appeared to experience a 'transmutation of their private emotional system' – 'emotional alienation' – were in a tiny minority at Flightpath. This 'incomplete transmutation' illustrates that, as a resource for the creation of surplus value, the emotional labour of service employees is 'a double-edged sword' (Filby, 1992). Employers claim that they want employees to interact with customers in a 'natural' manner. However, these claims are made as simultaneous training, supervisory and evaluative systems are developed which attempt to *prescribe* this 'natural' manner in line with *perceived* customer expectations. Managerial attempts to control such a private, personal realm – while claiming that they wish to 'unleash' it – appear to provoke strong resistance from employees.

Finally, I would like to argue that, on a structural level, the core propositions of 'labour process theory' can inform an analysis of emotional labour within the new workplace. These are fourfold. Firstly, that the employer–employee relationship necessarily involves relations of material exploitation and the extraction of surplus value. Secondly, that there is a 'logic of accumulation' to the capitalist labour process 'which forces capital constantly to revolutionise the production process' (Thompson, 1989:243) – levels of profitability cannot stagnate due to the 'forces of competition'. Thirdly, and shaped by the first two elements, there is a 'control imperative' in the relation between capital and labour. The exact nature of this control imperative cannot be specified without detailed empirical investigation into particular labour processes. Fourthly, 'the social relation between capital and labour is based on structured antagonism' even if this is not 'necessarily manifested in visible conflict' (244).

Throughout the chapter it has been implicitly argued that the first, second and third of these 'structural elements' or 'capitalist structures' to the telephone sales (and emotional) labour process have driven the *material implementation* – particularly in the form of training processes, supervisory and evaluative mechanisms and consequent attempted emotional control of employees – of discourses stressing the importance of employee/customer interactions (and the emotional labour this involves) to the creation of surplus value and capital accumulation in the light of competitive pressures in this sector of the economy. It has been explicitly argued that the power of managerial demands or 'discourses' for employees to engage in emotional labour resides in the way they are *embedded* within the inequitable employment relationship and manifest themselves within training, supervision and evaluation procedures. Discourses can be powerful when wedded to material power and embedded within material structures (Giddens, 1979). The acceptance of the discourse of enterprise by those with work organisational power means that the key to continuing capital accumulation within service delivery (as exemplified by Flightpath Telephone Sales) is seen to rest within managerial control of the employee/customer relationship. The 'control imperative' within service delivery is, along with other areas of contemporary western economies, increasingly pursued in a *normative* manner – through attempted control of the thoughts and feelings of employees (Thompson and Findlay, 1996). However, empirical investigation has shown how management 'control' of emotional labour can be partial, incoherent and often contradictory. This has been argued as inherent to managerial 'control strategies' in relation to the capitalist labour process more generally (Hyman, 1987; Watson, 1994). This research has also shown that employee internalisation of attempted normative and discursive controls must not be assumed *even when worker behaviour may indicate 'consent'*.[9] In the case of the telephone sales operation studied here, TSAs appeared to 'pragmatically' rather than 'normatively' (Mann, 1982) accept managerial prescription of emotional labour via the discourse of enterprise. Furthermore, this pragmatic acceptance has been primarily generated by material rather than discursive power. At the very least, it can be said that evidence indicating employee internalisation of the discourse of enterprise is inconclusive in this case.

The structural approach of labour process theory is, however, limited in terms of understanding and analysing how these structural forces impact upon the lived experience of employees within the workplace. The fourth core proposition can only serve as a *general framework* in understanding the varied, and often contradictory ways in which employees resist and consent to the emotional demands of the labour process – a task which is only beginning to be explored here. However, once an interrogation of the lived experience of the labour process is begun, the observation that 'gender relations are everywhere' (Pollert,1996:645) can be appreciated. Gendered power relations, which can only be revealed by investigating lived experience (Bradley, 1989; Pollert, 1996), both shape and are shaped by the structural properties of the labour process. At the level of lived experience, emotional labour is a distinctly gendered phenomenon (Filby, 1992). However, the concern in this chapter has been to reveal the way in which the deployment of emotional labour can be shaped by capitalist structures within paid work, and to begin exploring some of the ways in which employees can resist such forms of managerial control. It must then be recognised that the analysis of emotional labour, even within the telephone sales labour process at Flightpath, offered here is inevitably partial and limited. The gendered nature and experience of emotional labour within the service sector – and how this can involve a complex interplay of 'compliance, consent and resistance' to gendered power relations within the labour process (Pollert, 1996) – is explored elsewhere (Tyler and Taylor, 1997).

Acknowledgements

This chapter is an edited version of a paper – 'Emotional Labour and TQM: A labour process analysis' – originally presented to the *14th Annual International Labour Process Conference*, University of Aston, Birmingham in 1996. The author would like to thank Chris Warhurst and Paul Thompson for helpful comments on earlier drafts of this chapter.

References

Bolton, S. (1997) 'Emotion Here, Emotion There, Emotional Organisations Everywhere', paper to the *15th Annual International Labour Process Conference*, University of Edinburgh.
Bradley, H. (1989) *Men's Work, Women's Work*, Cambridge: Polity Press.
Brown, R.K. (1992) *Understanding Industrial Organisations: Theoretical perspectives in industrial sociology*, London: Routledge.
Cressey, P. and McInnes, J. (1980) 'Voting for Ford: Industrial democracy and the control of labour', *Capital and Class*, 11, 5–33.
Cressey, P. and Scott, P. (1992) 'Employment, Technology and Industrial Relations in the UK Clearing Banks: Is the honeymoon over?', *New Technology, Work and Employment*, 7:2.
du Gay, P. (1996) *Consumption and Identity at Work*, London: Sage.
du Gay, P. and Salaman, G. (1992) 'The Cult(ure) of the Customer', *Journal of Management Studies*, 29:5, 615–33.
Elias, N. (1987) 'On Human Beings and their Emotions: A process-sociological essay', *Theory, Culture and Society*, 4, 339–61.
Filby, M. (1992) 'The Figures, The Personality and The Bums: Service work and sexuality', *Work, Employment and Society*, 6:1, 23–42.
Fineman, S. (ed.) (1993) *Emotion in Organisations*, London: Sage.
Fineman, S. (1995) 'Stress, Emotion and Intervention' in Newton, T. (ed.) *'Managing' Stress: Emotion and power at work*, London: Sage.
Fineman, S. and Sturdy, A. (1997) '"Struggles" for the Control of Affect', paper to the *15th Annual International Labour Process Conference*, University of Edinburgh.
Fox, A. (1974) *Beyond Contract: Work, power and trust relations*, London: Faber and Faber.
Fuller, L. and Smith, V. (1991) '"Consumers" Reports: Management by customers in a changing economy', *Work, Employment and Society*, 5:1, 1–16.
Giddens, A. (1979) *Central Problems in Social Theory*, London: Macmillan.
Groonroos, C. (1984) *Strategic Management and Marketing in the Service Sector*, London: Chartwell-Bratt.
Hill, S. (1991) 'How Do You Manage a Flexible Firm ?', *Work, Employment and Society*, 5:1, 397–415.
Hochschild, A.R. (1983) *The Managed Heart: The commercialisation of human feeling*, Berkeley: University of California Press.
Hochschild, A.R. (1993) 'Preface' to Fineman, S. (ed.) *Emotion in Organisations*, London: Sage.
Howcroft, J. (1991) 'Customer Satisfaction in Retail Banking', *The Service Industries Journal*, 11:1, 11–17.
Hyman, R. (1987) 'Strategy or Structure ?: Capital, labour and control', *Work, Employment and Society*, 1:1, 25–56.

James, N. (1989) 'Emotional Labour: Skill and work in the social regulation of feelings', *Sociological Review*, 37:1, 15–42.

Kerfoot, D. (1995) 'The "Value" of Social Skill ?: A case from centralised administration in a UK bank', paper to the *13th Annual International Labour Process Conference*, University of Central Lancashire, Blackpool.

Kerfoot, D. and Knights, D. (1994) 'Empowering the "Quality" Worker ?: The seduction and contradiction of the total quality phenomenon', paper to the *12th Annual International Labour Process Conference*, University of Aston, Birmingham.

Knights, D. and McCabe, D. (1994) 'Total Quality Management and Organisational "Grey" Matter', presented to *Work, Employment and Society in the 1990s: Changing boundaries, changing experiences*, University of Kent, Canterbury.

Lewis, B.R. (1988) 'Customer Care in Service Organisations', *International Journal of Operations and Production Management*, 8:3.

McCabe, D., Knights, D. and Wilkinson, A. (1994) *Quality Initiatives in Financial Services*, Research Report, Financial Services Research Centre, Manchester School of Management, UMIST.

McCabe, D. and Knights, D. (1995) 'TQM: Reaches the subjectivity that other management initiatives cannot reach', paper to the *13th Annual International Labour Process Conference*, University of Central Lancashire, Blackpool, April.

Mann, M. (1982) 'The Social Cohesion of Liberal Democracy' in Giddens, A. and Held, D. (eds) *Classes, Power and Conflict: Classical and contemporary debates*, London: Macmillan.

Newton, T. (ed.) (1995) *'Managing' Stress: Emotion and power at work*, London: Sage.

Ogbanna, E. and Wilkinson, B. (1990) 'Corporate Strategy and Corporate Culture: The view from the checkout', *Personnel Review*, 19:4, 9–15.

Pollert, A. (1996) 'Gender and Class Revisited; or, the Poverty of "Patriarchy"', *Sociology*, 30:4.

Sewell, G. and Wilkinson, B. (1992) '"Someone to Watch Over Me": Surveillance, discipline and the just-in-time labour process', *Sociology*, 26:2, 271–90.

Sturdy, A. (1994) 'Smiling But Not (Always) Meaning It', paper to the *12th Annual International Labour Process Conference*, University of Aston, Birmingham.

Swan, E. (1994) 'Managing Emotion' in Morgan, T. (ed.) *Women in Management: A developing presence*, London: Routledge.

Taylor, S. (1995) 'Work and Autonomy: Case studies of clerical work and emotional labour', unpublished PhD thesis, Department of Sociology, University of Durham.

Thompson, P. (1989) *The Nature of Work: An introduction to debates on the labour process*, London: Macmillan, 2nd edition.

Thompson, P. and Findlay, P. (1996) 'The Mystery of the Missing Subject', paper to the *14th Annual International Labour Process Conference*, University of Aston, Birmingham.

Tyler, M. and Taylor, S. (1997) '"Come Fly With Us": Emotional Labour and Sexual Differentiation Within the Airline Industry', paper to the *15th Annual International Labour Process Conference*, University of Edinburgh.

Walsh, K. (1995) 'Quality Through Markets: The new public service management' in Wilkinson, A. and Willmott, H. (eds) *Making Quality Critical: New perspectives on organisational change*, London: Routledge.

Watson, T. (1994) *In Search of Management: Culture, chaos and control in managerial work*, London: Routledge.

Wilkinson, A. and Willmott, H. (1995) 'Introduction' to Wilkinson and Willmott (eds) *Making Quality Critical: New perspectives on organisational change*, London: Routledge.

Notes

1 Here, we are contributing further to an emerging critical literature examining the impact of quality initiatives (see for example Wilkinson and Willmott (eds) (1995)). However, even this critical paradigm has thus far failed to examine the nature and significance of emotional labour within such new working practices.

2 My emphasis.

3 Each TSA has an individual revenue target which he or she must surpass each month. Consistent failure to meet monthly revenue targets would, according to all levels of management, eventually result in dismissal. TSAs are only targeted on *direct* sales – when payment is received and the TSA can authorise the printing and dispatching of tickets by post. This does not include bookings which are reserved or merely 'keyed'. Surpassing the team's collective monthly revenue target earns the team a collective monetary award. Three-monthly and annual awards (money and holidays) are presented to teams which surpass their revenue targets. Recorded on a league table, individuals within the centre also compete for monthly and annual 'going for gold' awards (money and holidays). Similar team and individual awards are also made, and league tables constructed, on the basis of holistic, performance-related pay points accumulated.

4 Emphasis in the original.

5 My emphasis.

6 Emphasis in the original.

7 Emphasis in the original.

8 For full details, and a full defence, of the ethnographic approach adopted see Taylor (1995).

9 This is not to suggest that there was conclusive evidence of managerial normative internalisation of the discourse of enterprise at Flightpath. In fact, there was some evidence of managerial cynicism in relation to the TQM programme. This, in part, facilitated 'the incomplete transmutation' explored here.

6 Capitalising on Subjectivity: The 'New Model Worker' and the Importance of Being Useful

Jörg Flecker and Johanna Hofbauer

Introduction

The ever-new buzz words for the ideal worker, such as 'intrapreneur' or 'self-manager', can be seen as management rhetoric and fashions without major consequences for the labour process. But it can also be maintained that these notions and images shed light on the processes of social construction of the 'model worker', that is, the historically variable ideal of workers' subjectivity and behaviour. It is, for example, quite surprising that few demands are evident for the traditional virtues of work, such as reliability, performance of one's duties or obedience, in current managerial discourses, although these have been the cornerstones of the work ethic in capitalist societies. Instead, 'responsible decision makers', 'intrapreneurs', 'self-managers' and 'self-developers' have entered the scene. In contrast to conventional wisdom, such labels are not reserved for managers or workers in financial services and the like. The discourse embraces virtually every industry and occupation, blurring the differences, in socio-psychological terms, between the board of directors and the shop floor.

In a sweeping historical sketch the development of the image of the 'model worker' can be described as a corollary of the changes in the management of labour during the so-called three industrial revolutions (see Müller-Jentsch and Stahlmann, 1988). During the first industrial revolution, between 1780 and 1850, subcontracting and 'putting-out' systems were replaced by internal contracts establishing direct authority over work. The main management problem was the control of recalcitrant labour, the establishment of factory discipline and industrial time rhythms. Consequently the normative ideal of the factory worker put into practice disciplinary processes focused on punctuality, reliability and obedience.

The second industrial revolution, between 1880 and 1930, brought about big corporations and mass production of standardised goods. The autonomy of craft workers, their work rules and capacities for 'restriction of output', became one of the most prominent managerial concerns. Taylor's obsession with transferring all knowledge on the production process from the shop floor to the planning departments reflects the aim of coming to terms with the 'instinctively lazy' worker. The concepts of 'scientific management' disseminated by engineers and the parallel rationalisation movement undermined the then widespread view that the worker was the only creative factor of production; instead they dehumanised him and her to a passive element of a completely determined labour process (Müller-Jentsch and Stahlmann, 1988:14).

In the context of the strict separation of conception and execution, the will-less and opinionless 'man-as-machine' assumes the role of the 'model worker'. The active, generative part that workers play is conceived in mechanistic terms and in terms of physical power: the model of the 'human motor' (Rabinbach, 1992). Human labour is reduced to an executing organ – creativity and ingenuity are not only not wanted but are actively excluded on the grounds of reducing efficiency.

During the 'third industrial revolution', characterised by decentralisation, flexible production and new technologies, new management strategies aim at a flexible and overall utilisation of 'human resources'. In this context, the emergence of a new image of the 'model worker' reflects two interrelated tendencies: first, changing skill needs and attitudinal requirements, encapsulated in the term 'intrapreneur', and, second, the increased dependence of the labour process on workers' active and creative contributions. If divisions of labour and detailed rules governing work activities are abolished, allowing for a choice of means to reach pre-set targets, then organisations depend to a larger extent on self-reliant workers. In the attempt to capitalise on the 'subjective factor', Human Resource Management (HRM) moulds employees in the image of the new 'model worker' by way of selection, training and appraisal.

In this chapter we develop arguments about the relationship between organisational change and the social construction of ideals of workers' subjectivity. First, we sketch recent changes of the labour process in order to argue that in a process of 'reflexive restructuring' organisational spaces have been 'opened up' creating opportunities and obligations for self-reliant work activities. Second, against this background we describe the new image of the 'model worker' by referring to public discourses, notions of organisational membership, and the skill and training debate, which all to a certain extent play a role in the formation of subjectivity. The third part of the chapter contains arguments that qualify the seeming congruence between new forms of work organisation on the one hand and subjective potentials and work orientations in contemporary society on the other. The analysis of both the organisational features and the characteristics of subjectivity reveals limits and contradictions leading to new types of conflicts in the workplace.

Opening Up Organisational Spaces

Since the early 1980s, the concomitant structural characteristics of organisations – separation of conception and execution, strict horizontal and vertical division of labour, detailed work rules and bureaucratic employment relationships – have all been increasingly questioned and partly replaced. With reference to Beck's theory of 'reflexive modernisation' in the German debate, this tendency in organisational change is referred to as 'reflexive restructuring' (*reflexive Rationalisierung*) (Pries, 1991) because of its focus on the limitations of efficiency caused by previous rationalisation strategies. Among the most important reasons for this reorientation of organising principles are high levels of automation, changing market conditions, and the emulation of Japanese management.

Technology as a driving force of organisational change has long been underestimated because of the understandable desire to avoid technological determinism. In the last decade or so, however, a rather consensual view of changing labour utilisation as a consequence of rising automation levels has emerged. The much debated 'new production concepts' which were found in capital-intensive manufacturing industries include enlarged work roles and higher skills on the part of the production workers (Kern and Schumann, 1984). New manufacturing technology – it is maintained – can only be used efficiently if management abandons Tayloristic criteria of work organisation. Of course, not only technological requirements but also changes in management ideology are seen as reasons for the reorientation of restructuring strategies. The core of the argument is that new production concepts aim at a fuller utilisation of the capacities of human labour through reskilling and increasing the levels of discretion on the shop floor. While Kern and Schumann focused on what they called 're-professionalisation of production work', critics have argued that new production concepts remove barriers to labour utilisation and therefore lead to an intensification of labour (Düll, 1985; Deutschmann, 1989).

For our argument both points are important: in order to reduce down-times of complex technology the division of labour between machine operating and maintenance is reduced, while the self-reliance of machine operators, who of necessity are subject to less direct control, is increased. These new work roles are termed 'system regulators' or 'problem solvers' (Schumann *et al.*, 1994). Work itself takes the form of 'supervisory' or 'guarantee work' (*Gewährleistungsarbeit*) which indicates enlarged discretion and, as a consequence, increased importance of self-reliant judgement and competent intervention. It is well known from descriptions of Fordist production regimes that rules are double-edged: they are devices of management control and negotiated limitations on labour utilisation at the same time. It is therefore not surprising to see that the removal or replacement of some of the rules governing workers' activities makes them vulnerable to pressures to increase performance.

In the 1980s, new cost-cutting strategies which, in the name of flexibility, partly deviated from Taylorist principles, were first addressed in the debate on the development of the service sector. It was argued that the temporal and substantial uncertainty of demand makes it necessary to provide excess capacity. Thus work in the service sector and in many white-collar areas cannot be rationalised in the same way as in manufacturing. Personnel numbers can only be reduced by establishing *temporal and functional flexibility* which allows for adjustments of personnel capacities to business needs (Berger and Offe, 1981). Consequently, organisational change has aimed at increasing management discretion to assign tasks flexibly, and at enlarging options for the flexible deployment of labour both in temporal and functional terms. However, the task structure and the hierarchy of the organisation could remain unchanged.

The *integration of tasks* takes us a step further. Wherever there is uncertainty as to when a single task has to be carried out, the utilisation of labour can be intensified by enlarging the number of different tasks assigned to one employee (Baethge and Oberbeck, 1986). This principle is followed if, for example, auxiliary work is integrated into clerical work, if salespersons are assigned more products or customer groups, but also if indirect production work is integrated into direct production work. Task integration at the individual level includes some form of functional flexibility. However, in contrast to the principle mentioned above, it is the worker him and herself who 'redeploys' his or her capacities according to the requirements of production or business. This not only makes planning easier but also reduces the need for direct control by introducing a small degree of self-management.

Moving from the individual to the collective level leads us to *teamworking*. In this case, flexibility is enhanced through job rotation and flexible assignment of work within the team. Barriers to the utilisation of productive capacities of individual *and* collective labour are removed in order to speed up decision making on day-to-day production matters and to cut throughput times (Thompson *et al.*, 1995). Though taking different forms, this applies not only to capital-intensive but also to labour-intensive production. Some forms of teamworking, such as semi-autonomous groups, enlarge the scope of activities not only of individual group members but also of the group as a whole: the group assumes some of its superiors' functions as well as some specialist responsibilities (Berggren, 1991). The functional space occupied by production workers is therefore widened both vertically and horizontally.

In contrast, the concept of 'lean production' contains restricted group autonomy, though it is suggested that companies set up multifunctional teams in their effort to focus activities on the immediate production process (Womack *et al.*, 1990). The removal of barriers between management functions, and between specialists, aims at improving and speeding up the innovation process. Worker participation is oriented towards innovation and continuous improvement. Within the context of our argument here, such involvement strategies can be seen as enlarging the organisational space in an additional dimension: the monopoly on innovation held by engineers is broken up in order to allow workers to contribute to efficiency-enhancing measures. According to the concept of 'Toyotism', management not only utilises the ingenuity of skilled workers, but also of those carrying out repetitive tasks on the line: 'So in addition to workers being required to follow the "one best way", they are instructed to constantly ask "is there a better way?"' (Rinehart *et al.*, 1994:157). In companies applying participation programmes, the scope for workers' activities therefore includes design and planning tasks. While the primary aim is to utilise workers' experience and knowledge for the enhancement of efficiency, in addition, companies offer more interesting activities to workers doing repetitive jobs, and let them know that their ideas are important to the company.

The removal of barriers not only applies to functional and hierarchical division of labour within the organisation. Many companies aim at rendering their organisation more permeable to market pressures. By way of establishing profit centres and internal supplier–customer relations, managements attempt to apply the market principle internally. Continuous 'make-or-buy' decisions based on benchmarking also expose sub-units to external market pressures. Work roles at middle management level are thereby being changed considerably as they are 'enriched' by financial decision making and 'entrepreneurial' activities.

In our view, this brief overview of recent trends in organisational design suggests a blurring of internal delimitations as well as of the external boundaries of organisations. This argument not only refers to properties of the bureaucratic organisation, such as division of labour laid down in formal job descriptions, or to Taylorist–Fordist production organisation. It also reflects, for example, the diminishing influence of traditional demarcations between professions and trades which are defined by societal institutions external to the company. We would like to suggest that, since the 1980s, managerial concepts have aimed at removing formal, traditional and political structures of organisations, thus creating an open organisational space not only for deployment of labour but also for self-management by employees. At the same time, strict performance targets are being set for smaller and smaller organisational sub-units. This development is probably best encapsulated in a critical understanding of the term 'empowerment': in their attempt to meet pre-set organisational goals and targets, workers should be restricted by as few organisational rules – and as little protection – as possible.

In management writing and organisational analysis, this open space is theorised in various ways. Mintzberg's concept of 'adhocracy', for example, already included the flattening of hierarchies, informal and shifting division of labour and self-organising teams. In recent debates on Japanisation similar points have been stressed, in particular in describing 'information redundancy' in the 'learning organisation'. Instead of a clear division of labour, excess information should be created by, for example, overlapping departments or process phases. The open organisational space is presented as providing unrestricted opportunities for workers' individual or collective activities. In short, instead of carrying out well-defined tasks or following organisational rules, workers are required to do whatever is needed to reach organisational goals: their activities should be guided by a more general notion of rendering themselves 'useful' to the organisation.

It is obvious that with such far-reaching changes in organisational principles the role of workers' subjectivity and the image of the 'model worker' has changed dramatically. The ideal of an obedient yet energetic person compliantly following orders and rules has been replaced by the 'intrapreneur', a self-reliant, entrepreneurial yet loyal personality. Subjectivity is to a lesser degree addressed as a problem and more frequently as a resource. The increasingly unstructured and uncertain contexts of decision making enhance the demand for reflective abilities. As for the employee, research on 're-professionalisation' of work in manufacturing (Kern and Schumann, 1984; Schumann *et al.*, 1994), and on occupational orientations of skilled workers (Lappe, 1993), conveys the picture of a congruency between organisational needs for subjectivity and individual aspirations (Baethge, 1990). From a socio-psychological point of view, new workplaces are presented as being more acceptable to workers, the organisational change described therefore signals the end of alienation. Consequently, management overcomes conflicts typical of the workplaces of the past.

In the remainder of this contribution we would like to question the assumptions of current managerial discourse. Before developing arguments about the limitations of the congruency thesis a more detailed description of the changing image of the 'model worker' is required.

The Changing Image of the 'Model Worker'

We would like to describe the new image from different angles, looking at three arenas for the social construction of the 'model worker'. First, we have to take account of public discourses on the self-developing, entrepreneurial personality which is called for in contemporary society. These general images and norms act on the formation of subjectivity and can easily be taken up in work-related contexts. Second, the debate about organisational membership or citizenship addresses workers' attachments to the company they work for and aims at normatively integrating the self-actualisation stressed in public discourses. Third, management perceptions of skill needs and of necessary training activities directly reflect the characteristics of the 'new model worker' by 'operationalising' subjectivity.

'Entrepreneurial activism' and other fashionable notions go beyond mere management rhetoric intended to change attitudes and values within the company. They are promoted not only by management literature but also, in the guise of the 'pioneer spirit', or, more commonly, do-it-yourself attitudes, through commercials, movies and life-style magazines, often in a much more sophisticated and persuasive way. The media act as what W.I. Thomas described as 'defining agencies', producing images which incite strategies of imitation and pretension in our achieving, success-oriented society. Research on the novel social character of the 'self-developer' (Maccoby, 1989; '*neuer Sozialcharakter*': Baethge, 1990) also indicates that the image of the energetic, inventive sportsman or idealist, is becoming attractive, while the image of the bureaucrat is fading. Mixa (1996), in her study on career-women's checklists for success and manuals for self-design, shows how women are encouraged to overcome the mere 'housewife-and-mother' image and turn to 'everyday-life self-managers'.

Beyond instrumental rationality, political rhetoric refers to basic ideas of democracy and revives the positive image of the 'self-responsible member of society'. The idea of democracy, in this view, is that everybody contributes to the collective goal, that every citizen proves to be responsible, doing whatever is within his and her scope. Rose puts it in the following way: 'The citizens of a liberal democracy are to *regulate themselves;* government mechanisms construe them as active participants in their lives' (1992:10).[1] Neo-conservative discourse in western European politics furthermore contributes to the prevalence of entrepreneurial images. The gradual demolition of the welfare state, indeed, imposes a shift of political responsibilities from the state to the individual.

Du Gay (1996) states that, for Britain, the generation of the 'enterprising subject' within an 'enterprise culture' arose during the era of Thatcherism on the economic foundation of a so-called 'retail revolution'. This change in the economic structure, 'which extended well beyond the simple proliferation of shops and shopping centres', also brought about cultural changes. The role model of the retailer comprises not only specific skills, but also a range of social and mental dispositions such as the 'will to stay close to the customer', which, as du Gay notes, 'isn't simply a matter of "logistical engineering" since it also implies "engineering the soul" of the retail employee, to ensure that he or she automatically delivers the highly individualised quality service "demanded" by the enterprising consumer' (1996:116). The enterprise discourse disseminates the life order of the market which is imposed upon other spheres of life, to an extent that, 'multiple ethical selves constituted across the spheres give way to a singular conception of a human life as "enterprise of the self"' (192).

In a similar vein, Deutschmann (1989:276) describes the phenomenon of 'cultural imperialism of management' in Germany. In the course of a progressive enlargement of the territory of the market, the managerial discourse has gained hegemonic status throughout the 1980s. Almost all spheres of life are perceived in terms of this discourse's rationality (utility, efficiency, profitability). One of the major mechanisms which Deutschmann mentions to account for the establishment of this hegemony is personnel recruitment and new techniques of labour utilisation. In times of ever tougher competition on the labour market, personnel managers tend to select personnel according to attitudinal factors, such as unrestricted availability and overall flexibility, which renders the employee's life more dependent on work than ever before.

Theories of subjectivity lead us to an even clearer distinction between the public and the private realms. According to Schülein (1988), the individual does not act as an entrepreneur trying to cope with the increased demands of managing day-to-day life but, rather, is torn between different expectations and temptations of various institutions or social contexts. It is a specific competence of the modern subject to develop 'instant personalities' capable of reacting to divergent demands. Modern subjectivity must be flexible and differentiated, capable of adaptation, of coping with heterogeneous situations and, in particular, of 'balancing' diverse parts of the self (Schülein, 1988:401). In spite of the different conceptualisation of the phenomenon, these concepts nevertheless share an account of the new efforts of modern selves to cope with novel or contradictory expectations and to manage life – be it as entrepreneur of the self or as juggler of selves.

Organisational Citizens and Intrapreneurs

It is no coincidence that, at the same time as this notion of self-governing citizens is being promoted in public discourse, the notion of citizenship is entering the scene in management debates. Managerial discourse on 'organisational citizenship' or 'organisational membership' is aimed at making companies more inclusive again in relation to their employees' lives. On the other hand, loyalty secured by symbolic means is crucial to organisations in two respects. First, it is supposed to provide the 'glue' of flexible organisations. Second, it offers a source of meaning to the individual, which is needed in more open work situations requiring continuous self-reliant decision making. Consequentially, there are normative implications for the image of the 'model worker' and actual consequences for workers' day-to-day lives (Voß, 1994) which derive from these bonds established between organisation and member. Comparable to the public discourse referred to above, the talk about organisational membership conveys moral pressures. In the demand to devote themselves more fully to the aims of the company and to perceive of the latter as a community, in contrast to previous stages, management asks for enthusiasm, devotion, visions, motivation and emotions (Voß, 1994).

Organisation citizenship re-establishes and strengthens bonds between the economic and social systems, which are regarded as having been destroyed in the course of industrialisation. The concept of citizenship means an attempt to tie work life and life-world together more closely and makes one of the pillars of 'commitment-built organisation'. Critics accordingly state that it may pose a threat to the integrity of private life and intimacy. Parker puts it this way: '... it is as if we are being asked to weaken or relinquish wider (and increasingly contested) affiliations of nation, gender, occupation, ethnicity, profession, region and so on in favour of (putatively uncontested) organisational membership' (1997:77).

The significance of organisational offers of citizenship, furthermore, is to be seen in the context of changes in the mechanisms of social integration in wider society. Donzelot's (1991) findings, for example, concerning the discourse of 'pleasure in work' which gained importance in the 1970s in France, equally stress that the individual is construed as searching for meaning through experiences of participation, engagement, and sharing of responsibility at work. Work has been made 'the territory of the social, the privileged space for the satisfaction of social need' (Donzelot, 1991:253). It is noted by other writers that modernisation implies individualisation and relative isolation, and that people are thus rendered more receptive to social and normative integration policies of organisation (Knights and Willmott, 1989:550; see also Beck, 1986).

Hancock (1997) alludes to feudal or 'neo-feudal' relations and criticises Parker for implying that citizenship can mean a process of democratisation. He claims that the 'requirements of flexible, technology-driven organisations have produced the need for a neo-feudal version of the (male) vassal class, with incentives such as company health care, housing and profit sharing schemes, and even a "job for life"' (104). What is important for our argument here is that the new 'model worker' is not only self-reliant and entrepreneurial but seemingly an 'organisation man' (or woman) at the same time. Self-actualisation remains integrated to – and instrumentalised for – the aims of the organisation.

Skill Needs and Training Measures

At a different level, the image of the new 'model worker' is most prominent in the debate on new skill requirements. In spite of massive technological and structural change in Europe in recent years, both managers and academics seem to be less concerned about new or adapted technical skills than about 'tacit' and 'extra-functional'. The latter seem to dominate both the discussion and companies' selection strategies. Consequently, on top of educational and occupational qualifications, workers and job-seekers have to compete at the level of personality traits (Townley, 1991; Hohn and Windolf, 1988; Klinkenberg, 1994).

In German-speaking countries, the notion of *Schlüsselqualifikationen* ('key skills') has become a buzz word. Originally meant to denote abilities needed to 'unlock' other potentials, the term soon assumed a wider connotation of self-reliance, work-related virtues, social and communicative skills, and reflective abilities (Simoleit *et al.*, 1991). The term has also been seen as an 'operationalisation' of the concept of workers' subjectivity which is typical of open work situations (55).

There is, however, an additional angle to the same phenomenon: the new focus in the skill debate also means a shift from *abilities for* achievement, such as knowledge, dexterity or experience, to *willingness to* achievement manifested through motivation, engagement and identification with the company. The dissemination of the new image of the 'model worker' not only conveys the demand for particular skills and personality traits but, at another level, focuses attention on finding the right kind of person.

The area of personality training provides abundant examples of attempts at moulding the 'new model worker'. These include a large variety of topics ranging from time management and self-motivation to body control (Hofbauer, 1995 & 1996). It is a specificity of this area of training that participants cannot be forced to learn, rather they have to be motivated to voluntarily broaden their talents. The individual is incited to reposition his and her behaviour and to reshape his and her mental or emotional disposition. Techniques of self-discipline are offered that lead to the accomplishment of desirable goals. Such techniques may involve: self-examination by means of drawing up 'strengths-and-weaknesses charts'; goal setting and monitoring of goal realisation; ongoing self-monitoring by means of recording deficiencies and improvements; or the imagination of pleasurable experiences, and 'positive self-talk' aimed at self-motivation and reinforcement. Sims and Lorenzi (1992) refer to a self-management training programme for US state employees which taught them to write 'behavioural contracts' for themselves for administering self-chosen rewards and disincentives. They had to set 'proximal and distant goals', to 'self-monitor performance', to 'administer the identified consequences, and to brainstorm for potential problems and solutions for potential obstacles' (193).

Methods of organisational socialisation also include personnel appraisal. Though labelled as 'performance' appraisal, these methods are often oriented towards personality traits. Criteria used in such appraisal systems communicate to employees which attitudes and behaviour are desirable in the particular organisation (Townley, 1991). If repeated periodically, people are encouraged to reshape their dispositions in order to meet the standards.

Limits and Contradictions

Only on the surface is there a perfect match between the new image of the individual on the one hand and the characteristics of new organisational designs on the other. We would argue that such congruence can only be arrived at through undue generalisation. More detailed analyses reveal various problems, limitations and contradictions in this relationship and therefore in the instrumentalisation of subjective potential. In the following we want to address these limits and contradictions focusing on three aspects: first, formation of the self of necessity exceeds what organisations require from their 'subjective factor', an aspect we call 'superfluous subjectivity'; second, management is confronted with considerable and increasing diversity in subjective potentials and occupational orientations both in processes of organisational change and in sustaining new work structures; third, attempts at mobilising subjective potentials are inherently contradictory in that workers' self-actualising activities are unleashed and restrained or channelled at the same time.

The problem of 'superfluous subjectivity' and structural overcharge

The first reason for a mismatch between the formation of the self in contemporary society and organisational strategies of capitalising on the 'subjective factor' relates to the interplay between different societal subsystems and institutions. Various socialisation agencies create aspirations and expectations that necessarily exceed what working life can deliver for the vast majority of people. Paradoxically, cultural imperialism of management and 'enterprise culture' do not necessarily contribute to the instrumentalisation of private life. Not only work but also family life and leisure have become more demanding and objects of higher aspirations through the very process of generalisation of entrepreneurial and developmental attitudes. Depending on labour-market conditions, this can threaten the employers' monopoly on the exploitation of people's physical and psychological energies. The notion of 'superfluous subjectivity' is intended to stress that when management tries to utilise subjectivity, it will find that workers' orientations, aspirations and ingenuity are neither tailor-made nor reserved for their purposes. On structural grounds, therefore, subjectivity remains 'in surplus' even in relation to new organisational designs.

'Late capitalism' is characterised by increasingly complex social structures, caused by more individualistic designs for living which, in return, are rendered possible or even fostered by the system. Beck (1986) highlights the following contradiction: individuals are forced into geographic mobility in order to seize educational and work opportunities. Their educational and occupational aspirations and private interests regarding the establishment of durable relationships *structurally overcharge* the individual in co-ordinating life and establishing day-to-day routines. Partners, family and friends may then turn out to be somewhat troublesome as the individual is compelled and incited to put a substantial part of his and her energy into the job.

Pahl (1997) argues that private life is becoming increasingly demanding and points out problems of organisation and timing that people have to cope with nowadays. He illustrates the subject with the example of a man in his forties who may be divorced and remarried, thus having to meet his responsibilities to his first family, and possibly also to his step-children. His parents may need care. His wife has to meet equal responsibilities within her family. In this situation, life can become quite complicated. Weekends have to be organised with moving from here to there, time schedules have to be made, and daily routines to be found and managed (147). Different life situations have to be taken into account if management is to claim to consider the needs of the employees. In real life the abstractly construed 'model worker' turns out to be either man or woman, having different forms of family obligations and living different life stages with different consequences for the employment relationship. In moving from utilising labour power to capitalising on the whole person, companies can hardly avoid being confronted with other aspects of people's lives.

Thus one has to take into account the fact that people do not only try to be 'useful' to their employer. Society encompasses a variety of social institutions, each of which addresses the individual as responsible and committed (partnership, parenthood, leisure activities and so on) and may be in conflict with organisational goals. Research on attitudes towards work not only shows that the younger generation of employees is more determined in the search for meaning in work. They also strive for a more meaningful and intensive life outside work: 'Vivre le plus', in Camus' terms (Zoll, 1989; Trautwein-Kalms, 1995).

On the question of how 'superfluous' subjectivity is generated, the main argument also relates to education and the relationship between education and occupational system. Recent studies on education and vocational training have stressed the point that, compared to their parents' generation, people spend a considerably longer period of time in the expanded and easier to access education system. Baethge (1990) holds that a longer duration of education and training processes has a significant impact on people's expectations towards working life: their expectations as to how they imagine an attractive or unattractive job are more clear-cut. So are their views of what they may get in return for their investment in training, for having spent a longer period of their lifetime in education. An above-average job not only means higher job security and payment but also status and power. Having been educated for decision making, one eventually expects to become a decision maker. Yet Kadritzke and Baethge (1995) see a significant gap between these aspirations and actual possibilities. In their study on white-collar work in the engineering and chemical industries, they argue that professional life appears to be disappointing for many, for example, owing to the fact that they are denied strategic information, which restricts their ability to act out their role of experts (Kadritzke, 1997). New management fashions proclaim slogans like 'exchange of responsibility for trust' (*Vertrauen gegen Verantwortung*), while workers experience an unequal exchange of intensified efforts and stress for 'low trust', at best.

Hence there is an inherent tension between demands for higher levels of education and demands for adaptation to organisational structures. In fact it can be argued that this move towards more open spaces for self-reliant activities can, in part, be accounted for by individuals whose excessive aspirations created in the education system have been frustrated in traditionally ordered organisations (Baethge, 1990). If open spaces are only partial concessions to employees' expectations, we cannot assume a perfect match between aspirations and organisational realities.

In referring to these arguments we would like to highlight two interrelated points: first, if individuals are challenged and incited to develop 'entrepreneurial' attitudes and behaviour, they will turn out to be more inventive and strategic on their own behalf as well. Organisations, rather than having members, are confronted with calculating 'entrepreneurs of their own labour power' (Voß, 1994), which may, in turn, lead to increased difficulties in normatively integrating individuals' self-actualisation. Instead of an 'end of history' in organisational control struggles we can expect the perpetuation of 'old' conflicts, that is, conflicts over the subordination of individual orientations and behaviour to organisational goals. Furthermore, the debate highlights the possibility of 'new' conflicts stemming from structural overstrain. If subjectivity is seen as 'instant personality' forced to cope with many heterogeneous situations we can conceive of conflicts not only as stemming from antagonistic interests and limits to normative integration: additional, 'new conflicts' emerge as a consequence of excessive demand for coping with and balancing diverse situations (Schülein, 1988).

Limits to managing change and diversity

As a corollary of demands from various social institutions on the individual and of changing boundaries between the public and the private realms, we can see an increasing diversity of occupational orientations and of pressures stemming from different life situations. Therefore the problem is much more complex than simply matching the overall organisational design to individual aspirations. Generalisations, both about new forms of organisation and about new workers' attitudes and orientations, gloss over the fact that innovations that comply with the needs and wants of some may be detrimental to those of others. Furthermore, as the consequences of 'lean management' for middle managers show, organisational change does not affect all workers in the same way. Although it would be an exaggeration to present organisational change as a zero-sum game, the creation of opportunities for self-actualisation at the lower ranks of an organisation reduces the discretion hitherto enjoyed by superiors:

> ... dominant groups do have their own needs for autonomy, discretion and non-alienated activity. It is therefore probable that they will define other people's self-management as a threat to their identities and produce regulatory responses. (Thompson and McHugh, 1990:343)

We would like to illustrate the increasing diversity with recent empirical research on occupational orientations of managers and industrial experts in Germany (Baethge *et al.*, 1995). In contrast to the assumption of a congruence between organisational design and individual aspirations, the authors argue that subjective orientations on the one hand and behavioural standards of companies on the other are becoming increasingly irreconcilable. The findings include a typology of occupational orientations which is of particular importance to our argument. Apart from the 'self-developers' already mentioned, the study discerns the following types: 'professionally oriented', 'design oriented' and 'status oriented' persons. According to the survey, which covered a sample of 172 managers and experts in large manufacturing companies, the largest group, 32 per cent, could be classed as 'self-developers'. Traditional professional orientations, which includes esteeming scientific standards, trying to satisfy scientific interests at work and bonds with the scientific community, accounted for 25 per cent of the sample. Traditional status orientation, which combines loyalty to the company with clear career aspirations, was attributed to a further 25 per cent of the respondents. The wish to influence the organisation and, in particular, to innovate structures and processes is at the core of the 'design oriented' type, which was only found in 15 per cent of managers and experts.

The existence of distinct 'types of subjectivity' has severe consequences for companies, because personnel management is confronted with very different work and occupational orientations (Baethge *et al*, 1995:61). Traditional policies focus on distributing status, even though these bureaucratic methods of creating commitment only seem appropriate to a quarter of the occupational groups. According to these findings, the novel social character of the 'self-developer' is of considerable quantitative importance among the occupational stratum studied. However, given the fact that only one-third of managers and experts show these characteristics, companies cannot try to fully tailor their organisational structures and reward systems according to the desires and needs of self-developers.

In spite of efforts to create organisational cultures, people who desire to be 'useful' in working life use different criteria: those of the scientific community; those of organisational development and change; or those implicit in bureaucratic control. Strategies for capitalising on subjectivity would therefore need to include a great variety of structures and instruments, which is hardly to be found in today's companies.

Although 'managing diversity' is a proclaimed goal in many companies, the effects are questionable. Activities under the older term 'equal opportunities' on the whole failed to overcome the problems of reconciling work with family obligations (Papouschek and Pastner, 1997). It is therefore justified to expect other and contrasting strategies to bridge the gap between organisational requirements and diverse individual aspirations, for example HRM strategies to form homogeneous workforces. Careful selection of personnel is, of course, nothing new. What is new, according to Townley, is that such procedures are being applied not only to managerial staff and professionals but also to blue-collar workers. By way of personality testing in particular, those applicants are selected 'whose needs are seen as corresponding to the organisational ethos' (1991:93).

The 'new model worker' is, therefore, less diverse than managerial accounts allow for. It is diversity at *macro* level, in the sense of segmentation and regional variation of labour markets, that allows for strategies to build homogeneous workforces. 'There is plenty of evidence to show that large companies have often made their location decisions with specific cheap or controllable labour sources or stable industrial relations in mind' (Thompson and McHugh, 1990:108). Research on Japanese transplants in the US and the UK, for example, highlights the fact that the plants are deliberately located in areas with high unemployment.

Contradictions in the mobilisation of subjectivity

Even if we narrow our focus to processes internal to the company, we can discern important limits to the utilisation of the 'subjective factor'. By this we mean not only that old conflicts persist to some extent in the instrumentalisation of human labour, but also that new tensions are emerging between the demands for bringing in the 'whole person' and the conditions and opportunities for doing so. In the following we would like to illustrate both old and new conflicts with examples of new forms of work organisation on the shop floor.

As we argued earlier, against the background of Taylorist attempts to minimise the influence of workers' subjectivity on the labour process, participatory management on the one hand is making repetitive assembly work more acceptable to workers and, on the other, is attempting to utilise their experience and ingenuity for purposes of restructuring and cost reduction. While these strategies of 'reflexive rationalisation' are congruent with individual aspirations of workers, they do not necessarily overcome old tensions. Empirical findings on 'quality circles' and 'continuous improvement processes' (CIP) reveal the shortcomings of an 'end-of-alienation' argument (Flecker and Krenn, 1996).

The literature on 'Japanisation' contains examples of the persistence of old conflicts between management and labour stemming from the contradiction between involvement and openness on the one hand, and rigid economic targets on the other, which are likely to frustrate workers' expectations and to result in a calculative rather than committed participation. In their case study of the Canadian automobile plant CAMI, Rinehart *et al.* (1994) show how involvement in cost saving resulted in an open conflict of interests. In a competitive environment the innovative 'intrapreneur' always risks abolishing his and her own or his and her colleagues' jobs. A union leader at CAMI put it like this:

> They kaizened their area ... to create a floater among the team. The guy was moving around, helping everybody, unpacking stuff, and then the company turned around and started taking the person away when there were headcount problems. The team busted their ass to create the position within the team to make it a little easier for themselves. And then as soon as they did it the company started fucking them by taking it away all the time. And the team exercised its right to refuse unsafe work a couple of times as a result of that. (Rinehart *et al.*, 1994:164)

Turning to new conflicts, we would emphasise new forms of stress and strain caused by forms of work organisation that aim at instrumentalising the subjectivity of workers. Research on working groups in German engineering firms (Moldaschl, 1994) lists a number of causes for psychological burdens that basically stem from contradictory demands and tensions between what is demanded from workers and the working conditions they enjoy:

- the integration of tasks without adjustment of manning levels, for example, increases the work load and forces 'risky' behaviour on workers;
- the costs of flexibility in terms of settling-in time, for example, are left to the workers thereby stifling their willingness for job rotation. To management, workers then appear to be 'inflexible' or 'not willing to learn';
- responsibility is devolved on workers without giving them appropriate powers to influence the conditions of performance;
- increased group autonomy without appropriate training measures and systematic job rotation leads to 'pecking orders', leaving workers with lowest status with the most unpleasant work;
- stress is caused by unclear and contradictory competencies, in particular if the principle of responsibility and self-organisation is frequently broken by interfering superiors.

A worker being able to use his/her ingenuity to influence his/her immediate working environment certainly fits the common image of desirable working conditions. Participation schemes are therefore generally attractive. However, innovative action, and 'entrepreneurial' attitudes in general, are not necessarily in line with management expectations and organisational demands. It would be premature to conclude that the existence of socially-constructed individual needs as outlined above determine the outcome of involvement procedures. There is a wide range of possibilities: workers' commitment to organisational goals; partial congruence between individual or group aspirations on the one hand and management aims on the other; open conflicts of interest and opposition to managerial demands (see also, for example, McKinlay and Taylor, 1994; Deutschmann, 1989).

Involvement in continuous improvement processes is just one example of organisational contradictions and possible tensions. A similar argument can be developed with reference to profit centre organisation and budgetary control. While decentralisation of responsibilities creates space for individual decision making, the very same organisational design acts as a powerful control strategy, putting economic pressures on individual employees (Armstrong, 1996). What is usually obscured by the rhetoric of empowerment is the fact that the space available for individual commitment and ingenuity is surrounded by guiding mechanisms that are more than an organisation's safety net. Rather, they constitute a recycled iron cage: the necessities (*Sachzwang*) both of complex production processes and of budgetary control delimit workers' options tremendously. Research by Baethge et al., (1995) on industrial experts, showed that these enjoyed most discretion at the level of planning and executing their immediate work activities. More than a third, however, complained about a lack of decision-making powers in relation to the means and conditions of work, and nearly 50 per cent were dissatisfied with the low level of information on, and involvement in, the formation of company strategies. Concentration and internationalisation of capital tends to worsen this situation further.

At a more general level, the conspicuous contrast between the managerial literature on organisational membership or 'citizenship' and the trade union-oriented discussion on citizen rights within the company *(Bürgerrechte im Betrieb;* Müller-Jentsch, 1994) draws our attention to a similar aspect. Management addresses, and symbolically demands or offers, autonomy, responsibility and embeddedness of the individual within the organisation. However, can 'membership' remain detached from citizenship, duties from rights and responsibilities of workers for the 'community' from responsibilities of the 'community' for workers? There is at least the potential for workers to turn round management rhetoric or put forward demands for a realisation of messages conveyed in high-gloss mission statements and in training courses (Baethge *et al.,* 1995; Parker, 1997). This argument is not meant to ascribe a politically progressive effect to new management strategies but to highlight the persistently contradictory relation between mobilisation and instrumentalisation of subjectivity in work organisations.

Conclusions

The image of organisational change, on the one hand, and that of subjects that aspire to give meaning to their lives through work, on the other, seem to match perfectly well. But it becomes obvious that capitalising on subjectivity partly reproduces the old, and creates new contradictions and conflicts. Different areas of working life provide different interrelations between individual needs and orientations on the one hand and opportunities offered, and coercion exerted, by organisations on the other. Organisations that have, for example, to put up with strong professional cultures enjoy less discretion in determining the 'soft facts' of organisational behaviour.

On a theoretical level we can draw the conclusion that capitalism today is producing specific contradictions with particular effects on processes of formation of the self, rendering individuals useful *and* recalcitrant. As capitalist calculations and imperatives are gradually imposed on all societal subsystems besides the economic system, these systems enter into relations of competition with one another (Beck, 1986). For example, the expectations of private designs for living, desirable relationships, meaningful leisure-time behaviour and the like, are also exceedingly demanding and impose claims of propriety, pleasure and duty on individuals which 'overdetermine' identity, or, according to other notions leading to similar conclusions: they cause a 'fragmentation of identity' (Lasch 1978; Alvesson, 1990). Individuals establish 'partial identities' whose synchronisation remains necessarily incomplete as those expectations are contradictory (Schülein, 1988).

With this in mind we have argued that socialisation necessarily generates 'superfluous' subjectivity, that is, aspirations, desires for self-actualisation and so on, which exceed what is required in new forms of work organisation. Furthermore, several societal subsystems are acting on individuals, attempting to render them 'useful' within the realm of their respective logic. In their attempt to instrumentalise subjectivity therefore, business organisations face 'competition' from, for example, the leisure industry and institutions of private life.

Finally, there are, of course, tensions between the symbolic reality of mission statements and other artefacts of corporate culture on the one hand and the material reality of organisational relationships on the other, leading to obvious shortcomings in attempts at mobilising subjectivity. In the sociology of work and industry, individual aspirations and occupational orientations are still perceived against the background of bureaucratic and Taylorist forms of work organisation. Against the background of the exclusion of workers' subjectivity as well as the damage to personal identity, opportunities for self-actualisation in new organisational designs necessarily seem to meet workers' needs and wants. However, if we look at the increasing pressures and uncertainties of work situations, and conceptualise workers' subjectivity as 'instant personalities' and 'multiple selves', the workplaces of the future – freed of guiding and protecting rules – are easily conceivable as overstraining the coping and balancing capacities of individuals. The 'new model worker' is therefore subject to constraints from above and below in any capacity to capitalise on subjectivity.

References

Alvesson, M, (1990) 'Organisation: From Substance to Image?', *Organisation Studies*, 11:3, 373–94.

Armstrong, P. (1996) 'Management Accounting and the Casualisation of Labour' in Flecker, J. and Hofbauer, J. (eds) *Vernetzung und Vereinnahmung – Arbeit zwischen Internationalisierung und neuen Managementkonzepten*, Sonderband 3 der Österreichischen Zeitschrift für Soziologie, Opladen.

Baethge, M. (1990) 'Arbeit, Vergesellschaftung, Identität – Zur zunehmenden normativen Subjektivierung der Arbeit' in Zapf (ed.) *Die Modernisierung moderner Gesellschaften*, Verhandlungen des 25, Deutschen Soziologentages in Frankfurt a. Main.

Baethge, M., Denkinger, J. and Kadritzke, U. (1995) *Das Führungskräftedilemma. Manager und industrielle Experten zwischen Unternehmen und Lebenswelt*, Frankfurt und New York.

Baethge, M. and Oberbeck, H. (1986) *Die Zukunft der Angestellten*, Frankfurt a. Main.

Beck, U. (1986) *Risikogesellschaft. Auf dem Weg in eine andere Moderne*, Frankfurt a. Main, Suhrkamp.

Berger, J. and Offe, C. (1981) 'Das Rationalisierungsdilemma der Angestelltenarbeit' in Kocka (ed.) *Angestellte im europäischen Vergleich*, Göttingen.

Berggren, C. (1991) *Von Ford zu Volvo*, Berlin: Springer.

Deutschmann, C. (1989) 'Reflexive Verwissenschaftlichung und kultureller "Imperialisimus" des Managements', *Soziale Welt*, 3, 374–96.

Donzelot, J. (1991) 'Pleasure in Work' in Burchell, G., Gordon, C. and Miller, P. (eds) *The Foucault Effect: Studies in Governmentality*, London: Harvester Wheatsheaf.

Drucker, P. (1992) 'The New Society of Organisations', *Harvard Business Review*, 26, 95–104.

du Gay, P. (1996) *Consumption and Identity at Work*, London: Sage.

Düll, K. (1985) 'Gesellschaftliche Modernisierungspolitik durch neue "Produktionskonzepte"?', *WSI-Mitteilungen*, 3.

Edwards, R. (1979) *Contested Terrain: The Transformation of the Workplace in the Twentieth Century*, London: Heinemann.

Flecker, J. and Krenn, M. (1996) 'Double bind. Zur Gewährung von Autonomie in vernetzten Produktionssystemen' in Flecker, J. and Hofbauer, J. (eds) *Vernetzung und Vereinnahmung. Arbeit zwischen Internationalisierung und neuen Managementkonzepten*, Sonderband 3 der Österreichischen Zeitschrift für Soziologie, Opladen.

Hancock, P.G. (1997) 'Citizenship or Vassalage? Organisational Membership in the Age of Unreason', *Organisation*, 4:1, 93–111.

Hofbauer, J. (1995) 'Metaphern des Managens und Praktiken der Arbeitskontrolle' in Hofbauer, J., Prabitz, G. and Wallmannsberger, J. (eds) *Bilder, Symbole, Metaphern: Visualisierung und Informierung in der Moderne*, Wien: Passagen.

Hofbauer, J. (1996) 'Wenn Leistungsfreude zur Gewissensfrage wird. Über das Geheimnis der Selbstdisziplin und andere Mythen' in Flecker, J. and Hofbauer, J. (eds) *Vernetzung und Vereinnahmung – Arbeit zwischen Internationalisierung und neuen Managementkonzepten*, Sonderband 3 der Österreichischen Zeitschrift für Soziologie, Opladen.

Hohn, H.-W. and Windolf, P. (1988) 'Lebensstile als Selektionskriterien –Zur Funktion "biographischer Signale" in der Rekrutierungspolitik von Arbeitsorganisation' in Brose, H.-G. and Hildebrand, B. (eds) *Vom Ende des Individuums zur Individualität ohne Ende*, Opladen, Leske & Budrich.

Kadritzke, U. (1997) 'Hochqualifizierte Angestellte zwischen betrieblicher Herrschaft, Beruf und Lebenswelt' in Zilian, H.G. and Flecker, J. (eds) *Pathologien und Paradoxien der Arbeitswelt*, Wien: Forum für Sozialforschung.

Kadritzke, U., Baethge, M., 1995: '„ ... aber was sind Sehnsüchte gegenüber einer Beförderung?" Ein Versuch, die Welt der Angestellten zu begreifen' in Burkhart L. (ed.) *Großstadtmenschen: Die Welt der Angestellten*, Frankfurt a. Main.

Kern, H. and Schumann, M. (1984) *Das Ende der Arbeitsteilung? Rationalisierung in der industriellen Produktion: Bestandsaufnahme, Trendbestimmung*, München: C.H. Beck.

Klinkenberg, U. (1994) Persönlichkeitsmerkmale in Stellenanzeigen für qualifizierte Fach- und Führungskräfte: Eine Überprüfung ihrer Verwendung sowie der Selektions – und Akquisitionseffektivität', *Zeitschrift für Personal*, 4, 401–18.

Knights, D. and Willmott, H. (1989) 'Power and Subjectivity at Work: From Degradation to Subjugation in Social Relations', *Sociology*, 23:4, 535–58.

Lappe, L. (1993) *Berufsperspektiven junger Facharbeiter: Eine qualitative Längsschnittanalyse zum Kernbereich westdeutscher Industriearbeit*, Frankfurt a. Main, Campus.

Lasch, C. (1978) *The Culture of Narcissism: American Life in an Age of Diminishing Expectations*, New York: Norton.

Maccoby, M. (1989) *Warum wir arbeiten: Motivation als Führungsaufgabe*, Frankfurt a. Main and New York.

McKinlay, A. and Taylor, P. (1994) 'Power, Surveillance and Resistance: Inside the "Factory of the Future"', paper to the *12th Annual International Labour Process Conference*, University of Aston, Birmingham.

Mixa, E. (1996) 'Die neuen Heldinnen kommen' in Ernst, U. and Riedl, G. (eds) *Liebe, Technik und Ökonomie*, Wien: Service Fachverlag.

Moldaschl, M. (1994) '"Die werden zur Hyäne" – Erfahrungen und Belastungen in neuen Arbeitsformen' in Moldaschl, M. and Schultz-Wild, R. (eds) *Arbeitsorientierte Rationalisierung*, Frankfurt a. Main, Campus.

Müller-Jentsch W. (1994) 'Über Produktivkräfte und Bürgerrechte' in Beckenbach, N., and von Treeck, W. (eds), *Umbrüche gesellschaftlicher Arbeit, Soziale Welt Sonderband 9*, Göttingen: Verlag Otto Schwartz & Co.

Müller-Jentsch, W. and Stahlmann, M. (1988) 'Management und Arbeitspolitik im Prozeß fortschreitender Industrialisierung', *Österreichische Zeitschrift für Soziologie*, 2, 5–31.

Pahl, R. (1997) 'Nach dem Erfolg und dem Erfolg hinterher: Arbeit, Angst und Identität' in Zilian, H.G. and Flecker, J. (eds) *Pathologien und Paradoxien der Arbeitswelt*, Wien: Forum für Sozialforschung.

Parker, M. (1997) 'Organisations and Citizenship', *Organisation*, 4:1, 75–92.

Papouschek, U. and Pastner, U. (1997) *Im Dornröschenschlaf – Betriebliche Frauenförderung*, Wien: Wissenschaftsverlag.

Pries, L. (1991) *Betrieblicher Wandel in der Risikogesellschaft*, Opladen: Westdeutscher Verlag.

Rabinbach, A. (1992) *The Human Motor. Energy, Fatigue, and the Origins of Modernity*, Berkeley and Los Angeles: Unversity of California Press.

Rinehart J., Robertson, D., Huxley, C. and Wareham, J. (1994) 'Reunifying Conception and Execution of Work under Japanese Production Management? A Canadian Case Study' in Elger, T. and Smith, C. (eds), *Global Japanization?*, London: Routledge.

Rose, N. (1992) *Governing the Soul: The Shaping of the Private Self*, London: Routledge.

Schülein, J. (1988) 'Veränderungen der Konstitutions- und Reproduktionsbedingungen von Subjektivität', in König, H. (ed.) *Leviathan Sonderheft 9 'Politische Psychologie heute'*.

Schumann, M., Baethge-Kinsky, V., Kuhlmann, M., Kurz, C. and Neumann, U. (1994) *Trendreport Rationalisierung. Automobilindustrie, Werkzeugmaschinenbau, Chemische Industrie*, Berlin: Sigma.

Simoleit J., Feldhoff J. and Jacke N. (1991) 'Schlüsselqualifikationen – betriebliche Berufsausbildung und neue Produktionskonzepte' in Braczyk H.-J. (ed.) *Qualifikation und Qualifizierung – Notwendigkeit, Chance oder Selbstzweck?*, Berlin: Sigma.

Sims, H.P. and Lorenzi, P. (1992) *The New Leadership Paradigm: Social Learning and Cognition in Organisations*, Newbury Park.

Thompson P., Wallace T., Flecker J. and Ahlstrand, R. (1995) 'It ain't what you do, it's the way that you do it – Production Organisation and Skill Utilisation in Commercial Vehicles', *Work, Employment and Society*, 9:4.

Thompson, P. and McHugh, D. (1990) *Work Organisations – A Critical Introduction*, London: Macmillan.

Townley, B. (1991) 'Selection and Appraisal: Reconstituting Social Relations?' in Storey J. (ed.) *New Perspectives on Human Resource Management*, London: Routledge.

Trautwein-Kalms G. (1995) *Ein Kollektiv von Individualisten? Interessenvertretung neuer Beschäftigtengruppen*, Berlin: Sigma.

Voß, G. (1994) 'Das Ende der Teilung von „Arbeit und Leben". An der Schwelle zu einem neuen gesellschaftlichen Verhältnis von Betriebs- und Lebensführung' in Beckenbach, N. and von Treeck, W. (eds) *Soziale Welt Sonderband 'Umbrüche gesellschaftlicher Arbeit'*.

Womack J.P., Jones, D.T. and Roos D. (1990) *The Machine that Changed the World*, New York: Rawson Associates.

Zoll R. *et al.*, (1989) *Nicht so wie unsere Eltern! Ein neues kulturelles Modell?*, Opladen.

Note

1   Emphasis added.

7 The Times They Are A'Changing: Dividing and Recombining Labour Through Computer Systems

Joan Greenbaum

Introduction: From Automated to Distributed Systems

Computer information systems, like systems of work organisation, are designed. Sometimes the designers are computer systems analysts working for the same company for which they are developing information systems, developing for example new inventory control programs. At other times the designers may be consultants or outside vendors who develop systems for the general public such as general accounting packages. Whatever the method of system development, computer information systems are ordered to meet certain sets of requirements and such requirements generally reflect the organisational philosophy and objectives of upper management.[1]

In the earlier days of computer system development – from the late 1950s through the first half of the 1980s – systems were generally ordered to fit in with the objective of *automation*. In general, such systems tried to mimic older industrial models of automation by 'streamlining' production and feeding pieces of data – as if they were pieces of products – into computer systems. Typical systems in this period of automation included insurance claims processing, routine payroll processing and large bank accounting systems. Such systems were called *data* processing systems, rather than the current term of information systems or information technology, because the focus on automation tended to reduce everything into small individual units of data which then had to be fed or processed through a series of computer programs before it would come out as chunks of information.[2] Automated data processing systems were designed to fit with routinised and rationalised systems of vertically divided labour; fitting well with the types of deskilled jobs that Braverman (1974) described.

By the second half of the 1980s, however, most large organisations had shifted their operational strategies away from the sequential orientation of automated systems and had begun to spell out requirements specifications for systems that allowed for more *distribution* of information. The newer systems were designed, for example, so that customer service representatives, whether they worked for insurance companies, telecommunications firms, or banks, could look up wider varieties of information in random data bases and handle assorted questions rather than step-by-step customer queries. In the 1980s some authors optimistically predicted that distributed systems and flatter organisations would foster more 'upskilled' jobs (Adler, 1986; Zuboff, 1988) but, as the next section illustrates, horizontally divided labour and more integrated jobs and information systems have not necessarily resulted in enhanced pay or security for workers with such jobs.

This chapter lays out a framework for better understanding how the design of information systems is closely linked with the design of work organisation; specifically systems for dividing labour. In analysing how the division of labour is reflected in the design of computer systems I focus on the ways that the management functions of *control and co-ordination* are introduced into the technical specification process. The chapter does not answer the question of who (which specific level of management[3]) orders changes in work and technology, nor does it present evidence that management objectives are necessarily met, but it does focus on some of the reasons why changes are planned and some of the effects of the new designs. The interplay between technical and work system design, particularly in regard to control and co-ordination of labour, is not always a smooth one. Even with the clearest of strategic plans, top management is not able to control a smooth integration of work and technical systems for a variety of reasons which are discussed in the following sections.

Although computer and social scientists routinely pay lip-service to the social roots of technology, pronouncements about the introduction of what appear to be totally new concepts, like the Internet and distributed computing, once again come from the direction of technologically determined statements. In order to avoid such discussions, the analysis presented here outlines the ways that computer systems design reflects social and economic goals and, in some cases, conflicting practices. In addition it highlights the circumstances under which computer systems have been constrained by prior technical developments as well as the way labour was organised in producing earlier computer systems (Kraft, 1977; Friedman, 1977; Greenbaum, 1979).

Technical system design, like organisational design, is laden with contradictions – contradictions clearly between the needs of workers and the objectives of managers, as well as contradictions between the objectives of organisational redesign and the objectives which can be successfully carried out by technical systems. In the case of the design of newer information systems there is at least one more level in the complexity of contradictory processes, for the newer distributed systems are being ordered to replace, or at least try to replace, lower- and middle-level managers. As the following sections illustrate, newer information system design has been fairly successful in pulling together formerly divided tasks and embedding the co-ordination functions of management in software and networked applications. The control functions of management however, while specified in technical requirements, are harder to 'capture' in hardware and software: indeed it is an open question whether the contradictory nature of control over labour power could be embedded in technical systems.

Changing Times

In the US it is now clear that jobs and work have changed, but in the beginning of the 1990s the recession masked structural job shifts – shifts that were to bring: huge cuts in the number of 'payroll' or formerly full-time jobs; a compression of job titles in the remaining full-time jobs; and a surge in the 'contingent' or 'off the payroll' workforce. These three changes were coupled with the increasingly common phenomenon of people working from home, both as 'telecommuters' (those on staff or payroll) and as freelancers. Church, in *Time* magazine, put it succinctly:

> By now, these trends have created an 'industrial reserve army' to borrow a term from Karl Marx – so large that a quite extraordinary and prolonged surge in output would be required to put all its members to full-time, well-paid work. (1993:35)

Many of the changes have been propelled, in part, by upper management's belief in Business Process Re-engineering, which was used to flatten organisational hierarchies, reorganise work processes, redefine required skills and introduce new technologies under the banner of fighting the new world order of global competition (Greenbaum, 1995). Indeed a key debate among the leading industrial nations and a central concern in the EU, is the issue of how to steer a course that avoids the unstable labour conditions that American, and to some extent British, workers face following the wave of political deregulation which supported work and technology designed for work speed-up.

Jobs, however, do not change overnight. Patterns of reorganisation build on prior structural changes. In the 1960s and 1970s, structural change took the form of rationalising and dividing labour and developing computer systems that cemented, separated and divided labour in place (Kraft, 1977; Greenbaum, 1979). This was a clear attempt to control costs and workers: within known economic circumstances; within the limitations of expensive mainframe technology; and given management's reliance on bureaucratic principles. Now economic circumstances are less predictable, yet computer hardware and software is much more so, giving rise to a reliance on using technology to solve, by design, some of the control and co-ordination problems management had in prior periods.

Just as jobs do not change overnight, technical change is slowed by the ways the design of the technology fits with work organisation. Current changes which facilitate the imbedding of control and co-ordination into computer software and network technology give upper management more flexibility in changing skill and job requirements. Computer applications like Lotus Notes or Microsoft's Office 97 are examples of software that support geographically dispersed tasks that can be recombined and managed through information accumulated in the software systems. Workers using these applications and using an enhanced range of job and computer skills would probably be considered as having 'upskilled' jobs, but their wages and working conditions do not necessarily reflect this enhancement. New management strategies of so-called flexibility attempt to accomplish the same objectives that the old bureaucratic ones based on rationalised labour did – controlling wages and limiting labour's control of the work process. In many cases, the new flexibility results in jobs which contain a wide range of skills but do not have wages which reflect these increased skills. It also can result in work tasks that are designed to be so flexible that far fewer workers are needed to get the same amount of work done (Head, 1996; Herzenberg, 1996).

Changing occupations

This chapter uses examples of white-collar work in the US. Given the current emphasis on development of a world-wide technical infrastructure – including fax, voice mail, email, information technology and Internet standards – the global redivision of labour can increasingly be supported by the same technology and can take on characteristics such as those found in the deregulated economies of the US and Britain. Understanding the way the technology is designed to support deregulated and so-called flexible labour is important for finding ways to combat the increasing stress and pace of work that workers are facing under these conditions. It is also critical for better addressing the facts of declining or stagnating wages in white-collar work.

According to the US Department of Labor, occupational categories that commonly fall within the white-collar sphere include: (1) executive, administrative and managerial, (2) professional specialties, (3) technical and related support and (4) administrative support, including clerical (*Employment and Earnings*, 1995). It is argued that these occupations represent the new 'knowledge industries' and the growth of knowledge workers (see Warhurst and Thompson's opening chapter in this volume). While knowledge work is a convenient title to apply to work that is largely based on gathering, applying and communicating information, I find it less useful than the older category of white-collar work which at least differentiated jobs which were typically found in offices. Indeed the characteristics of so-called knowledge work can also be found in a growing number of service sector jobs including package delivery, telecommunications repair services, and of course sales. A central argument presented here and elsewhere in this volume is that as labour is redivided geographically and horizontally, the older definitions of jobs and occupational categories are becoming blurred. A few examples of the ways that white-collar categories are fading in the move to more horizontally divided labour are presented so that the specific ways pieces of jobs are being recombined and integrated with technology can be better understood.[4]

The job of editorial assistant is one categorised as administrative support, yet workers are expected to have at least a bachelors degree and knowledge of a large number of computer applications. Editorial assistants, while carrying the 'assistant' title, frequently make a number of decisions about production and prepare contracts and other professional documents associated with manuscript publication. Traditionally in the US the job was considered as a low-waged stepping stone to other editorial work, but now as more senior level editors are expected to take on a larger number of manuscripts and more responsibilities, there are fewer slots to which these assistants can vertically rise. In addition, as the number of computer applications editorial assistants are expected to know increases, and as their responsibilities expand, salaries have been kept in check by publishing firms as they merge and expand in attempts to take on broader markets. The editorial assistants near the bottom of the old status hierarchy bear the brunt of increased labour flexibility – more responsibility, more skills and yet wages as low as $17 000 (barely above the official US poverty line for a family).

Customer Service Representatives are a growing job category[5] as large organisations such as banks, telecommunications companies and insurance firms move more of their 'in-person' services to remote telephone operations. Service 'reps' typically answer telephones and use a number of computer data bases and applications to look up information at customers' requests. In banking, for example, they help bank customers, often by solving problems that lower- to mid-level bank officers used to handle.

Similar to editorial assistants, they represent jobs where pieces of older, divided labour have been put back together into work that is more 'upskilled' but where wages have been suppressed by the same merge-and-expand strategies of deregulated financial institutions. And as the large financial institutions move toward flatter organisational structures, customer service representatives are finding it difficult to find rungs on a job ladder to which they can move.

In one case study I found that the ratio of service representatives to supervisors was 1:20; a ratio that had been expanding as more and more of the work was monitored via telephone and computer systems with performance statistics accumulated in data bases for review by supervisors and higher-level management. In that institution, a megabank on the East Coast of the US, there were no middle managers – service representatives reported to supervisors who in turn reported to the vice president in charge of operations. Computer and telephone monitoring, along with an upskilled workforce where each representative was to 'act professionally' toward the customers, played roles in increasing productivity per worker. And the swell of well-educated laid off white-collar workers in the region kept the labour market flooded with potential recruits while leaving wages at the very low level (compared to skill) of $19 000. The fact that the telephone service center – the epitome of geographically distributed work – could be relocated anywhere at the flip of an electronic switch, acted as a further lid on wages.

While workers at the lower-status end of white-collar work are most seriously affected, professional and managerial work is also pressed under the flatter organisational structures and expected increases in skills, responsibilities and output. The work of computer systems analysts is often looked at as indicative of high status, 'high tech', knowledge work, and indeed it combines professional, technical and managerial responsibilities. Yet systems analysts, often functioning as project managers, talk of having to juggle several projects at the same time, a marked increase in work load and pace of work. Along with their technical duties their managerial responsibilities have increased as more projects have to be co-ordinated and more reports accumulated and supplied to upper management. Although there are a large number of computer tools to support these technical tasks, such as Computer Assisted Software Engineering (CASE) programs, and specialised project administration and tracking systems to aid in the project co-ordination functions, systems analysts that I interviewed complained that the existence of software support was used as an argument for them to produce more reports and co-ordinate more projects and staff. It is difficult to find average salaries for systems work since it, like customer service jobs, represents a wide range of former job categories from programmer through second-level managerial titles. However, industry studies indicate that salaries are not increasing, particularly in regions where there are a large number of 'downsized' technical workers (*Computer World*, 1996).

Not Under One Roof

The reasons for current economic change have been discussed elsewhere in this volume and are not the focus of this chapter, but it is useful to point out a few of the highlights of earlier periods that contrast sharply with current economic developments in order to see how these characteristics have influenced information system development. The change in technical design focus from automated systems to distributed ones reflects changes in the economic characteristics of the current period and the way strategic management views have switched gears to keep up with them. Specifically, management theory now advocates a flatter, more horizontal organisation of work, at least for service sector industries that are the cornerstone of post-industrial work (see, again, Warhurst and Thompson). Automated computer systems that were designed to process the flow of data were developed under the assumption that most information flowed top–down and that organisations should be structured in a more rigid, vertical manner. Distributed systems, on the other hand, acknowledge that many pieces of jobs that had been carved up in the earlier period are now being recombined. Thus the intent behind the newer systems design is to take work that is spread out geographically, physically and temporally and reintegrate it horizontally using distributed networks and multi-purpose software. This reintegration often falls under the rubric of systems designed for enhanced 'communication' since the central management function of communicating information is now considered part of the technical design specifications.

Industrial division of labour and automation

Since rationalised division of labour and automated technical systems were concepts that grew out of the industrial period it is useful to take a brief look at the function of these concepts then and now. Table 7.1 highlights some of the major characteristics of the industrial period, contrasting them with post-industrial factors – specifically those that computer systems are designed to support. One of the ways of characterising early industrial capitalism (late 1700s–early 1800s) was the fact that workers were brought from small home-based workshops into larger factory units. The guiding economic principle was that of *economies of scale* – where profits were derived from creating larger units of operation. This implied that work which was situated under one roof, such as that of factories, would be more efficient than small-shop enterprises. Economies of scale formed a basis for work organisation and the beginning of managerial practices. In the early period this meant that in order to bring workers out of their small enterprises and off farms, *labour contracts* were needed to compel workers to work in one place and work for set periods of time (Marx, 1867; Thompson 1968).

   The use of labour contracts which specified wages and hours reinforced economies of scale through managerial practices aimed at disciplining and supervising large numbers of workers into producing standardised products at a faster pace. Over the course of the nineteenth century and throughout the first half of the twentieth, labour was *divided and rationalised* along lines that led to the need for *close supervision* and a *hierarchical* structure of control for management. The technical systems that were introduced to support this form of divided work organisation were based on *sequential flow of products* leading to systems of *mechanisation and automation*.

Post-industrial division of labour and distribution

Industrially developed countries in North America and Europe experienced a major break-up of these industrial characteristics by the 1980s. The principle of economies of scale proved not as effective in the face of increased global competition and politically deregulated economies. In the 1980s this situation was becoming clear in office work where detailed division of labour, centralised offices and bureaucratically centralised decision making were cited as management failures (Peters, 1982). Additionally it was possible to base computer hardware on miniaturised circuits and new mass production techniques which had been developed to microcomputers, and to produce them inexpensively (Friedman, 1989).

Table 7.1   Historic overview of characteristics influencing design of work and technical systems

Industrial period	*Post-industrial*
Economic Characteristics:	**Economic Characteristics:**
• centralised workplace	• distributed workplaces
• economies of scale	• flexibility of scale and place
Organisational Characteristics	**Organisational Characteristics**
• labour contract	• temporary agreements
• rationalised division of labour	• partial reintegrated labour
• close supervision	• individual/group responsibility
• hierarchy (later bureaucracy)	• flatter structure–professionalism
• vertical integration	• horizontal integration
Technical Characteristics	**Technical Characteristics**
• mechanisation (later automation)	• communication
• product based	• information based
• sequential flow	• distribution

The economic shifts were becoming visible in computer system specifications by the late 1980s when companies began to call for information systems that could handle *communication* functions and *distributed* work (Greenbaum, 1996). These changes in technical requirements reflected the economic change toward flexibility of scale and place as well as distributed workplaces. These in turn were evidenced by organisational changes which stemmed from the separation of work from place and the delinking of labour contracts from employment, resulting in an increasing reliance on *temporary agreements* rather than employment contracts. This is borne out by both the increasing unemployment rates in the US and Europe and the noticeable impact of part-time, freelance and leased-work relations.[6]

By the 1980s the post-industrial economic and political landscape was shifting out of the workplace and away from the fixed time and place arrangements of industrial relations. Thus the design focus for computer systems was shifted from systems that automated flows of products produced under one roof to systems that needed to co-ordinate and control workers and information spread out over time and space.

Building on the Old

Young people entering the US labour market today have a hard time imagining that corporate bureaucracy was the theme song of the 1970s. The rhetoric that they now hear about the ways that companies need to be 'lean, mean, market machines' stands in stark contrast to the prior period. Yet the ground rules of bureaucratic functioning – from its reliance on rule-based decision making to the rationalistic way computer systems were designed – are still with us. Three levels of control functions from this period have become the building blocks of newer management strategies and act as behind-the-scene assumptions in information system design. These are:

- corporate managerial control was based on getting workers to internalise the rules (Edwards, 1979);
- division of labour was focused on separating tasks and dividing the head from the hands (Braverman, 1974);
- computer system design, in the form of systems analysis procedures, mirrored corporate practices of control and division of labour (Greenbaum, 1979).

The analysis presented here will highlight some of the major changes since the 1970s in management strategies of control on these three levels. Mainframe computer systems for automated data processing and bureaucratic corporate procedures were in place in the 1960s but the 1970s represent an important starting place since all three control systems were well-entrenched by this time.

The 1970s: vertical division and bureaucratic control

On the overall corporate level, Edwards, in *Contested Terrain* (1979), describes what made bureaucratic controls tick: 'The defining feature of bureaucratic control is the institutionalisation of hierarchical power. "Rule of law" – the firm's law – replaces "rule by supervisor command"' (21). Now in the 1990s, the rule of 'professionalism' is supplementing strict bureaucratic control, yet its fundamental principle rests on getting the worker, particularly the white-collar worker, to shoulder the responsibilities for getting the work done the way the firm wants it. Professionalism is a way where the 'rule of law' is internalised even further, so that, in theory, hierarchical levels of managers do not need to be around to enforce it. The internalisation of rules through professionalism plays an important role as increasing numbers of workers are but rarely do coding or testing. At a lower level in professional and corporate hierarchies, there are many other IS workers who are far more closely managed and less well paid, officially permitted to make few decisions about the technology they use, the programmes that they work on or the direction of their organisation.

Reinforcing this sense of division, numerous recent surveys on IS occupations confront the monolithic image of IS staff as those who deal with managing, developing and programming new systems. Labour force surveys in the sector delineate distinct areas of IS jobs, including systems management, network support, systems development, technical support, operations, PC end-user support and help-desk operators (National Computing Centre, 1997; *Computerworld*, 1995). The nature of the work (its routinisation or focus on hardware or software, for instance), status, pay and the job controls experienced by these different groups vary greatly. UK surveys show a shifting composition of the IS workforce, with the most rapid growth (up to 10 per cent yearly) among network staff and end-user support, moderate growth in development, and a sharp decline in the number of operations staff. These developments reflect the rising importance of open systems and the reduced role of central IT departments, resulting in decentralisation of computing functions from the centre towards end-users, or alternatively towards outsourcing (National Computing Centre, 1993 & 1997).

There is also a growing degree of fragmentation and stratification of activities and responsibilities in software development itself. The *Computerworld* (1995) survey in the US found nine different types of job being performed within this field alone. Developers tended to become highly specialised (for example as COBOL or C programmers), usually working on different kinds of applications. In our own research, we found repeated references to differences of culture and outlook among these different groups, which were often also generational, reflecting tensions arising from the rapid pace of change and the constant threat to long-term job security. These workers are divided between organisations which are heavy IS users, such as banks or public services, and specialist software houses. The latter are gaining ground, especially as outsourcing grows and as downsizing hits employment in user organisations (Thomasson, 1994) .

This points to another remarkable feature with regard to the nature of IS occupations today, namely the shift from a simple labour market to an amalgamation of various distinct sectors, including technical experts, engineers, business consultants and clerical staff, for example (Orlikowski, 1989). This shift has implications for the nature of skills, knowledge and experience required, while signifying that computing jobs are found in an ever-widening variety of organisations. In skill terms, the corollary is that IS staff may be required not only to maintain and develop their technical abilities in line with advances in technology and applications (Currie *et al.*, 1993), but concurrently to enhance their organisational and business development skills to meet the strategic requirements of clients and employers.

Such developments amount to an extension of established tendencies towards more communicative and collaborative ties with users. The importance and difficulties of connecting programmers and other developers with users has long been recognised, at least for the preliminary work in agreeing systems specifications. As with developers themselves, users are often treated as an homogeneous group. Friedman and Cornford (1989) provided an early attempt to introduce greater clarity here, differentiating between six categories of user: (1) the patron, initiator and champion of the system, (2) the client, for whom the output is intended and who will pay the bills, (3) design interactors, that is, people involved in system specification and design, (4) end-users – the individuals who will operate the installed system, (5) those involved in maintenance and enhancement of the system and, (6) secondary users, including people displaced by the new system, people whose work is changed by the system, those whose non-work life is affected and proxy-users such as departmental managers and union representatives. More recently, Fincham *et al.* (1994) identified two critical variables which affect the proximity of users to IS workers, namely, their level of computing literacy and degree of organisational power.

These attempts to provide a more grounded understanding of user encounters and relationships with IS workers present an image of systems development as a highly complex social, organisational and professional bridging process (Quintas, 1991). Yet this is compounded by another aspect which has been even further out of focus in orthodox accounts of the development process, namely the emergence of gender stratification and segregation.

Studies of gender careers in IS (Baroudi and Igbaria, 1995) have shown that women are mostly found in the non-managerial group of IS staff. Men are more likely than women to be project leaders, IS managers and consultants while women tend to be concentrated in roles such as systems analyst, designer and programmer. According to the *Computerworld* (1995) US Salary Survey, only 17 per cent of chief information officers were women. In the UK, this percentage is even lower. Ordroyd (1996) reports that since 1991, women have made up just over 20 per cent of the UK IS workforce, while only 4 per cent were heads of IS departments.

Clearly, the overall nature of computing work remains complex and variable, and subject to diversification as far as skills requirements are concerned. The following section examines the powerful rationalistic tendencies in this area of work, and so the application of managerial strategies pursuing labour control. Subsequently, we will examine the limitations of such strategies, and the contrary tendencies within computing.

Rationalising the Computing Labour Process

The official history of software design work is one of progress through the application of engineering principles to systems programming and analysis

(Somerville, 1989; Pressman, 1992). In the 1960s, so the story goes, the growing ascendancy of software bottlenecks over hardware limitations created a sense of 'crisis', intensified by the pressures of the Cold War and of business demands for systems of increased complexity. Previously, the main constraint on systems performance, and the dominant cost, had been hardware. Software development was regarded as a creative and esoteric task, with mathematicians and other individualist staff recruited and given high degrees of autonomy (Friedman and Cornford, 1989).

Software productivity levels were low and failing to rise in a way which matched the demand for systems, while the nature of the work seemed to demand highly skilled labour which was in short supply, making it hard to retain key staff and even harder to restrain salary costs (Quintas, 1991). For the last thirty years or so, many of the new strategies which have been proposed for organising and managing software production can be seen as attempts at rationalisation, acceleration of productivity growth and the assertion of control from above. These initiatives have been aided by the shift of power in the 1980s from IS departments to marketing and finance which has left IS more vulnerable to the demands of senior management in user departments (Friedman and Cornford, 1989; Knights and Murray, 1994).

For one group of writers in the labour process tradition these management objectives have been largely achieved:

> The making of computer programs has been subject to a process of intellectual industrial engineering, a scientific management of mind work. In every important respect these techniques are identical to those applied in the production of cars and cornflakes. (Kraft and Dubnoff, 1986:194)

These authors chart a progressive degradation of software knowledge work, a slide from the status and autonomy of the skilled artisan to the regimented task-structures of Taylorised clerical labour. Since the mid-1970s, the time and motion brigade is seen as having subjected yet another area to the debilitating impact of 'divide and conquer' rationalisation (Kraft, 1977; Greenbaum 1979). By the most pessimistic accounts, new software technologies have separated conception from execution, diluting skills and transferring them to a combination of non-specialists and machines (Kraft, 1987; Kraft and Dubnoff, 1986). The resulting stratification of jobs has allegedly reproduced a conventional hierarchy of power and rewards, of highly paid senior managers dealing with policy, technical direction and user communications while under-managers allocate, supervise and evaluate clusters of technical 'detail workers' who perform the fragmented tasks of coding, programming, testing and so forth. The result is a proletarianisation thesis, and a scenario of deskilling and degradation.

A contemporary assessment does indeed reveal a number of rationalising elements. The first involves the *automation of programming*. When third generation languages (3GLs) such as COBOL were developed in the 1950s and 1960s, they made contingent and therefore dependent on the ideology of professionalism in order to hold on to their current contract or hope for the next piece of work, even if their salaries and lack of security stand in direct contrast to the well-paid, secure image of professionalism.

At the level of division of labour, the 1970s was a period when, at least in theory, strictly divided tasks were a cornerstone of bureaucratic functioning. Edwards describes how it is used to stratify work and motivate workers along the corporate path. He explains, 'work becomes highly stratified; each job is given its distinct title and description; and impersonal rules govern promotion. "Stick with the corporation", the worker is told, "and you can ascend up the ladder"' (21). Now, of course the ladder is being pulled away in white-collar work and the strict stratification of jobs is being loosened in favour of workers who do more all-around tasks. Yet it is still the impersonal rules that govern work practices, and these are not only reinforced by professionalism but also built into computer and telephone systems that, for example, monitor telephone-based bank representatives to make sure that they give out the most up-to-date and accurate information, and give it in the least amount of time. My argument here is that management is able to extract more productivity, and at lower wages, than with the stratified and specialised division of labour in the 1970s and 1980s, in part because the prior periods of rationalisation laid the groundwork for stretching the impersonal rules, and in part because the division of head and hands can now also be stretched to a new global level.[7]

To understand how divided labour can be put back together in new forms it is useful to briefly go back to Braverman's (1974) analysis of the 1970s. While the period he was studying was clearly characterised by divided, rationalised and separated tasks and workers, he warned us that this can take many forms, including those where, for example 'office rationalisation has in part been taking place under the banner of job enlargement and the humanisation of work' (37). The same warning is true for the flexibility arguments management puts forth today, for while the newer jobs, such as bank customer service representative, include a good deal of job enlargement, the pay is low compared to the skill level, and the intensity of work, with its accompanying stress, is reminiscent of assembly-line jobs (Greenbaum, 1995).

In describing how in the 1970s consultants were called on to cut labour costs and 'enlarge' jobs, Braverman says; 'In a typical case, a bank teller who is idle when the load at the counter is light will be pressed into service handling other routine duties such as sorting checks' (1974:39). Now, of course, banks are encouraging customers to use cash machines as they cut down on the number of branch banks and the number of tellers, and cheque sorting has, since the late 1970s, been outsourced to service bureaus which use high-speed machines for such processes. In banking, as in other financial and service sector industries that had undergone intense prior rationalisation, newly integrated jobs can be built around the pieces that remain.

A third level of control was that of the design of computer systems. In the 1970s computer systems were large, mainframe-based programs which were programmed to process data in batches. The idealised form of computer system design was of course modelled after factory automation where parts were processed in a sequential and linear fashion and where all rules and controls were centralised. During the 1970s, mainframe computers became a fact of organisational life, although very few companies had more than one. Most of the 'bugs' or programming problems in the mainframe operating systems had been ironed out by this time and management was beginning to rely on mainframes to develop applications that could handle large volumes of transactions. Insurance companies, banks, airlines, securities firms and government agencies had high volumes of data and a large amount of repetitive work, characteristics that made them candidates for computer processing.

A key characteristic of the factory model of automation was that work had to be rationalised and data standardised *before* programming could be attempted (Greenbaum, 1994). In order to accomplish this rationalisation and standardisation, management tried to gain control over data and procedures by centralising all data processing. Standard bureaucratic management practices were used in supervising the development of software programs to do this work. Systems analysis – the process of designing and developing programs – reflected both its engineering roots in Operations Research during the Second World War and its managerial predecessors in isolating problems and separating tasks. The emphasis was, as it still is, on managing quantitative data so that management could review the numbers and accountants could record them. This was a continuation of bureaucratic practices, which emphasised standardisation of work, only with computer systems it was also applied to the more detailed level of standardisation of information, turning decisions about the organisation into routine and standard chunks of data. The combination of routinising tasks and standardising data led to computer systems that recorded only routine transactions, such as accepting or rejecting insurance claims, processing payrolls at regular intervals and ordering flight reservations by destination – routinisation of data and procedures that are still with us today, even though computer system development and computers have changed a great deal.

The 1980s: building on bureaucracy

In retrospect it is clear to see that centralised computer system design fits well with centralised bureaucratic practices and in co-ordinating and controlling the divided, rationalised labour of the early post-industrial period. By the 1980s, however, market conditions had begun to change and upper-level managers began to change their tune about the handling of all three levels of controls. Management theories of the 1970s had relied on two industrial concepts underpinning their bureaucratic practices: economies of scale and extensive division of labour. By the end of the 1970s different and indeed counter technologies such as early Personal Computers (PCs), mini computer networks, timesharing mainframe systems and stand-alone word processing machines were all in use, yet the predominant use of computers followed the still-dominant management theory of large, centralised mainframe systems. Both the reliance on economies of scale and on centralised control were to bend to the winds of economic change in the 1980s. Bend, but not break, for the echoes of bureaucratic practices, detailed division of labour and computer system design that are based on central and vertical control, are still with us today.

By most management accounts, the factory image of automation in the 1970s did not result in faster document production or enhanced office productivity. In fact, while it produced sharp divisions between back and front office jobs and thus between salary patterns, the outcome of the 1970s was rapidly growing office employment (see US Congress Office of Technology Assessment, 1985). By the early 1980s it was becoming clear to what was being called 'strategic' management, that rigid bureaucratic practices, the extensive division of labour, and standardised data-processing applications were leading to worker and customer dissatisfaction, as well as to lack of productivity gains and lack of control over data and service output. Popular literature claimed that the 'Japanese were doing it better' and phrases from 'leaner and meaner' to 'flexibility' were borrowed from loose translations of what was believed to be the basis of the Japanese success story. Thus, decentralised management functions began to replace centralised ones and job enhancement and upskilling were advocated in place of rationalisation and deskilling for front office jobs (Peters, 1982). In the arena of computer support, the Personal Computer, or stand-alone computer, was touted as the technical answer that fitted with the newer decentralised, more skill-based strategies.

In practice, however, the 1980s was a period of management stumbling, on both a theoretical and practical level, to adapt previous strategies to much more rapidly changing conditions. Indeed the term 'office automation' a catchword of the first half of the decade, along with the concept of the 'paperless office', were in many ways hold-overs from the centralised policies of the bureaucratic period. Office automation systems stayed within the automation paradigm, being based on a smooth 'flow' of information from managers and professionals down to clerical workers. Work organisation and available technology were out of sync with what upper management thought it wanted to accomplish. According to a mid-decade report by the US Congress Office of Technology Assessment:

> Where organisational issues like job redesign and workflow restructuring have not been properly managed, organisational costs can more than offset productivity gains expected from new technology. (1985:117)

In fact PCs were not machines designed to smooth out the 'flow' of data, since the software for each machine was geared to single users doing more comprehensive tasks. Nor did the existing division of labour fit the expected patterns of professional workers doing more administrative work such as word processing, and administrative workers such as secretaries being expected to do data base administration and similar 'professional' tasks. While upper management began to favour decentralisation of functions, computer support in the form of PCs was far too decentralised to help managers pull information together for the purposes of co-ordination and control. It is interesting to note that spreadsheet programs, which were widely marketed as the fastest way to produce budgets and financial statements, were difficult to co-ordinate on separate PCs running different versions of software.

In 1986 *Fortune* magazine ran a cover story claiming that 'US business has spent hundreds of billions of dollars on them [office computers], but white-collar productivity is no higher than it was in the late Sixties. Getting results usually entails changing the way work is done and that takes time' (Bowen, 1986:20). It was clear that there were massive misfits between the three levels that management needed to keep in tandem: overall control functions; division of labour and computer systems. On the overall level, calls for decentralised planning had not shaken off the well-entrenched practices of bureaucratic rule-based behaviour, nor were they supposed to. Corporations had to find a way to make decisions more rapidly while still keeping some form of control over centralised rules – the basic building block of bureaucracy. At the level of division of labour, calls were made for new forms of work organisation – forms in which some work would be divided while other tasks could be integrated into broader job categories. And in the area of technology, the gap between older centralised mainframe processing and totally decentralised PC-based computing had to be filled with networked systems, at least in the form of local area networks (LANs).

The 1990s: Co-operation, Control and Contradictions

By the 1990s, Business Process Re-engineering offered upper-level managers the vocabulary to blend the three levels of control into one overall 'strategic' plan, and to do so with plans that called for work redesign along with technical system design. Hammer's (1990) famous phrase 'obliterate work, don't automate it', was seen as a call to break down old patterns of work and technical design. In management strategy circles and in the academic branch of the computer field two concepts began to replace the guiding principles of the prior period. The first, 'communication', emphasised that computer systems and management policy should tilt in favour of communication between workers, managers, departments and customers, rather than be based on 'automation' or routine functions. In part this shift was one of rhetoric, but in terms of computer system design it has, to some degree, influenced the development of network-based computer packages so that distributed operations and workers can use computers as a means of communication. The second, 'co-operation', puts the focus on how groups and teams of workers need to take part in co-operative work, rather than be part of a system of extensive division of labour. Again, on the level of work organisation this has been a mechanism that is often used to induce more competition and thus output between 'co-operative' teams, but in the area of computer system design it has meant developing software for sharing files, data and documents; something that had been sorely lacking in the 1980s. And by making files and documents accessible over distances, it has also meant that upper-level managers have access to more information without the intermediaries who used to provide the middle-management functions of compiling and analysing this information. What C. Wright Mills (1951) called 'the enormous file of the office', made up of layers of people, each cranking out separate sets of numbers and accounts, can now be handled, at least in theory, by 'co-operation' among groups who 'communicate' using shared computer files and networked applications.

The design of computer systems that could move in the direction of communication and co-operation began in the latter part of the 1980s, with some of the theoretical work growing out of a field called Computer Supported Co-operative Work (CSCW). This field emphasised the need to design computer systems that would support non-routine work practices, paying particular attention to the co-operative and distributed nature of work (Greif, 1988; Grudin, 1994). For academics in the design field there was a progressive flavour to it because it offered the possibility of breaking with automation and the design principles of repetition and routine. Indeed the field was in the right place at the right time for it supported upper-management's intention of combining tasks and jobs and co-ordinating work that was being distributed out over time and space. It should come as no surprise, however, that co-operative work is an extension of the social character of production. Marx saw this and explained it this way:

> When numerous labourers work together side by side, whether in one or the same process, or in different but connected processes, they are said to co-operate, or to work in co-operation. (1967:325)

But the real nature of co-operation, he argued was:

> The direct motive, the end of the aim of capitalist production, is to extract the greatest possible amount of surplus-value, and consequently to exploit labour-power to the greatest possible extent ... Moreover, the co-operation of wage-labourers is entirely brought about by the capital that employs them. (331)

The focus on the co-operative nature of work by computer system designers was for management not an interest in co-operation *per se*, but rather an extension of viewing how divided labour processes could be reassembled through management practices co-ordinated by computer systems. In the industrial period, as indicated earlier, detailed division of labour had two main benefits for management: it heightened productivity through specialisation, repetition and routine; and it created divisions in the working class which kept people apart. During the current period, the detailed division of labour has proven too slow to respond to rapid market changes. But the second function of division of labour – that of divide and conquer – is very much alive in current labour market and labour process restructuring. Professional and administrative support workers may be closer together in the range of tasks they perform, but new divisions split the labour force by: full-time versus part-time status; payroll versus contract work; and corporate offices versus home office among others. And for all occupational groups, the pressure from 'temps' and out-sourced groups keeps the lid on wage growth (Head, 1996). Thus computer systems can be designed to support 'co-operation' among groups of workers in different places and under different contractual arrangements but it is very much a co-operation that feeds into the mechanism that bureaucracy used to provide – control and co-ordination of diverse forms of labour which are divided more horizontally and geographically.

In the 1970s the labour process debates inspired by Braverman's analysis focused primarily on the degrading and deskilling aspects of labour process change. In the 1980s, particularly growing out of sociology, studies tended to favour a view of an 'upskilled', more integrated labour process where 'knowledge workers' would, particularly with desk-top computer tools, get to do more 'informated' and interesting work (Zuboff, 1988). Obviously if we are to avoid this type of 'talking past each other', the larger issues, not the specific trends, need to be put back in context. The past two decades have shown that computer systems can be designed to support both deskilled and upskilled work. What is at issue now is the ways computer systems can be designed to absorb lower-level management functions and the extent to which such systems create new contradictions by doing so.

The 1990s has been a period of regrouping. The ideology of professionalism has supplemented the shortcomings of bureaucracy, making workers individually respond to internalised rules rather than relying on the corporation as a whole to do so. This has heightened competition in both the labour market and the labour process. Detailed division of labour has been supplemented with broader job definitions and pressure is on groups to 'get the job done', again intensifying competition and speeding up the decision making process. And computer systems of repetition, based on the assumption that work was routine and thus could be automated, have been supplemented by systems which spread work over time and space through distributed communication technology. The assumptions behind the newer systems rest on the concept that office work is not necessarily routine, although the individual tasks that make it up have been woven together after decades of routinisation and standardisation.

The current period is also riddled with contradictions which make upper-management's objectives open to pressure points of change. The ideology of professionalism, for example, was based on people earning significant salaries for their devotion to their tasks. Administrative, professional and managerial salaries have not been growing, and in fact, the increase in the number of freelance and contingent workers puts an increasing number of professionals on an insecure footing in relation to the labour market (Kilborn, 1994; Head, 1996). Thus professionalism might not necessarily offer upper management the obligations and rule-following behaviour that bureaucratic corporate practices did, because so-called professionals are not necessarily experiencing the benefits of the label.

At the level of changes in work, the flexibility that the new integrated labour processes offer management also offers a potential flexibility for labour. In the US most workers in all white-collar levels, from administrative support through managerial, are expected to have and learn wide ranges of skills and take on greater amounts of responsibility. Should the conditions of the labour market change or should people accept the actual 'co-operative' nature of their work, this could result in new forms of organising, just as divided factory labour gave rise to industrial unionism. The communicative and co-operative aspects of the technology that is used in workplaces and homeplaces can be seen as a double-edged sword: for just as it gives management the ability to put the pieces together, it also gives people in their roles as workers, citizens and customers the chance to communicate with each other about what they are experiencing and what they think could be done about it.

Computer systems can be designed to co-ordinate more horizontally divided labour. This has been evidenced through the success of networked software like Novell and Windows NT systems as well as through the hardware and software links supporting the Internet. The co-ordination aspects of software design can also be seen in commercially available applications such as Lotus Notes and email, fax, calendar and 'communication' packages. Custom-designed systems for individual companies which are tailored for integrating and co-ordinating distributed labour, such as those used by telecommunications firms and financial institutions, are developed not only to co-ordinate tasks done by different workers but to assemble the data about the tasks into supervisory monitoring reports and management-level statistical analysis.

Nevertheless, it is not at all clear whether the principles of *co-ordinating* horizontally divided labour through technical design can be expanded to *controlling* labour through technology. In the current period it appears that hardware and software can be designed to absorb many of the co-ordinating functions of lower-level management, particularly those that concern gathering and routine analysis of information. In addition, communication aspects of management, at least at the level of sending, storing and receiving messages, documents and files, are being designed into systems. Still, managerial functions include more than these routine definitions of co-ordinating information and routing communications. To the extent that managers need to control labour and the labour process – and there is no reason to believe that this function could wither away – the making of computer chips into managers can not be brought about by technical design.

References

Adler, P. (1986) 'New Technologies, New Skills', *California Management Review*, 29:1.

Bowen, W. (1986) 'The Puny Payoff from Office Computers', *Fortune*, 26 May.

Braverman, H. (1974) *Labour and Monopoly Capital: the degradation of work in the twentieth century*, New York: Monthly Review Press.

Church, G. (1993) 'Jobs in an Age of Insecurity', *Time*, 22 November, 35.

Computer World (1996) 'Salary Issues', 7.

Edwards, R. (1979) *Contested Terrain: the transformation of the workplace in the twentieth century*, New York: Basic Books.

Friedman, A. (1977) *Industry and Labour, Class Struggle at Work and Monopoly Capitalism*, London: Macmillan.

Friedman, A. (1989) *Computer Systems Development: History, Organisation and Implementation*. New York: Wiley.

Greenbaum, J. (1979) *In the Name of Efficiency*, Philadelphia: Temple University Press.

Greenbaum, J. (1994) 'The Forest and the Trees', *Monthly Review*, Special Issue on Braverman, November.

Greenbaum, J. (1995) *Windows on the Workplace – Computers, Jobs and the Organisation of Office Work in the Late Twentieth Century*, New York: Monthly Review Press, Cornerstone Books.

Greenbaum, J. (1996) 'Back to Labour', *CSCW Proceedings*, ACM, November.

Greenbaum J. and Kyng, M. (eds) (1991) *Design at Work: Co-operative Design of Computer Systems*, Hillsdale, NJ: Erlbaum Associates.

Greif, I. (ed.) (1988) *Computer-Supported Co-operative Work: A Book of Readings*, Calif: Morgan Kaufmann.

Grudin, J. (1994) 'Computer Supported Co-operative Work: History and Focus', IEEE, Computer, May.

Hammer, M. (1990) 'Re-engineering Work: Don't Automate, Obliterate', *Harvard Business Review*, July–August .

Head, S. (1996) 'The New, Ruthless Economy', *New York Review of Books*, 29 February.

Herzenberg, S., Alic, J. and Wial, H. (1996) *Better Jobs for More People: A New Deal for the Service Economy*, Washington: Twentieth Century Fund.

Kilborn, P. (1994) 'Low pay and closed doors greet youth in job market', *New York Times*, 13 March.

Kraft, P. (1977) *Programmers and Managers: The Routinisation of Computer Programming in the United States*, New York: Springer-Verlag.

Marx, K. (1967; 1867) *Capital* vol.1, New York: International Publishers.

Mills, C. Wright (1951) *White Collar*, Oxford: Oxford University Press.

Peters, T. (1982) *In Search of Excellence*, New York: Knopf.

Peters, T. (1992), *Liberation Management: necessary disorganisation for the nanosecond nineties*, New York: Knopf.

Thompson, E.P. (1968) *The Making of the English Working Class*, London: Penguin.

US Congress Office of Technology Assessment (1985) *Automating America's Offices*, Washington: Government Printing Office.

US Department of Labor Bureau of Labor Statistics, see Tables 11 & 39, yearly, see also *Employment and Earnings*, January 1995, January 1996 and January 1997.

Zuboff, S. (1988) *In the Age of the Smart Machine: The Future of Work and Power*, New York: Basic Books.

Notes

1 While systems are in fact ordered by managers there are and have been attempts to design systems from the viewpoint of workers. See literature on Participatory Design and Co-operative Design, for example Greenbaum and Kyng (1991).

2 Standard US introduction to computing textbooks still defines data as raw material to be processed and information as the finished product of an information system.

3 Upper-level management here refers to the conceptual and strategic plans that are made by corporate directors or top officials in government organisations. Central to the argument here is the fact that as borders blur between professional/managerial and administrative job categories, an operational definition of upper management is not possible at this time.

4 Unless otherwise indicated the examples and illustrations used here are taken from the research studies presented in Greenbaum (1995).

5 Spokespersons for the US Department of Labor Bureau of Labor Statistics have confirmed that these jobs are increasing, but it is as yet difficult to record the numbers since service representatives are a new job title and encompass many former jobs in the administrative support area as well as formerly professional jobs such as bank officials.

6 In the US, the Bureau of Labor Statistics developed new categories for counting underemployed and involuntary part-time workers. When these categories are added to the press-cited low unemployment percent of 5–6 per cent, the official unemployment figures come to 10–11 per cent. This is comparable with many West European countries and counters the claim that 'free market'-styled deregulation would lower Europe's unemployment rates.

7 Management claims about increased productivity in the service sector are of course difficult to quantify, but at least from a worker's perspective, studies show that workers in most occupational categories experience speed-up, increased pace of work and increased hours (Herzenberg *et al.*, 1996).

8 Developments in Computing Work: Control and Contradiction in the Software Labour Process

Martin Beirne, Harvie Ramsay and Androniki Panteli

Introduction

The labour process literature has tended to show interest in computing not in its own right, but as something which affects its true concerns. It is the embodiment of 'new technology' which captures attention, impacting upon (and more likely than not afflicting) work organisation, and potentially threatening to eliminate employment altogether. A distinction between 'hardware' and 'software' may be vaguely noted, with hardware being 'the bit you can kick'. The nature of the production system which creates not the machinery but the programs which run on the machinery, so potentially shaping the work of others, has remained a black box in all but a few exceptional studies.[1]

Yet on reflection, the nature of the work performed in producing and operating software should be a matter of great curiosity to labour process analysis. Firstly, it is an expanding and increasingly important field of employment, in an era when other jobs are vanishing. Hence, the nature of the labour processes in computing work are likely to assume increasing significance in the future. Secondly, as an occupational category it has emerged largely since the 1960s, and so does not carry the baggage of a long history of skill definition, status, or gender stereotyping, for instance. As such, it could be seen as a test-bed for different accounts of forces shaping the trajectory of the capitalist labour process. Thirdly, as already noted, the 'output' of this labour process has direct and potent implications for the future of work more generally.

This chapter focuses largely on those who work in computing itself, leaving the exploration of the impact of computerisation on work organisation more generally to Greenbaum's contribution to this volume. Because the boundary between computing and non-computing is inevitably increasingly blurred by the diffusion of information technologies, however, there will also be some shared territory in the two discussions. For example, one of our main concerns here is to challenge the conventional privileging of expert 'designers', despite the sympathy now lavished on the long-suffering 'end-user'. As we shall demonstrate, design is a fragmented and divided labour process among those formally credited with its achievement. Moreover, in practice, a redesign of systems is undertaken by users 'after the fact' of expert design, though often this is well hidden (Beirne *et al.*, 1996); to ignore this reality merely recreates the head and hand presumptions that labour process accounts set out to challenge.

In what follows we draw upon a disparate literature little known outside computing researchers, relating this to our own research on the Scottish software sector. Following a well-founded labour process tradition, we adopt a view of software development which is consistent with the conceptualisation of systems design and application as a process of social contention, and political as much as technical determination (Noble, 1984; Thomas, 1994). In this sense, we forecast possible futures for computing work by extrapolating from the emergence of current work regimes, examining nascent divisions of labour and management strategies to rationalise and deskill or devalue software production labour, and the problems and nature of resistance these encounter.

Computing Work

The following quotation presents a common image of the prototypical computing worker:

> ... the programmer is challenged to combine, with the ability of a first-class mathematician to deal in logical abstractions, a more practical, a more Edisonian talent, enabling him to build useful engines out of zeroes and ones alone. He must join the accuracy of a bank clerk with the acumen of a scout, and to these add the powers of fantasy of an author of detective stories and the sober practicality of a businessman. To top all this off, he must have a taste for collective work and a feeling for the corporate interests of his employer. (Ershov, 1972:502)

There are a number of notable features to this account which merit attention here. Firstly, we challenge the simplistic image of *the* nature of computing work that it articulates, initially by examining internal divisions of computing labour. Secondly, we will look at the forces which have been exerted in an attempt to rationalise information systems (IS) work and subject it to closer management control. Thirdly, we will explore forces undermining detailed control. These partly reflect the fact that the skills required for successful development go far beyond mathematical and 'technical' proficiency, and partly the capacity of IS workers for resistance. Finally, in the course of all this we address the presumptive image of the IS worker as a male.

Ershov's statement presents programming work as monolithically a craft-based, creative form of work. This ignores divisions of labour within IS work itself, and also its contact with, or segregation from, users. Traditional differences between those who manage and others who are managed persist in IS work in many ways. There is typically an elite group of IS staff who advise corporate managers and other executives on 'feasible' ways to exploit current technology, but rarely do coding or testing. At a lower level in professional and corporate hierarchies, there are many other IS workers who are far more closely managed and less well paid, officially permitted to make few decisions about the technology they use, the programmes that they work on or the direction of their organisation.

Reinforcing this sense of division, numerous recent surveys on IS occupations confront the monolithic image of IS staff as those who deal with managing, developing and programming new systems. Labour force surveys in the sector delineate distinct areas of IS jobs, including systems management, network support, systems development, technical support, operations, PC end-user support and help-desk operators (National Computing Centre, 1997; *Computerworld*, 1995). The nature of the work (its routinisation or focus on hardware or software, for instance), status, pay and the job controls experienced by these different groups vary greatly. UK surveys show a shifting composition of the IS workforce, with the most rapid growth (up to 10 per cent yearly) among network staff and end-user support, moderate growth in development, and a sharp decline in the number of operations staff. These developments reflect the rising importance of open systems and the reduced role of central IT departments, resulting in decentralisation of computing functions from the centre towards end-users, or alternatively towards outsourcing (National Computing Centre, 1993 & 1997).

There is also a growing degree of fragmentation and stratification of activities and responsibilities in software development itself. The *Computerworld* (1995) survey in the US found nine different types of job being performed within this field alone. Developers tended to become highly specialised (for example as COBOL or C programmers), usually working on different kinds of applications. In our own research, we found repeated references to differences of culture and outlook among these different groups, which were often also generational, reflecting tensions arising from the rapid pace of change and the constant threat to long-term job security. These workers are divided between organisations which are heavy IS users, such as banks or public services, and specialist software houses. The latter are gaining ground, especially as outsourcing grows and as downsizing hits employment in user organisations (Thomasson, 1994) .

This points to another remarkable feature with regard to the nature of IS occupations today, namely the shift from a simple labour market to an amalgamation of various distinct sectors, including technical experts, engineers, business consultants and clerical staff, for example (Orlikowski, 1989). This shift has implications for the nature of skills, knowledge and experience required, while signifying that computing jobs are found in an ever-widening variety of organisations. In skill terms, the corollary is that IS staff may be required not only to maintain and develop their technical abilities in line with advances in technology and applications (Currie *et al.*, 1993), but concurrently to enhance their organisational and business development skills to meet the strategic requirements of clients and employers.

Such developments amount to an extension of established tendencies towards more communicative and collaborative ties with users. The importance and difficulties of connecting programmers and other developers with users has long been recognised, at least for the preliminary work in agreeing systems specifications. As with developers themselves, users are often treated as an homogeneous group. Friedman and Cornford (1989) provided an early attempt to introduce greater clarity here, differentiating between six categories of user: (1) the patron, initiator and champion of the system, (2) the client, for whom the output is intended and who will pay the bills, (3) design interactors, that is, people involved in system specification and design, (4) end-users – the individuals who will operate the installed system, (5) those involved in maintenance and enhancement of the system and, (6) secondary users, including people displaced by the new system, people whose work is changed by the system, those whose non-work life is affected and proxy-users such as departmental managers and union representatives. More recently, Fincham *et al.* (1994) identified two critical variables which affect the proximity of users to IS workers, namely, their level of computing literacy and degree of organisational power.

These attempts to provide a more grounded understanding of user encounters and relationships with IS workers present an image of systems development as a highly complex social, organisational and professional bridging process (Quintas, 1991). Yet this is compounded by another aspect which has been even further out of focus in orthodox accounts of the development process, namely the emergence of gender stratification and segregation.

Studies of gender careers in IS (Baroudi and Igbaria, 1995) have shown that women are mostly found in the non-managerial group of IS staff. Men are more likely than women to be project leaders, IS managers and consultants while women tend to be concentrated in roles such as systems analyst, designer and programmer. According to the *Computerworld* (1995) US Salary Survey, only 17 per cent of chief information officers were women. In the UK, this percentage is even lower. Ordroyd (1996) reports that since 1991, women have made up just over 20 per cent of the UK IS workforce, while only 4 per cent were heads of IS departments.

Clearly, the overall nature of computing work remains complex and variable, and subject to diversification as far as skills requirements are concerned. The following section examines the powerful rationalistic tendencies in this area of work, and so the application of managerial strategies pursuing labour control. Subsequently, we will examine the limitations of such strategies, and the contrary tendencies within computing.

Rationalising the Computing Labour Process

The official history of software design work is one of progress through the application of engineering principles to systems programming and analysis

(Somerville, 1989; Pressman, 1992). In the 1960s, so the story goes, the growing ascendancy of software bottlenecks over hardware limitations created a sense of 'crisis', intensified by the pressures of the Cold War and of business demands for systems of increased complexity. Previously, the main constraint on systems performance, and the dominant cost, had been hardware. Software development was regarded as a creative and esoteric task, with mathematicians and other individualist staff recruited and given high degrees of autonomy (Friedman and Cornford, 1989).

Software productivity levels were low and failing to rise in a way which matched the demand for systems, while the nature of the work seemed to demand highly skilled labour which was in short supply, making it hard to retain key staff and even harder to restrain salary costs (Quintas, 1991). For the last thirty years or so, many of the new strategies which have been proposed for organising and managing software production can be seen as attempts at rationalisation, acceleration of productivity growth and the assertion of control from above. These initiatives have been aided by the shift of power in the 1980s from IS departments to marketing and finance which has left IS more vulnerable to the demands of senior management in user departments (Friedman and Cornford, 1989; Knights and Murray, 1994).

For one group of writers in the labour process tradition these management objectives have been largely achieved:

> The making of computer programs has been subject to a process of intellectual industrial engineering, a scientific management of mind work. In every important respect these techniques are identical to those applied in the production of cars and cornflakes. (Kraft and Dubnoff, 1986:194)

These authors chart a progressive degradation of software knowledge work, a slide from the status and autonomy of the skilled artisan to the regimented task-structures of Taylorised clerical labour. Since the mid-1970s, the time and motion brigade is seen as having subjected yet another area to the debilitating impact of 'divide and conquer' rationalisation (Kraft, 1977; Greenbaum 1979). By the most pessimistic accounts, new software technologies have separated conception from execution, diluting skills and transferring them to a combination of non-specialists and machines (Kraft, 1987; Kraft and Dubnoff, 1986). The resulting stratification of jobs has allegedly reproduced a conventional hierarchy of power and rewards, of highly paid senior managers dealing with policy, technical direction and user communications while under-managers allocate, supervise and evaluate clusters of technical 'detail workers' who perform the fragmented tasks of coding, programming, testing and so forth. The result is a proletarianisation thesis, and a scenario of deskilling and degradation.

A contemporary assessment does indeed reveal a number of rationalising elements. The first involves the *automation of programming*. When third generation languages (3GLs) such as COBOL were developed in the 1950s and 1960s, they were intended to replace abstract mathematical manipulation with English-like statements that would remove the programmer from the need for direct contact with the code, which was generated by a complier through which their program was processed. For this reason they were referred to as 'high-level' languages (Martin and Powell, 1992). Those who promoted these new languages were hopeful that they were the first step to the replacement of programmers and eventually all but managerial systems design roles, although this possibility was to prove far more difficult than they anticipated. In the 1980s 4GLs appeared, followed by still more powerful software such as ORACLE, using object-oriented programming. It was intended that these languages would be more easily used by less computing-literate staff. However, their complexity and abstraction made them difficult for non-experts to approach. Potentially, however, their impact on programming and on systems design more generally, offered a considerable potential to raise productivity.

Still more ambitious moves to automate or at least routinise the work of the programmer and systems analyst also began to emerge in the late 1980s in the form of Computer-Aided Software Engineering (CASE). CASE is a general term used to describe a range of innovations from particular tools for simplifying programming to full integrated project support environments (IPSE) which aim to link together methods for automating numerous aspects of systems design. For the moment, though, the greatest impact is probably with regard to the use of specific programming tools such as 'visual' programmes. By using menu-driven options to design options and with the lines of code needed in a library in the programming system, these programmes provide a further interface between the programmers and the codes they produce. Productivity can be enormously increased by this means, especially where measured by output of lines of error-free code in a given period.

In this respect, our research came across claims of massive routinisation of work in a fairly large software house which had specialised in standardised adaptations of generic systems for clients. The work was described as repetitive and highly pressured. The environment was also non-union, and it was reported that the company required staff to work unpaid overtime to meet demand, or else risk losing their jobs. Many of those employed were not highly qualified but the nature of the task was such that individuals with limited computing knowledge could be trained fairly easily to perform it. For example, youngsters on work experience projects were used to generate standard screen colourings.

Another development has been described as the *'industrialisation' of software production*. Bansler and Havn (1996) argue that there is a long-term shift from in-house systems development towards generic applications and systems. These are developed by outside suppliers, usually large software houses, and seek to offer as wide a functionality as possible, though their fit with specific user requirements is often poor. Nonetheless, the economies of scale and powerful options built into generic software make it an attractive proposition for increasing numbers of companies.

Bansler and Havn also consider some of the consequences for in-company IS functions. They suggest that traditional programming and systems analysis will be greatly reduced, and the number of IS staff is likely to be cut. However, they argue that certain high-skill staff will still be required in-house, focusing more on user requirements relative to available options, negotiating with vendors, and carrying out integrative analysis to fit the new software with other bought-in systems. They also claim that this should entail greater user influence over purchases and adaptation, and declare themselves supporters of user participation.

It is not clear, however, that companies themselves will recognise the need for such highly skilled staff or the increased role for users. Downsizing opportunities have a tendency to be taken beyond their optimum point under current management ideologies, and the remaining employees are expected to cover the (underestimated) amount of work that still has to be done internally. The result could be more akin to the intensification and lack of skill recognition predicted by Greenbaum (1995). The nature of work in producing generic software is not considered in Bansler and Havn's analysis, the focus of which is within the customer only. Our research, however, suggests that the routinisation and intensification of the labour process in large software houses is higher than is the case in-house.

The rationalisation of IS work has also been pursued by seeking to impose tighter *bureaucratic controls* on software developers. The crisis of the 1960s led to an attempt to shift software development from being an esoteric and unregulated, highly individualistic activity towards a 'software engineering' discipline (Shapiro, 1992). The implication is that software development is an applied science, driven by issues of practicality, adequacy and efficiency. For labour process analysis, the link to Taylor(ism) is evident. Thus the focus has shifted to getting programs produced on time, at low cost, with low error counts, and on measuring progress of development more closely. Quintas (1991) describes state and management efforts to establish this orientation, especially in the UK through the Alvey programme of the 1980s.

Two closely linked manifestations of the software engineering (SE) approach have emerged as the dominant (official) means for organising software development work: the application of formal methodologies, and the various associated definitions of a software development life cycle. There are numerous formal structured methodologies in use,[2] but there are strong family similarities between most of them. Each lays down the procedures and protocols to be followed in development, the tools and techniques to be used at each stage, the timing and extent of user consultation at various points, and the required documentation. Even those methodologies which challenge the conventional assertion of software professional expertise (as against potential user contributions) implicit in these methods, such as the 'Soft Systems Methodology'

(Checkland and Scholes, 1990) or ETHICS (Mumford, 1996), remain highly structured. At the same time, such methods find it all but impossible to handle any subjective or micropolitical issues (even where, as in the case of SSM and ETHICS they do give some cognisance to these issues), since these cannot be prescribed for or measured neatly in a way that fits the engineering frame of reference (Beirne and Ramsay, 1988).

Alongside this omission, and inscribed on most structured methodologies, is a picture of the sequence of the software engineering process, predominantly in a 'waterfall' format. This format presents systems development as a cascade through some variant of requirements specification, outline and then detailed design, testing and implemention, with occasionally debugging and maintenance added at the end. Some variants seek to increase 'user-involvement' through prototyping phases, with adjustments to requirements and design in a 'spiral' model. Genuinely participative content is still marginal in these models, however. Indeed, the general approach not only constrains the designer and limits any interaction with users; it also intensifies the 'top–down' feel of systems design in the prevailing software engineering ideology (Avergou and Cornford, 1993b).

In more recent times, a further layer of bureaucratic control has been added to officially approved development procedure: the general spread of the quality management fashion. Again there are a number of variants but the dominant ones are those derived from the ISO standards (ISO 9001 as elaborated for the software industry in ISO 9000-3; applied as TickIT in the UK) and the Capability Maturity Model (CMM) developed at the Software Engineering Institute at Carnegie Mellon University in the US. The latter is founded directly on the five levels of maturity defined by the mainstream TQM guru, Philip Crosby (1980). Our research in Scotland did reveal a parallel and growing dissatisfaction with some aspects of it, however. The phenomena which were found to be driving this discontent will be familiar to those versed in the TQM debate: bureaucratisation of work; obfuscation of the real problems; overly rigid procedures; lip-service to user involvement whilst actually reducing the space for any user role, or making any input less effective; and so forth. In short, quality management often seemed more like a control device than an enabling approach.

Finally, as with other areas of organisations, IS has been seen as a prime area for *commodification*, wherein the application of market pressures are seen as means to enhance efficiency and cut costs, imposing self-discipline on IS staff to make their own savings. This may be done internally by creating a separate IS unit 'selling' its services into the larger organisation, possibly in competition with outside suppliers. We encountered this strategy in finance, distilling and telecommunications enterprises.

Such a shift is a common outcome of Business Process Re-engineering programmes, where IS seems an obvious candidate for restructuring to those charged with demonstrating change. On the face of it the software sector is particularly vulnerable to this type of initiative. Since its output is entirely constructed in digital form, it is ideal for transmission over small or large distances, maximising the flexible options apparently open to management.

A more radical solution, therefore, is outsourcing. The use of outside contractors to carry out IS functions for an organisation has a long history, but its take-off point is usually traced to the decision of Eastman-Kodak to outsource its data handling to IBM, Businessland and DEC in 1989 (Loh and Venkatraman, 1992; Lacity and Hirschheim, 1993; Gurbaxani, 1996 respectively). Outsourcing may cover a range of activities of IS staff, including data capture and management, network support, and software design and operation. A number of large corporate players are emerging to assume these tasks, such as the General Motors-owned Electronic Data Services (with 85 000 employees, and huge contracts *inter alia* to run Inland Revenue and other public-sector computing operations in the UK), or the Computer Sciences Corporation (which already handles large contracts with BAe and Lucas). By the mid-1990s a large proportion of American companies were investigating or already engaging in IS outsourcing. While the take-up has apparently been slower in the UK,[3] it has been estimated that by the end of the decade up to 80 per cent of the top 400 UK firms will be buying in some or all of their IT services. Certainly in our own research we have encountered plentiful evidence of a steep rise in both the amount of outsourced work and the number of contract staff on site in the last couple of years.

How Taylorised Are Software Jobs?

The vision of rationalisation and Taylorism invoked above has sparked intense controversy over the past decade, not least for its Bravermanian connotations. Sometimes critiques of Braverman have been 'read-off' and applied to Kraft and Greenbaum in unforgiving terms (Orlikowski, 1988). The attribution of craft status to early programming and the identification of labour control as the key driver towards deskilling have been taken as signals of Bravermanian absolutism, prompting more cautious discussion, and even a less charitable view of the plight of software workers. Where 'corrections' have focused on the ambiguous class position of computing staff in refining technologies that control the work of others, it is possible to detect a sense that 'they get whatever they deserve'. Since they seem happy to rationalise other jobs, why should we empathise with their apologists in lamenting the ironical loss of influence by such willing agents of capital (Orlikowski, 1988; Martin, 1984)?

Such a reaction risks mirroring the rigidities of those it criticises, downgrading contingencies and obscuring the totality of the computerised workplace. The experience of software workers is neglected, as more 'deserving' attention is paid to their supposed victims. At the same time, the limits and contradictions of rationalised software production are underplayed, providing limited purchase on empirical material which seemingly 'cuts against the grain' of envisaged outcomes and forecasts. Yet there is a requirement to account for developments which inform more optimistic scenarios.

Though Kraft takes the language of industrialisation to be indicative of tendencies towards software 'production' (from craft programming) the newer techno-speak of 'systems-builders' and 'analyst-programmers', which suggest a recomposition of development tasks, has received only limited critical scrutiny. Greenbaum, one of the progenitors of the proletarianisation thesis, has acknowledged that 'new twists in programming work have reintegrated some programming, analysis and management functions' (1995:92) albeit with equally debilitating consequences. By intensifying work and absorbing additional activities into broader career bands, Greenbaum regards any job enlargement as continuing, rather than departing from, long-run rationalistic tendencies towards more oppressive managerial control. Ostensibly, the net result is a converging experience of misery for users and developers alike.

In practice, the impact of the changes we have outlined on the work of developers remains ambivalent. We have spoken to individuals who welcomed the greater ease of completing standard routines in large systems brought by forms of automation, for instance, while others (generally lower in the hierarchy and/or less skilled) complained of routinisation of work.

There are clear signs, too, that the diffusion of generic software is prompting a change in the structure of IS provision and, correspondingly, the nature of development jobs, both in supplying and purchasing organisations. In-house developers are seeing a significant shift in the balance of their work, with a growing incidence of small-scale projects, upgrading, amending and customising existing or acquired applications. From our own research on IS departments in a range of industries from finance to computer manufacturing, it was increasingly rare for staff to be involved with more than three or four fellow developers, and common for them to have a number of their own, one-person, projects running concurrently with any collaborative work. As those with established knowledge and experience were focusing on mainframe legacy systems, others, frequently newer graduates versed in currently popular languages, were concentrating on client-server adaptations, refining marketing information systems or vendor networks, for example.

In each area, the traditional distinction between new development and maintenance was blurring, both in terms of job demarcations and work content. Staff from hitherto separate functions were finding their work reclassified and reintegrated, sharing out the various 'enhancement' projects. In the finance sector, for instance, a project would be classed as maintenance if it required less than a one-person month's worth of effort; otherwise it was a new development. The portfolio carried by individual developers incorporated a mix of long and short, team and individual assignments, the balance influenced by seniority and experience. In common with other sectors, the emerging trend signalled some enlargement of work roles, and possibly also job enrichment for those previously confined to 'bug fixing' or to incorporating minor amendments such as interest rate changes in financial information systems, for example.

Rather than fulfilling an ineluctable Tayloristic logic, these changes point to some fluidity in the composition of software jobs. Instead of a linear trend towards tightening demarcations with attendant routinisation and deskilling, variable job controls are apparent, along with a widening of some tasks and a de facto skill mix which renders rationalistic strategies problematical. The importance of situated knowledge, of local experience and a grounded understanding of priorities within particular application areas, confirms that software development is still a highly interpretative process, at least for large numbers of on-site workers (Fincham *et al.*, 1994). The most effective developers in our own case studies were often considered to be those who could network informally with users, and lay claim to organisational and commercial knowledge as well as technical expertise. The arrival of 'end-user computing' has reinforced such a view, in theory devolving development capabilities and requiring IS staff to work more directly with users, enabling them to create their own enquiry and reporting systems in tandem with existing databases. *Pace* Kraft and Dubnoff, it seems that user contact is no longer the prerogative of upper-level managers and design specialists. Instead, it often broadens the work roles, interests and expertise of grassroots staff working independently or collectively on 'enhancement'.

While challenging any simple deskilling thesis, it would be folly to overplay the extent of developers' influence over the conduct of software work. Any compensations that can be found in the evolving work roles must be set against the less palatable consequences of entrenched rationalism. While IS managers encourage and expect their staff to adopt a more rounded approach to their work, synthesising contextual knowledge and technical expertise, it is far from clear that this translates into formal recognition, upgrading or autonomous control, either of work pace or the terms governing collaborative encounters. On the contrary, there is a ceiling on managerial approval of informal interactions and expressions of developer autonomy.

Indeed, far from welcoming end-user consultation as a way of improving the usability of software, a high proportion of IS managers in our own research saw it as destabilising, undermining the consistency and rigour of development practices and storing up compatibility and maintenance problems for the future. Retaining a conventional engineering approach, they sought to formalise (and so contain) user-involvement via quality assurance and project monitoring procedures, at the same time imposing tighter controls on developers, restricting their scope for informal contact and inhibiting their 'organisational learning'. Sanctions were frequently applied, usually in the form of verbal or written warnings, when software staff overstepped their authority on user contact, even for incorporating subtle corrections or improvements to specifications. In the most striking example, two developers were reprimanded for executing a short program which corrected a recurring error identified by one of their designated users but was not passed through the official conduit for authorising system upgrades.

Such an attachment to bureaucratic controls was often justified as a means of protecting developers from intrusive interruption. However, it was also apparent in practices that have fewer recognisable advantages, and more direct costs. 'Critical performance metrics' represent a growing area of interest for many software companies and departments, demonstrating an obvious continuity with more conventional labour control strategies. Monitoring tools, including log sheets and status reporting procedures, provide a means by which managers aim to distinguish fast from slow developers (Blackburn *et al.*, 1996). Many claim that these are not taken to extremes or applied directly to performance appraisal, rather providing more of a project planning resource, helping them to schedule workloads and signal reliable completion dates to clients. However, it is difficult to separate scheduling from acting on staff in some way, and there is evidence that developers perceived and, in some cases, experienced a connection between metrics and management discipline.

In most of our research sites staff were juggling projects to 'keep up appearances', to give the impression of making progress on all fronts, fearing sanctions if this were not the case. The pressure bearing upon staff was intense. Interview respondents in the financial sector indicated that every minute of development time was now logged and counted into costs against targets, so it was difficult to encourage staff to settle, even with explicit management clearance and a formal release of time. One department manager was candid in his view that, with quality assurance, staff knew what was expected of them, and could be (and occasionally were) 'bawled out' for playing 'silly buggers' with the project controls.

The potential to extend and enact such direct control is currently rising, again as a consequence of the shift in favour of generic software and concomitant proliferation of enhancement projects. Despite the traditional image of software teams reinforcing informal group ties, supportive social interaction and expressions of autonomy, developers in commercial contexts are experiencing a fragmentation of project teams and more individualised working, albeit in the broader collective context of an application or business area. Their individual tasks, although predicated upon the work of others, are less interdependent, spatially and temporally separated from contributors to the generic systems and other upgrades and amendments that interface with their own programs. Even those with experience of the collective development of legacy systems can find themselves working with documentation, with manuals of recorded involvement rather than human collaborators, encountering more episodic briefing communications and fewer shared assignments.

As a corollary, more hierarchical arrangements are emerging to cover the allocation and organisation of enhancement work. A vertical division of labour is apparent in the changing role of project managers, a small proportion of them moving beyond team leadership to the more conventional human resource responsibilities of departmental 'under-managers'. Liaising with senior managers, this second tier is more active in controlling the workflow of a wider pool of developers: allocating projects, evaluating performance, authorising overtime, planning holiday cover and so forth. Remaining project managers can find themselves reporting to these individuals, carrying a mixed portfolio, though perhaps receiving less detailed program outlines and conducting more of the analysis and design themselves as a concession to their standing and experience. Despite such recognition, the net result is a share in the common experience of having their knowledge and abilities compressed into a larger number of small-scale projects, with visible productivity metrics increasingly applied to indicate their effectiveness in making progress on all fronts. In addition, traditional opportunities for translating team leadership and authority into promoted managerial posts have been reduced by downsizing and outsourcing, trends which compound the intensification of work that results from being more formally managed.

Judging by numerous press reports and evidence from our own research sites, redundancies have taken their toll of a large number of software workers in recent years. Managerial grades have been among the major casualties in terms of job loss, especially as career positions have been removed in favour of contingent workers, part-timers and contractors on fixed-term assignments. 'Body shopping' for temporary contract staff is a growing business in its own right, with many displaced workers operating as independent freelancers or through placement agencies. Although the accompanying rhetoric has presented an image of re-engineered autonomy, nurturing entrepreneurship, self-supervision and even the freedom of teleworking (ironically echoed by the conjecture of critical theorists),[4] the reality presents a much starker picture of the consequences visited upon remaining and hired staff.

From our own studies, 'temps' are usually integrated into existing managerial control structures, confronting much the same diet of enhancement projects and individualised work as full-time developers. Although staff from independent software contractors were more likely to have short periods of placement working on specific, contracted projects, agency and freelance developers were juggling portfolios in the same way as regular employees, often with recurring six-month or year-long contracts. The latter was typically the result of IS having a sanctioned core complement of staff that was insufficient to deal with the outstanding workload, itself due to organisational politics or downsizing beyond the optimum staffing point for 'total project management'.

Either way, it was common for all categories to be working long hours, regularly into the evenings and weekends to complete projects, and without additional compensation by way of financial inducements or time in lieu. Working longer and harder was seen as a consequence of the times, of coping with available budgets and demands while counteracting an historical image of poor productivity and software quality. We found a general experience of intensifying pressures on software developers, with time spent on tasks being logged in increasing detail.

From the available evidence, the pressures of rationalised working are undoubtedly bearing heavily upon software workers. There are strong continuities with established traditions of labour management in the efforts to tighten bureaucratic controls, to alter working practices and terms of employment, despite the recent delayering of hierarchies and enlargement and formal enrichment of some jobs. However, the precise impact remains mixed and ambivalent. The next section addresses managerial problems which help to explain this uncertain outcome.

Limits and Contradictions

The previous two sections have, with some qualification, demonstrated the potency of the efforts to subjugate computing work to the same disciplines as other parts of organisations. Yet just as we know such strategies have met resistance from workers and circumstances in other areas of work, so have they in computing. As the fallout from 1970s Bravermania confirmed, outcomes cannot be anticipated with confidence or 'read-off' from management's rationalistic ambitions or declarations. There are countervailing tendencies, including work-based practices which challenge the wisdom, pursuit and realisation of these ambitions and declarations. Our own research has shown numerous reasons why the forces of rationalisation may founder.

In practice, despite drives to formalise, structure, monitor and capitalise the development process, evidence points to persistently high levels of frustration, continuing problems with 'usability', and departures from authorised methods to improve outcomes. Some have been spectacular, such as those reported in recent years at the Stock Exchange, London Ambulance Service and the Performing Rights Society (Flowers, 1996). Yet complaints that software falls spectacularly short of what people want or envisage are commonplace across a whole range of organisations (Sauer, 1993). Costly amendments and organisational adaptations have typically been found necessary to secure barely acceptable levels of performance with new systems. These unintended and unforeseen outcomes prompt a basic questioning of the assumptions that inform rationalistic approaches.

The limits to rationalisation may be seen firstly by looking at the activities of those officially designated as designers, and secondly at the way demands on them are generated and their products implemented. It is also useful, thirdly, to examine the ways in which end-users actually operate systems, since this group often challenge the notion that development is an exclusively 'expert' activity by revising systems in significant ways to make them workable.

Considering firstly those in software development posts, the departure from official methodologies in all but final documented behaviour has been observed by several studies (Bansler and Bødker, 1993; Fincham *et al.*, 1994; Guidon and Curtis, 1988; Harding and Gilbert, 1993). Some custodians of 'good practice' have lamented the prevalence of ad hoc and chaotic practices in the management of software projects both in the US and Europe (Fenton, 1991; Paulk, 1993). Others have cautioned that quality practices are not penetrating to the lower levels of software organisations, that developers are not demonstrating the take-up of 'mature' methods (Wilson *et al.*, 1996). Similar woes can be heard from champions of automated programming, CASE tools and fourth generation languages (4GLs). Although a growing range of development technology is now available, evidence suggests a very low and limited usage (Livari, 1996; Fincham *et al.*, 1994) – a feature that we also observed in our case studies.

Instead of criticising developers for their intransigence, some commentators question the formalised, hierarchical methods themselves, since the context and target environment of 'live' software projects display a complexity and subtlety that is beyond rationalistic models. The established ideal of structured, top–down design is at odds with the reality of incremental software development in which key aspects and decisions are negotiated as the process unfolds (Curtis, Krasner and Iscoe, 1988; Bansler and Bødker, 1993). Such accounts welcome the space for, and acknowledge the advantages that arise from, tacit skills and informal practices that are considered inappropriate by advocates of rationalistic control. Departures from rationalistic prescriptions are seen as necessary to 'get things done'.

Our Scottish research conveyed a clear sense of the resilience of developers in negotiating their way around formal methods that were felt to be hampering their efforts. For example, many of those employed by independent software companies were marshalling knowledge and cultivating an image of expertise from placements in client IS departments with the intention of resisting tighter engineering process controls. By appearing sensitive and responding to (even *seeming* to accommodate) client concerns in the field, developers could shift attention from adherence to a rule-book to the personal input of 'tried and trusted friends'. This became the basis for repeat business and for the retention or even expansion of existing job controls. The purchase to 'pull this off' came from the commercial context in which they operated, in fact from a general 'squeeze' on costs and completion dates which could be turned against the logic of rationalism to avoid project controls and defined procedures.

These developers were in effect playing on a contradiction between engineering and commercial variants of software rationalisation. Though ostensibly complementary, engineering and managerial drives to control the software process are not necessarily congruent. In software engineering, the guiding principle is adherence to strictly defined procedures that provide an orderly route from specifying user requirements to implementing operational systems. However, for commercial software providers development issues are not confined to the internal logic of engineering methodologies. Indeed, a frequent criticism is that these methodologies lack a meaningful grasp of business problems, a particular drawback when success in the software marketplace means containing costs and providing a responsive service.

This contradiction is reinforced by a second consideration, the impact on computing of the micropolitical reality of organisational life (Knights and Murray, 1994; Salzman and Rosenthal, 1994). In this view, software specification, design and implementation are all matters of contestation between different individual and group interests. It follows that to negotiate the treacherous waters of competing demands from different managerial and user groups, a developer needs political skills as well as ones of systems analysis. In many ways, this problem was particularly acute for outside vendors, and we found greatest concern with the need for this aptitude in supplier companies. Within larger organisations, we saw various efforts by developers to manage these tensions, some by distancing themselves and using formal specifications and methods to keep the users at arm's length, as in one public sector organisation, others by identifying with either user-buyers or end-users and resisting other allegiances, as in a finance-sector company with customer-dedicated design teams. All these responses solved some problems at the expense of creating others.

Where rationalistic controls have been incorporated in development projects, there is evidence also of user resistance to counteract unpalatable consequences and, perhaps more surprisingly, to improve the resultant software. User interventions to defeat monitoring functions have been recognised for some time, recent examples including bank staff penetrating security screens and field engineers disabling productivity controls (Salzman and Rosenthal, 1994). Recent research has also drawn attention to the development role of users in accomplishing de facto design tasks by rendering generic software packages useful for their own work and in their own terms. Clement (1993) and Nardi and Miller (1991) provide illustrative case examples of clerical workers extending software design on an incremental basis with local adjustments and collaborative problem solving to establish spreadsheet templates, construct databases and devise wordprocessing conventions.

Our research in further education colleges found even more direct evidence of user intervention in technical design and programming (Beirne *et al.*, 1996). Staff employed on short-term contracts to input data to a new, though seriously flawed, student records system redefined their job boundaries to include programming and development work, securing positive results which eluded in-house IS managers and suppliers of the applications software. Two users who had some computing training were particularly creative, experimenting with unfamiliar query languages and, through trial and error, devising a way of delivering useful reports to administrators, lecturers and senior managers. These de facto designers were motivated by a sense of disenchantment with the pressures they were confronting in their work, and which they eventually felt compelled to tackle by overstepping the terms of their employment contract.

Their interventions remained unofficial, though when news spread about their effectiveness managers turned a 'blind eye', even prompting them to attend training courses to refine their illicit skills.

This case also illustrated issues familiar from other work contexts, as it displayed particular gender dynamics in its outcomes for those involved. End-users in this and a majority of other information system settings were female, their managers male. Eventually, these women found themselves with a (male) systems manager appointed above them, and lost much of their control over the situation as their methods were officialised. Our visits to four other colleges uncovered variants on this theme, including its gendered aspect, in each case.

Conclusions

Although we began by identifying numerous seemingly ineluctable forces for rationalisation and work degradation in the computing labour process, our investigations have eventually brought us to a more contradictory and indeterminate conclusion. In this respect, IS work echoes most other areas of labour in capitalist systems.

Commercial pressures, which are often seen as the engine of degradation, can turn against the logic of tight engineering process control. In the dynamic context of client relations, grassroots development staff may find space to assert themselves, taking the initiative and developing their own resources to create viable software. Examples of user and developer activity beneath the surface of structured and over-rationalised methodologies highlight the reflective creativity of social actors and the significance of their various interventions. As with accounts of unfettered managerial control over labour in other spheres of working life, images of subordination in computing frequently obscure the more subtle processes of human interaction and micro-politics. Yet counteracting notions of passivity and programmed behaviour should not detract from recognition of the pervasive influence of rationalistic prescriptions or attachment to formalised models of management within modern organisations. Caution is required to avoid romanticising the informal, or making too much of the capabilities and *relative* autonomy of users or software workers. Informal interventions and concessions unfold within a structural context, with a real potential for constraints, contradictions and tensions to take their toll of the actors involved.

Gender was a variable which we suggested could be particularly important in the working through of these alternative possibilities. Despite the limitations discernible in the proletarianisation case presented by Kraft and Dubnoff, their safest conclusion is that female software workers are found in the lower reaches of task and pay structures. This situation remains, with even more visible evidence of ghettoisation in the 1990s as women are increasingly concentrated in low status 'specialities' such as merging and tidying databases or writing summary report programs. Although important for effective functioning, the rationalisation and automation of such work into routine and monotonous jobs is promoting a recomposition of software labour along gendered lines (Panteli *et al.*, 1997; Grundy, 1996).

The informal practices we encountered were located within managerial regimes where an enthusiasm for more direct control, and frustration at its elusiveness, were nonetheless readily apparent. Developers were acutely aware of rationalistic leanings in management, detecting an intensification of their work as managers aggressively reduced costs and timescales in tendering for contracts yet pushed them to be ever attentive to client needs. Cynicism in this regard was coupled to worries about employment and conditions, concerns that were heightened by apparent trends towards subcontracting and outsourcing. Gauging a realistic sense of emerging outcomes thus requires broader attention to the dynamic context in which rationalistic inclinations and tendencies are crosscut by mixed emotions and responses, prevailing conditions and contingent events. Software jobs can neither be seen as rationalistic constructions or as ad hoc clusters of formal and informal activities. Hence the future of software work is unlikely to match straightforward and unambiguous images of deskilling and degradation, or enskilling and job enrichment.

It seems equally difficult to avoid the conclusion that rationalistic ambitions towards orderly and predictable work performance are as strong as ever. Software labour is more circumscribed, and liable to encounter continuing processes of intensification. These are not uncontested, nor are they always effective, predictable outcomes flowing routinely from software technologies or the expressed intentions of autocratic IS managers. Yet despite the significance of informal behaviour and the job controls retained through organisational knowledge, traditional hierarchical boundaries and distinctions between different categories of labour exhibit an unfortunate longevity. We may not have found reason for unalloyed pessimism on degradation, but there is no sign either that any collapsing of job ladders, outsourcing or recomposition of tasks will create equality of opportunity or durable 'empowerment'.

Currently, a debate is raging in business computing circles about the likely impact of a paradigm shift in systems configuration towards network computing and away from networked individual PCs. The most public protagonists are Bill Gates, head of Microsoft, and Larry Ellison, head of Oracle, with Ellison championing the new approach. For him, network computing cuts costs and restores the possibility of closer centralised monitoring of users and designers; for Gates and more radical defenders of stand-alone machines, this pathway leads to the reassertion of control from the centre, and so an attack on individual freedom and flexibility. The foregoing analysis would lead us to see the latter view as credible, but to expect that its progress will be patchy and unstable in practice. The contradictions of rationalisation strategies will continue to haunt IS workers and management alike.

Acknowledgements

This chapter is based partially on research funded by the Economic and Social Research Council, award reference number R000235289. The authors gratefully acknowledge the support of the ESRC for this project.

References

Avergou, C. and Cornford, T. (1993a) *Developing Information Systems: Concepts, Issues and Practice*, London: Macmillan.

Avergou, C. and Cornford, T (1993b) 'A Review of the Methodologies Movement', *Journal of Information Technology*, 5, 277–86.

Bansler, J.P. and Bødker, K. (1993) 'A Reappraisal of Structured Analysis: Design in an Organisational Context', *ACM Transactions on Information Systems*, 11:2, 165–93.

Bansler, J.P. and Havn, E. (1996) 'Industrialised Information Systems Development: Procurement and Customization of Generic Software', *Centre for Tele-Information Working Paper*, Technical University of Denmark.

Baroudi J.J. and Igbaria M. (1995), 'An Examination of Gender Effects on Career Success of Information Systems Employees', *Journal of Management Information Systems*, 11:3, 181–201.

Beirne, M. and Ramsay, H. (1988) 'Computer Redesign and "Labour Process" Theory: Towards a Critical Appraisal' in Knights D. and Willmott, H. (eds) *New Technology and the Labour Process*, London: Macmillan.

Beirne, M., Ramsay, H. and Panteli, A. (1996) 'Participating Informally: Opportunities and Dilemmas in User-Driven Design' in Blomberg, J., Kensing, F. and Dykstra-Erickson, E. (eds) *Proceedings of the Fourth Biennial Conference on Participatory Design*, Cambridge, Mass.

Blackburn, J., Scudder, G. and Van Wassenhove, L. (1996) 'Improving Speed and Productivity of Software Development: A Global Survey of Software Developers', *IEEE Transactions on Software Engineering*, 22:12, 875–85.

Checkland, P. and Scholes, J. (1990) *Soft Systems Methodology in Action*, Chichester: Wiley.

Clement, A. (1993) 'Looking for the Designers: Transforming the "Invisible" Infrastructure of Computerised Office Work', *AI and Society*, 7, 323–44.

Computerworld (1995) '9th Annual Salary Survey: Unequal Opportunities', 4 September, 1, 70-72, 74, 78.

Crosby, P. (1980) *Quality Is Free: The Art of Making Quality Certain*, New York: Mentor.

Currie, W., Fincham, R. and Hallier, J. (1993) 'Strategy, Evaluation and Career Development in the Management of IT Projects: A Research Framework' in *COST A3 Proceedings*.

Curtis, B., Krasner, H. and Iscoe, N. (1988) 'A Field Study of the Software Design Process for Large Systems', *Communications of the ACM*, 31:11, 1268–87.

Ershov, A.P. (1972) 'Aesthetics and the Human Factor in Programming', *Communications of the ACM*, 15:7, 501–5.

Fenton N (1991) *Software Metrics: A Rigorous Approach*, London: Chapman-Hall.

Fincham, R., Fleck, J., Procter, R., Scarbrough, H., Tierney, M. and Williams, R. (1994) *Expertise and Innovation: Information Technology Strategies in the Financial Services Sector*, Oxford: Clarendon Press.

Flowers, S. (1996) *Software Failure: Management Failure*, Chichester: Wiley.

Friedman, A.L. and Cornford, D.S. (1989) *Computer Systems Development: History, Organisation and Implementation*, Chichester: Wiley.

Greenbaum, J. (1979) *In the Name of Efficiency*, Philadelphia: Temple University Press.

Greenbaum, J. (1995) *Windows on the Workplace*, New York: Monthly Review Press.

Grundy, F. (1996) *Women and Computers*, Exeter: Intellect Books.

Guidon, R. and Curtis, B. (1988) 'Control of Cognitive Processes During Design: What Tools Would Support Software Designers?' in *Conference Proceedings of CHI*, Washington DC, Chicago: ACM Press.

Gurbaxani, V. (1996) 'The New World of Information Technology Outsourcing', *Communications of the ACM*, 39:7, 45–6.

Harding, S. and Gilbert, G.N. (1993) 'Negotiating the Take-Up of Formal Methods' in Quintas, P. (ed.) *Social Dimensions of Systems Engineering: People, Processes, Policies and Software Development*, New York: Ellis Horwood.

Jayaratna, N (1994) *Understanding and Evaluating Methodologies: NIMSAD, A Systemic Framework*, Maidenhead: McGraw-Hill.

Knights, D. and Murray, F. (1994) *Managers Divided: Organisation Politics and Information Technology Management*, Chichester: Wiley.

Kraft, P. (1977) *Programmers and Managers: The Routinisation of Computer Programming in the United States*, New York: Springer Verlag.

Kraft, P. (1987) 'Computers and the Automation of Work', in Kraut, R. (ed.) *Technology and the Transformation of White Collar Work*, New Jersey: Lawrence Erlbaum.

Kraft, P. and Dubnoff, S. (1986) 'Job Content, Fragmentation and Control in Computer Software Work', *Industrial Relations*, 25:2, 184–96.

Lacity, M.C. and Hirschheim, R. (1993) *Information Systems Outsourcing: Myths, Metaphors and Realities*, Chichester: Wiley.

Livari, I. (1996) 'Why Are CASE Tools Not Used?', *Communications of the ACM*, 39:10, 94–103.

Loh, L. and Venkatraman, N. (1992) 'Diffusion of Information Technology Outsourcing: Influence Sources and the Kodak Effect', *Information Systems Research*, 3:4, 334–58.

Martin J. (1984) *An Information Systems Manifesto*, Engelwood Cliffs, N.J.: Prentice-Hall.

Martin, C. and Powell, P. (1992) *Information Systems: a Management Perspective*, London: McGraw-Hill.

Mumford, E. (1996) *Systems Design: Ethical Tools for Ethical Change*, London: Macmillan.

Nardi, B. and Miller, J. (1991) 'Twinkling Lights and Nested Loops: Distributed Problem-Solving and Spreadsheet Development', *International Journal of Man-Machine Studies*, 34, 161–4.

National Computing Centre (1988, 1992, 1993 & 1997) 'Salaries and Staff Issues in Computing', *Annual Reports*, Manchester.

Noble, D. (1984) *Forces of Production: A Social History of Industrial Automation*, New York: Knopf.

Ordroyd, R. (1996) 'Is the IS industry a turn-off for women?', *Sunday Business*, 26 May, 9.

Orlikowski, W. (1988) 'The Data Processing Occupation: Professionalisation or Proletarianisation?', *Research in the Sociology of Work*, 4, 95–124.

Orlikowski, W. (1989) 'Software Work', *Industrial Relations*, 25:2, 184–96.

Panteli, N., Ramsay, H., Stack, J. and Atkinson M. (1997) 'Women in the UK software industry – how much do we know?', paper to *Women Into Computing Conference*, De Montfort University, Milton Keynes.

Paulk M. (1993) 'Mapping from ISO 9001 to the CMM', *SEI Memorandum*, June.

Pressman, R.S. (1992) *Software Engineering: A Practitioner's Approach*, New York: McGraw-Hill (3rd edition).

Quintas, P. (1991), 'Engineering Solutions to Software Problems: Some Institutional and Social Factors Shaping Change', *Technology Analysis and Strategic Management*, 3:4, 359–76.

Salzman, H. and Rosenthal, S. (1994) *Software By Design*, New York: Oxford University Press.

Sauer, C. (1993) *Why Information Systems Fail: A Case-Study Approach*, Henley-on-Thames: Alfred Waller.

Shapiro, S. (1992) 'Its Own Worst Enemy: How Software Engineering Has Fallen Victim to Engineering Mythology', *CRICT Discussion Paper no. 25*, University of Edinburgh.

Somerville, I. (1989) *Software Engineering*, Wokingham: Addison-Wesley (3rd edition).

Thomas, R.J. (1994) *What Machines Can't Do: Politics and Technology in the Industrial Enterprise*, Berkeley: University of California Press.

Thomasson, K. (ed.) (1994), *Key Note Market Review: UK Computer Market*, Middlesex: Key Note (4th edition).

Tudor, D.J. and Tudor, I.J. (1995) *Systems Analysis and Design: A Comparison of Structured Methods*, Oxford: National Computing Centre/Blackwell.

Willcocks, L.P. and Fitzgerald, G. (1996) 'IT Outsourcing and the Changing Shape of the Information Systems Function' in Earl, M.J. (ed.) *Information Management: The Organisational Dimension*, Oxford: Oxford University Press.

Wilson, D.N., Petocz, P. and Roiter, K. (1996) 'Software Quality Assurance in Practice', *Software Quality Journal*, 5, 53–9.

Notes

1   Noteworthy exceptions include Friedman and Cornford (1989), Knights and Murray (1994) and Fincham *et al.* (1994).
2   For descriptions and discussion see Tudor and Tudor (1995), Avergou and Cornford (1993a) and Jayaratna (1994).
3   Willcocks and Fitzgerald (1996) report very few large outsourcing contracts.
4   See, for example, Orlikowski (1988).

9 'Bright Satanic Offices': Intensification, Control and Team Taylorism

Chris Baldry, Peter Bain and Phil Taylor

Introduction: Office Work and Office Buildings

From the outside, the contemporary office certainly looks good: curtain walling of smoked or reflective glass, a marble-floored entrance area, perhaps an atrium with luxuriant plants (some of them real). It is a built environment clearly designed to impress the passer-by or the visiting client with the suggestion of corporate or organisational prestige and modernity. The office worker, however, sees none of this. For her it is the place where, day after day, she endlessly repeats a series of familiar routines as she handles the mortgage application, the personal loan, the insurance premium, the welfare benefit, or the customer complaint. To do this she will use the telephone, the keyboard and the computer display screen, with few breaks during the working day. Her work is rigidly structured around a sequence of tasks dictated by the software, and to tight time and performance schedules in which she is answerable to her team leader or supervisor. The office space in which this work is done, and which she shares with maybe forty or even a hundred other workers, is likely to be open-plan and will deliver what somebody has decided are acceptable or optimum levels of fresh air, working temperature and lighting. If she experiences these environmental conditions as unpleasant, or if they adversely affect her work, there is no respite as, by design, the windows are sealed and unopenable and she is forbidden by management to bring in a fan or portable heater. In this sealed environment she may experience repeated coughs, stuffiness, sore throat and headache to compound the stresses of the job. For this worker, the office can be hell.

This chapter has two dimensions. It is first an examination of the contemporary intensification of white-collar work and of the experienced reality of routine clerical work processes in the modern office. On another level, however, it is also saying something about the use of space and the built environment and should be read as an argument for the reincorporation of the physical work environment into any analysis of the labour process.

This plea is necessary as, for historical reasons which we examine later, it is customary in both social science and management literature to view the work building – the factory, office, hospital, warehouse – as merely a neutral shell, independent of, and unconnected with, the social dynamics that create particular labour processes. But, if this is true, we are left with the task of explaining why such labour processes take place in quite specific environments: offices, factories, warehouses, and hospitals look different from each other. Their respective semiotic codes tell us what kind of building they are as we step through the door and also suggest what kind of behaviour is appropriate to each (Baldry, 1997).

Work buildings are structures of control – they both house the labour process and, in so doing, facilitate control over it by the way that space is organised. As Marglin (1976) pointed out in his examination of the origins of management, it was control over the labour process rather than the necessity for housing any new technology, that underpinned the origin of the 'factory' or 'mill'. These were locations to house and encompass the new social relations of production, the dominant characteristic of which was the exchange of labour power and its control for money. The office is a later addition to this building typology but, as a work building, one which we would expect to share the same socio-economic priorities. The way such work space is then socially ordered reproduces and reinforces hierarchical authority relationships within the organisation as, for example, the further up the hierarchy you are, the more space you are allocated, the more lavishly it will be decorated and furnished and, essentially, the more control you will have over its operation.

As an illustration, let us compare our ideal-typical model of the contemporary office worker, with that of a male Senior Clerk of around 1860 – Lockwood's 'black coated worker' (Lockwood, 1958). His labour process was marked by a high degree of autonomy and task discretion, his relations with the employer by high trust and his social status was an ambivalent mix of salaried labourer and aspirant bourgeois. His physical work environment closely resembled his home in its furniture, its open fire, curtains and, by the end of the century, gas lighting. He had the same degree of control over this environment as in his home – he could call for the office junior to put more coal on the fire, he could open or close a door, pull the curtains, or open a window.

How did we get from A to B? We are by now familiar with the account of the changing white-collar labour process with its sub-themes of feminisation, mechanisation and Taylorisation, the decline in status and the debate over proletarianisation (Klingender, 1935; Crompton and Jones 1984; Smith, Knights and Willmott, 1991). But what of the office building? Are we to believe that, while office work has become progressively routinised and controlled, architects have simply presented organisations with a series of improved designs for offices which are completely neutral or independent of the priorities of capitalist production? We no longer accept that this is the case for technology and there is no reason to assume that it is the case for buildings.

Returning to our first example, say a call-centre worker in 1997, it is evident that these changes in white-collar work have been paralleled by remarkably synchronous developments in the working environment. Just as our modern clerical worker's labour process is characterised by the low task discretion, specified performance targets, visual and electronic surveillance and low-trust relations associated with Taylorised work, so also has she lost any ability to control her environment. The building is entirely dependent on a computerised building management system (BMS) for heating and ventilation. To alter the temperature she probably has to complain to the supervisor, who contacts the departmental manager, who rings down to the maintenance engineer employed by the development company who owns the building, who might be able to tweak the software for the BMS to deliver more heat in one or two more hours time.

Essentially we can say that, as white-collar work has become progressively routinised, feminised and stripped of its early attendant aspirations to bourgeois status, the workspace in which it is conducted has become less personalised, more subject to hierarchical delineation and structuring and less open to immediate control by its occupants. There are many examples which illustrate this historical process. When women first entered offices their segregation into the routinised areas of clerical tasks created by the new technologies of the typewriter, the adding machine, telephone and telegraph, was reinforced by segregated work space. The new women office workers were located in separate rooms, often entering by a different door from the men and working different hours (Crompton and Jones, 1984). The reason for this gender apartheid, while justified in terms of decorum and the maintenance of seemly behaviour, was actually so that women would not be able to see and envy the more interesting work of the men (Dohrn, 1988) and, in this, the use of space must be seen as an instrument of managerial control.

The early application of scientific management to white-collar work was frustrated until the late 1920s by a reliance on windows for natural lighting and ventilation, which ensured that most offices remained relatively small and/or shallow. Technical developments in heating and ventilation systems eventually allowed the construction of the large 'deep' spaces required to implement Leffingwell's advocacy of centralised accommodation of such support services as typing and filing. The early 'bull-pen' offices were noticeable for the first appearance of Taylorised space: regimented desks all facing the same direction to facilitate visual supervision and the hierarchical use and control of work space. On the periphery of the building and around the central area of the 'pool' were the managers' and supervisors' offices. Only managers retained the prerogative of controlling a window for ventilation and light and a door for privacy, while the pool workers were reliant on increasingly centralised mechanical delivery of the ambient environment.

The development of fully open-plan offices occurred in the late 1930s in the US but not until the 1960s in the UK because of the later development of the capital concentration necessary for companies of a size able to lease a whole floor of a building. Open-plan offices held out major advantages to management. They were cheaper to build and fit out with heating and ventilation systems, there was less wasted space and they greatly facilitated visual surveillance of the labour process and the establishment of flow-line processes. The consequences for workers, however, were the elimination of visual or acoustic privacy, a constant perceived surveillance, and lowering of a sense of self-worth (Manning, 1965; Oldham and Brass, 1979).

We can refer to this historical development as the scientific management of space, in the sense that control over the built environment has been steadily removed from the hands of the office worker and the use of space has been increasingly delineated by divisions of function, gender and hierarchy. Should this be seen as a somewhat fanciful label when applied to past developments, it assumes a more concrete reality with the advent of the so-called 'intelligent building' or IB.

The Rise of the Intelligent Building

The growing complexity of equipping office buildings for both internal office automation and external telecommunications facilities meant that newly constructed buildings such as the Rank-Xerox headquarters in Marlow in Britain, could contain some 3700 miles of cabling for communications alone (Greig, 1988). Heavily promoted in the US by the telecoms companies that resulted from the break-up of AT&T (Aronoff and Kaplan, 1995), the IB attempts to integrate not only all computing and communications systems but also the building's own control systems such as heat, light, ventilation, water, security and fire. Such buildings, it is claimed, offer the prospect of virtually unlimited IT expansion into the foreseeable future, substantial savings on operating, maintenance and labour costs and the provision of a safe, healthy and comfortable working environment (Atkin, 1988).

The IB's 'brain' is the computerised BMS whose outstanding claimed characteristic is control over energy requirements. Lighting, for example, can be controlled by means of movement sensors, only coming on when someone is present in the area and/or regulated by placing sensors at windows so that internal lighting acts as a 'top-up' to natural light. Temperature levels and ventilation rates are set centrally, resulting in considerable cost savings. Other services such as fire and security can also be programmed into the BMS, with an additional saving on staffing costs (although this may have been underemphasised for diplomatic reasons).

The 1980s saw such state-of-the-art buildings under construction in the major economic centres in the US, Japan and Western Europe and the emphasis was frequently not just on savings in the construction of integrated systems but on some hoped-for effect on productivity. When the US Government launched an 'advanced office technology' project it focused on 'employee productivity as affected by office automation, advanced communications systems, space flexibility and improved service reliability' (Wright, 1988). The federal General Services Administration's new building in Portland, Oregon was used to test features to be incorporated in future federal offices and to record their effects on productivity.

Managing the Intelligent Office

The combination of the increasing complexity of the built environment and concern with its contribution to productivity produced the new management function of facilities management, responsible for co-ordinating all efforts related to planning, designing, and managing buildings and their systems, equipment and furniture. In the self-promotion of facilities management there has been much talk of understanding the organisational culture and the basis on which decisions are made, and how it views its employees and its business market, and the task of:

> ... transforming an organisation's building ... from an overhead into a company resource ... (for) where once office work was for the most part stable and unchanging, the equipment base low, and the amount of capital invested in each office worker minuscule (compared to blue-collar counterparts) today there is change on all fronts. (Wilson, 1987:91)

This quote usefully draws our attention to the fact that such intelligent buildings have been developed and promoted at the same time as the management offensive that has given us HRM, TQM, team working, empowerment, performance targets and all the other varied neologisms and euphemisms for intensification in the increasingly competitive business environments in the private sector and a budget-curtailed public sector. If we take a holistic approach to the office, which puts these two developments together, we find that the outcome for the workers' experience of the labour process is doubly significant.

Three Offices in the 1990s

The cases referred to in this chapter form part of a research project on Sick Building Syndrome (SBS). The locations were chosen not specifically because of their work organisation but because workers, unions and/or management felt that there was something about the way the building operated that was producing high and repeated levels of ill-health complaints and sickness absence. We do not intend to discuss SBS here (see Baldry, Bain and Taylor, 1997a & 1997b) but in the course of this research it became apparent that there were some significant similarities between these offices, both in the developing white-collar labour process and in the utilisation of office space and how the office working environment is experienced by office workers. The data comes from working environment surveys carried out in the three office locations, observational visits and, wherever possible, interviews with representative employees, union officials (both workplace and full-time), senior management and supervisors.

Two, referred to as 'State Office' and 'The Department', are public sector locations, while the other, 'Finance Bank', is a private sector financial institution. Each has around 300 employees, has a high usage of IT and is housed in a modern office location in Glasgow's central business district. Each of these buildings, which we will refer to respectively as Polar House, Forth House and Clyde Wharf, was first occupied by these organisations within a six-year period from the late 1980s to early 1990s and the story of these relocations sheds some light on the criteria by which workspaces are initially selected.

Each organisation commenced looking for new premises because of a planned major restructuring of the labour process and was initially drawn to its new location by the heavy emphasis placed by the developers on the incorporation of IT use. The publicity brochures for all three buildings drew attention to the raised access floors incorporating trunk cabling and all stressed the flexibility of open-plan floor-plates. At Forth House, the column-free floor-plate offered tenants maximum space flexibility, and higher staff densities: 'By diligent space planning up to 50 per cent extra staff can be accommodated on each floor, thus providing excellent potential to reduce occupational overheads.' Both Finance Bank and The Department wanted open-plan space suitable for accommodating multi-functional teams, while the 'production-line' process of document production at State Office seemed to fit the long and rather narrow structure of Polar House.

A closer look at State Office provides some additional detail about locational decisions. With the lease on their old building also due to expire, the organisation commenced searching for a new building in the mid-1980s because they were about to computerise their operations and expand the workforce from 80 to 200. Polar House was one of three or four on the shortlist of potential sites and was chosen, according to the regional manager, because it was advertising itself as the first IB in the West of Scotland, and ' ... the other factor was the cost. The fact that it was less than ten pounds per square foot caused a frisson of excitement in the PSA [Property Services Agency].'

The Rise of Team Taylorism

While the services provided by each organisation are very different, such contrasts are dwarfed by the striking similarities in the labour process. Contemporary HRM rhetoric counterposes the empowering and collective effort of teamworking to the linear process and individual effort that is historically associated with Taylorism. The evidence of the case studies presented here demonstrates that, appearances notwithstanding, workers experience such forms of team organisation as being no less coercive than classically understood Taylorism. In the following analysis we use the term 'Team Taylorism' to bridge this alleged dichotomy between classical Taylorism and supposedly new forms of work organisation.

The work of State Office (a government agency) was described by the manager as 'basically a production line process'. Correspondence from individual members of the public passes through a sequence of stages in batches and culminates in the production of a personal document. Each demarcated stage of the process is undertaken by workers organised nominally in teams, although adherence to HRM, team-based nostrums and practices is far less developed than in our private sector case.

In Finance Bank, operations are a direct consequence of the deregulation of the sector produced by the 1986 Financial Services Act and the 1987 Building Societies Act. The labour process is a classic expression of IT-based reintegration, where tasks previously separate in the functional division between HQ, back office and customer face-to-face offices, have been centralised through electronic information flows under the one roof. In contrast to State Office where functional teams perform successive stages from application and information entry to the final physical production of the document, teams in Finance Bank handle all stages of an application, granting a mortgage loan, monitoring the account and following up queries.

The final case office, The Department, is closer in organisational style to that of Finance Bank than State Office. The business involves the registering of public complaints and the processing of cases leading, ultimately, to the authorisation or rejection of claims for financial compensation. In most cases, even though the time period may be extensive, individuals working in multi-functional teams will see a case through to completion.

In all three cases the work load can be defined as customer driven, though in the case of Finance Bank, high street branches act as intermediaries, relaying applications between customer and team member.

Information Technology

Notwithstanding diversities of business and sector, one common and pervasive feature of the three cases is the fundamental importance of IT to the labour process. The arrival of each organisation at the new location coincided with a managerial decision to transform the way in which work was organised. The computerisation of functions was integral to Finance Bank's move from Biscay House to Clyde Wharf in 1992. Multi-functional team working based on geographical areas was made possible by the recently introduced information technology. The basic sedentary team task involved answering the phone, dealing with queries, checking details on a VDU and entering data.

The arrival of State Office at Polar House in May 1987 marked an explicit attempt to make budgetary savings through the installation of complete IT systems. The Glasgow office was to be the testing-ground for a new computerised work system. Early stages in the document processing involve workers alternating between routinised VDU data entry and post opening. Later stages see further intensive screen work as the actual document is compiled through a word processing template. Inbound and outbound telephone operations are also performed as operators deal with customer queries and pursue information necessary for validation. With 35 per cent of documentation requiring further contact with the public, a key IT innovation is an Automatic Call Distribution (ACD) system, employed to stack and record incoming telephone calls. Operators then oscillate between screen and phone.

Similarly, senior management in The Department decided that computerisation and a new method of claim assessment should accompany relocation at Forth House in 1994. In the words of a CPSA representative: 'The nature of work basically changed from a manual process to a computer process with the introduction of the new scheme ... It affected everything. There was a knock-on effect.' The early stages of the labour process on new applications essentially consist of data input, although management does not like this term. Later tasks are essentially word processing, 'filling in shells', and updating the progress of claims. Once again, screen operations are combined with extensive and, mainly outbound, telephone queries.

We can make four important points. Firstly, the decision to move and the choice of location involving an assessment of the suitability of the building for the computerisation of previously manual operations are managerial judgements which have massive consequences for the labour process. The new buildings which host these organisations are not just conveniently situated boxes. The computer cabling and trunking and the internal configuration of office space are determining factors in the way work is to be organised.

Secondly, whilst variations exist in the extent of IT across the different case offices and, at the same time, between different jobs at differing stages of the labour process, the overwhelming and common impression is of a fundamentally high level of IT use in the three locations. A question in our environmental survey, which asked employees to record their perceptions of the frequency of VDU/PC use, makes this explicit.

The results, shown in Table 9.1, were subsequently confirmed by observation. In Finance Bank, where the percentage reporting all-day VDU use is lower than for the other two offices, continuous screen work is more interrupted by phone calls and by reference to filed hard copy documentation, the utilisation of which ran in tandem with screen template operations. It must be remembered that these are overall percentages which do not directly reflect the different stages but it would seem that, in both the State Office and The Department, there are a greater number of tasks and a proportion of employees who are engaged *solely* on data entry-type operations. These amount to differences of degree within a total picture of extensive VDU operation.

Table 9.1   Percentage of employees in the three offices reporting frequency of VDU/PC and telephone use

	Finance Bank	State Office	The Department
VDU/PC			
All day	26.0%	41.7%	43.7%
Often	37.8%	37.1%	25.9%
Sometimes	27.6%	16.7%	23.7%
Telephone			
All day	39.4%	21.2%	19.3%
Often	40.9%	23.5%	39.3%
Sometimes	15.0%	43.9%	32.6%

Thirdly, an evident characteristic of these offices is the oscillation between repetitive screen tasks and telephone work, in which a frequent observation was the performing of these operations simultaneously. Workers might have a phone receiver wedged between ear and shoulder, speaking and listening, whilst translating information onto the screen through keyboard manipulation or typing.

Fourthly, recognition that the work of this nature can be mind-numbingly monotonous is confirmed by both the statements of managers and also the articulated experiences of the workers in our surveys and from our observations. In State Office, job rotation is incapable of ameliorating the intrinsically boring nature of daily work, so that the office manager permits the widespread use of personal stereos to relieve the monotony of data entry, since 'the job's so boring you need some music to take your mind off it'. But repetitive tasks are not easy as Tony, a Finance Bank Mortgage Processor, explains: 'Psychologically, I would say that it is a difficult job in here because it is basically very boring. You are doing the same thing every day.' The evidence is that inherently uninteresting, repetitive manual clerical work has become more monotonous through the widespread introduction of IT systems in the modern office, even where the basic unit of work organisation is a multi-functional team.

External Benchmarking, Production Targets and Intensification

In each of the three offices external business and organisational pressures contribute to internal target-driven work intensity. In Finance Bank, internal pressure derives from the highly competitive financial services sector in which step gains in efficiency are measured by comparison with market rivals. The merger of Finance Bank with another major bank led to managerial injunctions to outperform other mortgage companies in order to secure a competitive advantage for an unpredictable future. In State Office, performance is subject to the discipline of continuous comparison with the department's other dispersed offices while, in referring to The Department, a CPSA national official summarised the competitive pressure:

> I think the London office is playing a large part in the work of the Glasgow office increasing. They do the same work as us but they only cover the London area. We do all the complaints from the rest of Britain. And if you compare the staff levels, Glasgow should have more staff than it does.

Evidence that these pressures and the IT-driven labour process have generated significant and perceived increases in the volume, speed and intensity of work is confirmed by the surveys completed by employees at the three organisations. The results can be seen in Table 9.2 and were given graphic form in the interviews:

> With the state of the Civil Service at the moment, it does not really matter what modifications are made to the building. All management want is figures, they don't care about quality. Therefore that leads to added pressure, which in turn leads to stress – basically, the work will kill you in the end. (Administrative Officer, State Office)

Public or private sector, the impact is similar when these pressures are translated into work load pressure in the labour process. The outcome is an organisational obsession with targets and measurements of output which would have delighted F.W. Taylor.

The effect on team members is similar whether production targets are formal and specific or informal and general. In Finance Bank there is considerable tacit pressure on the performance of work loads where an unwritten agreement between the Glasgow office and the branches specifies that new applications will be turned round in twenty-four hours and the rest of business is completed on a five-day cycle irrespective of the current volume of work. In State Office the pull of public demand is the decisive driving force. Although management can not predict exact demand because of seasonal variations, with 18–25 000 individual cases completed weekly in peak periods, they organise the work process on 'just-in-time' lines with consequent reductions in document material held in stock. In The Department, with a more complex journey from case application to conclusion, output is measured by the number of completions. These brief descriptions of the pressures and measurements emanating from customer demand need to be fleshed out by more detailed analysis of the impact on workers themselves, for as one respondent testified, 'The pressure comes down the line. It's at the bottom that the pressure is greatest.'

Table 9.2   Percentage of employees in the three offices reporting increases/decreases in aspects of job over the last two years

	Finance Bank	State Office	The Department
Volume of Work			
Increase	70.9%	46.2%	76.3%
Decrease	2.36%	0.0%	7.4%
Speed of Work			
Increase	62.2%	37.1%	64.4%
Decrease	3.2%	0.76%	5.2%
Intensity of Work			
Increase	60.6%	33.3%	71.9%
Decrease	2.36%	0.76%	2.2%
Stress and Pressure			
Increase	64.6%	36.4%	71.1%
Decrease	0.8%	4.55%	1.5%

Shona, a Mortgage Processor in Finance Bank, makes explicit how these general pressures lead to extensive monitoring and detailed measurement of individual and team work effort:

> There is so much pressure with the phone calls from the branches ... In a way the real pressure comes from the daily statistics sheet. They can not measure how much we work from the screens but they can from the daily statistics sheets. Throughout the day every time you finish a job you are supposed to enter it on the statistics sheet.

Statistical data are collated and summarised by supervisors and used at the weekly team brief by managers to encourage or discipline individuals although, ostensibly, they only measure team performance. Each team receives a sheet with times allocated to all possible tasks in microscopic detail. For example, in 1995 a team was expected to average 28.16 Application telephone calls, 21.77 Redemption telephone calls, and/or 22.98 Application Logged On operations per hour. Information from the statistics sheets are computerised and form the basis for work intensification as times are revised upwards. Similar controls exist in Forth House where, in the words of one Administrative Officer:

> The worst aspect of working in The Department is the management pressure to meet the output targets which are increased by the management almost every year without giving thought to an individual's capability. This puts the clerical staff under tremendous pressure since the pay is linked to annual box markings, which in turn is a reflection of the output.

The ramp-up of workloads and targets and a seemingly arbitrary connection to financial reward leads to complaints that some staff might get no pay rise or even be dismissed through poor box marks. As the above respondent continued: 'These kind of pressures cause unnecessary stress-related illness, both mental and physical.'

In State Office, each individual document is allocated a unique identification number which enables management to track progress and assess workers' performance at each successive stage through daily numerical targets. The ACD equipment allows for the visual display of numbers of waiting calls and can both calculate the number of calls per operator and their average duration. In these ways the general customer-driven pressure is magnified through the use of these acute measurement devices.

Human Supervision and Teams

IT leads to both intensification of work and more sophisticated monitoring of effort. Yet, in the modern office this does not mean the diminution of active *human* supervision of employees as surveillance and control continues to take both technological and human forms. Where IT is used to monitor employees' output the data is still required to be interpreted by supervisors and line managers and utilised in disciplinary or other ways 'to encourage the others'. Additionally, the modern office is characterised by cellular or team forms of organisation in which supervisors or team leaders, or other HRM equivalents, perform the important role of continuous visual surveillance. In two of our cases, Finance Bank and The Department, similar arrangements of work stations and physical layout were to be found.

In Finance Bank, twenty or so team members sit in front of VDUs surrounding an elongated rectangular table. Although team members can talk to each other, the job of team member is a fairly static one involving sitting at the desk answering phones, dealing with queries, checking the details on a VDU in front of them and processing forms. When they leave their desks it is to retrieve files or to go for refreshment but there is no formal work break and teas and coffees are usually consumed at the work station. The overall impression is of uninterrupted and intensive working and the only time everyone stops at the same time is for the weekly team briefing.

The Team Manager is positioned at the head, with two team supervisors on either side of the table. The close proximity of either supervisor or manager to all team members is striking and, while one or another might leave the table for managerial briefings, the team is never left unsupervised by someone. Although they have no disciplinary powers, the pivotal role of the controllers is underlined by, as one of them put it, their responsibility to watch for an employee's personal problems or 'quiet' attitude. This contributes to considerable tacit pressure on work performance.

The supervisors perform similar tasks to team members but, as experienced employees, are called upon by team members to answer complex problems. They might intervene to direct the work of individuals or allocate specific phone calls or tasks. Their most significant role seems to be that of a permanent presence ensuring that members are not distracted from application to their tasks. Altogether, surveillance and intervention form a continuous process in which supervisors and managers define the limits of acceptable non-work social interaction between team members.

In The Department the configuration is similar if on a smaller scale, due in part to the more partitioned layout of the original open-plan space. One former employee described team arrangements at Forth House:

> The team structure is one line manager, five or six case workers and a couple of support grades. The line manager sits at the top and rules the roost. Although they sit in teams it's not really team work because everybody is responsible for their own casework. You don't feel that everyone is pulling their weight and you're all mucking in. It's not like that. It's misleading to call it team work.

Team working suggests collective effort, increased job satisfaction and a degree of autonomy and discretion for members in the conception and execution of tasks. This evidence, especially from Finance Bank which is awash with HRM declarations of employee commitment and empowerment, is the opposite: individual output devoid of conceptual content, job dissatisfaction and tight physical and technological surveillance. Closer to Taylor than Hawthorne, the configuration of work, atmosphere and level of surveillance is more akin to a light manufacturing assembly plant than to conventional images of office work. The daily experience, then, of the majority employed in these white-collar factories is not of enrichment but of 'Team Taylorism'.

Lean Staffing

Team working can also be seen from a managerial perspective to perform, at least rhetorically, the function of sharing (and thus increasing) the workload in a period of cuts and lean staffing. Both of the public sector organisations exhibit lean staffing driven by budget cuts. Scottish Office policy led to both compulsory and voluntary redundancies in The Department and at State Office. There was also a freeze on permanent appointments. In addition there has been the more widespread moratorium on permanent promotions throughout much of the Civil Service, contributing to reported decreases in staff morale and motivation. A national CPSA official, talking to the Branch AGM in 1996, described management's intention as 'trying to create a culture whereby workers internalise the vicious circle of heavier workloads, increasing levels of stress'.

Management at private sector Finance Bank has a different starting point but the desire to seek competitive advantage leads to similar consequences for the workforce. Tony, the Mortgage Processor, commented: 'Some of the complaints that people are making could be psychological in that a lot are dissatisfied with their jobs. There is a real lack of motivation because there are no promotion prospects. That is why I am leaving to go to Direct Line.' A labour turnover figure of 17 per cent in that year confirms that this is not an individualised grievance. Thus, frozen staffing in the public sector contrasts with labour turnover in the private sector, as low morale and lack of motivation impact upon workers' perceptions of the labour process.

What lean staffing means in terms of work intensification is shown in two of our cases: Finance Bank and The Department. In neither organisation do workers take tea breaks but sit at their desks and have a drink whilst continuing to work. In Finance Bank an unauthorised break would be promptly noticed by a supervisor. At The Department it appears that management has reneged on a previous tea-break agreement. An Administrative Officer commented:

> I feel staff would give more if they were allowed to take tea breaks away from their desk. Facilities even for eating lunch are non-existent and 90 per cent of staff eat lunch at their desk ... Having raised the point of tea breaks, management are totally against staff taking a break away from their desk.

Although not physically chained to the VDU, workers are compelled by management to remain at their work stations for periods which may exceed legal limits.

The Built Environment

What part does the physical built environment play in the intensification of white-collar work? It may seem up to this point that we are arguing that there is a straight functional relationship between a given labour process and the way space is constructed to house and facilitate it: the three organisations were looking for flexible space which would facilitate IT use around team working, and this facility is what the three buildings claimed to provide.

This is only true up to a point however, as buildings are also sold or leased on the basis of their appeal to other priorities of capitalist organisation. The 'Premises of Excellence' study by Building Use Studies of how twenty-two leading UK companies managed their offices (Wilson, 1987) concluded that organisations can view their buildings' relationship to working conditions and performance in five ways:

(1)   as a container of minimal significance to performance. Here expenditure on premises will be at a minimum;

(2)   as a prestige symbol. The exterior is the key factor rather than the internal working conditions;

(3)   as a vehicle for industrial relations. A healthy work environment with, for example, recreational facilities, will be an expression of concern for the workforce;

(4)   as an instrument of efficiency. Work investment expenditure will be high but geared to return on money, not staff welfare;

(5)   as an inspirational force: a functional and symbolic role reflected in management and design.

Companies in categories 1 and 2, it was suggested, would hold that working conditions would have no effect on performance, while those in categories 3 and 4 believe that good working conditions can only make things better, not worse. Category 5 companies would say that good working conditions positively enhance productivity.

Speculative building developers, of course, do not know which particular view of office premises their likely tenants have in mind, so they will suggest several features at the same time, such as their ability to minimise running costs by saving money on energy, and their potential to enhance the standing of the company through the combination of an impressive external facade, interior fitments and being in a prestige location.

Thus we find in the promotional material for our three locations such statements as :

> The assurance of greatly reduced running costs, fitting out and management charges combined with increased business efficiency and staff productivity gives a building's true economic value to a tenant ... The sophisticated heating systems which can save up to 40 per cent energy costs and balanced lighting systems which can save up to 80 per cent energy costs ... (Polar House)

> All services are monitored and optimised by a sophisticated building management system which provided occupiers with total control of the working environment thereby minimising running costs. (Forth House)

and, for prestige:

> Solar reflective double glass curtain walling gives initial impact ... Although what goes on inside a building is ever more important, the building itself must be of the best possible quality and appearance to project a progressive and business like image. (Polar House)

> Probably the most prominent HQ location in Scotland ... The location and nature of the building is ideal for companies seeking strong corporate presence. (Forth House)

Clearly, work buildings such as these offices are promoted as simultaneously meeting differing management priorities. However, because these will usually be the responsibilities of different management *functions*, it is quite possible for there to be a clash of priorities between, for example, saving on fitting-out and running costs and the provision of a healthy ambient working environment. In addition, because in the management hierarchy, personnel and human resources issues are generally subservient to the claims of cost accountancy, there is always a strong tendency for cost considerations to take precedence. This priority can be manifest even before the building is occupied.

The Workers' Story

How are these high technology prestige workplaces actually experienced by the workers themselves? Vischer (1989: 132) has identified seven dimensions in office users' judgements of their work environment: air quality, noise control, thermal comfort, privacy, lighting comfort, spatial comfort and building noise control. In the comments in our working environment surveys and interviews we find office workers in our three locations commenting adversely in most of these areas.

In all three locations occupants made a clear distinction between temperature and air quality. A common description of these offices was 'stuffy'. Shona described how, in Clyde Wharf:

> It does get stuffy very quickly. I am beginning to find it stuffy already [9.30 am]. You can come in when it's freezing outside and within minutes you can hardly breathe in here. By lunch-time you are nearly gasping for breath.

Temperatures in State Office's Polar House building had been a constant source of complaint from the moment of occupation. This seemed largely the product of the unique heating and ventilation system which, in the words of a consultant, 'defied the laws of physics', providing hot spots and cold spots at the same time, and proving incapable of combating solar gain in the summer and low winter temperatures. Respondents commented:

> The atmosphere varies from hot and stuffy to extremely low temperatures (the need to wear outdoor coats and jackets is often required).

> The logic behind the blowers is difficult to understand. They seem to operate in a most arbitrary manner, often at times when the temperature does not warrant their use. Cold air blowing down your neck can be very uncomfortable, especially when the nature of the work does not permit you to move.

Almost identical comments were voiced in Forth House: 'There seems to be no middle ground: the temperature is either too cool or too hot and the atmosphere is often stuffy', 'Having to suffer cold air from the ceiling all day is not a comfortable environment.' Similarly, at Finance Bank, Jackie, a team manager, commented :

> The problem is, if you heat the periphery to make the temperature bearable, the people in the middle tend to cook. When we were freezing on the third floor Charlie would come up with the thermometer and show us the temperatures, which were in the mid-80s. It did not feel anything like that. I think they've fixed the thermometer to read a hotter temperature than it is. There is something not right with the air circulation. The top half of your body can be hot, too hot in fact, and at the same time your legs can be cold.

The work areas at Polar House were a mixture of open-plan and enclosed offices. According to the CPSA official, the open-plan areas could prove very distracting to workers engaged on individual cases due to phones ringing, background noise and movement, while some of the other offices were experienced as quite confined. Comments from the employee survey included 'there is not enough space to work comfortably in. The work stations are positioned badly, meaning you have to twist and turn your neck to the side far too often.' At Forth House, the partitioning of the original open-plan floor-plate had created overcrowding in areas such as the typing pool, with subsequent perceived high temperatures and deterioration in air quality. At Finance Bank an interviewee who had moved with the company into the new building commented 'for all that it is open-plan in here it is not a natural openness ... When I first started here ... we would come in before this place was occupied and the feeling I got then was one of claustrophobia.'

Lighting in Polar House was variously felt to be too bright and contributing to migraines and headaches. Its most prominent feature, however, was that it was operated by movement sensors in the ceiling with no manual override switches: 'The lighting system is extremely irritating. Our job consists of sitting in more or less the same position and because of lack of movement the lights switch themselves off.' Comments about the lighting in Finance Bank have to be interpreted in the context of that building's smoked glass windows: 'It's difficult to put your finger on what's wrong because the lights do seem bright in here. But when you go out of the building you feel like you're getting out of prison. It's so bright you're almost blinded by the light.'

Running beneath all the complaints was a perceived lack of control. With the move to each of the new locations the workforce had experienced a decline in their ability to control their environment. At Forth House 'All I know is that in the previous building it was not air conditioned and you were able to open windows, you could also control heaters yourself.' At Finance Bank there were a number of thermostatic controls on the pillars and walls throughout the floor area, which were supposedly able to deliver temperature changes of plus or minus one degree on a grid matrix. However, as Shona commented in an interview: 'We were told not to touch them because, I think, we were causing havoc. What we were supposed to do is to phone and complain to Charlie if the temperature gets too hot or too cold. He then comes up to adjust them.'

Buildings and Control

But, the reader may ask, why do these buildings not behave in the way in which they were supposed to? We can identify a number of possible reasons. Firstly, there can be specific structural causes of malfunction, such as cost cutting in both building and maintenance processes. The Office Environment Survey (Wilson and Hedge, 1987) found that the most common cause of poor air quality in offices was management cost cutting on maintenance programmes. Secondly, sometimes sensors and controls fail to operate as planned, as in the case of a fire in a 62-storey Los Angeles office block in 1988. As is commonly the case where there is heavy computerisation, there was no sprinkler system and the computer-controlled doors remained open instead of closing, enabling the flames to spread up the stairwell from the 12th to the 16th floor. In addition, the lifts, instead of automatically returning to the ground floor as they had been programmed to do, carried on operating and delivered a maintenance man to his death on the 12th (Gregerson, 1989).

Thirdly, additional problems can be created by the actions of tenants. Forth House had been designed as an open-plan configuration but The Department had decided to create separate office areas by floor to ceiling partitioning. This is not uncommon as, in a speculative property market, there is almost no communication between architect and end-user as to the organisational demands on the space provided, and it is still the rule that management prefer personal offices as a badge of status. This partitioning drastically interfered with the functioning of the ceiling fancoil units (which were found to be defective anyway).

Fourthly, it is claimed (Mill, 1988) that the expectation in building design is that only about 80 per cent of occupants will find the environment reasonable, which suggests that there will always be 20 per cent who may find aspects of it disagreeable. However, the *main* reason for the discrepancy between the buildings' external image and the experienced reality of working in them is that, in a sense, the buildings *are* working as designed, because, as we have seen in our three cases, they are marketed primarily as energy (cost)-saving structures, with an implicit, or hoped for, assumption that this will somehow also provide a pleasant and healthy working environment.

A building is not just a technical system but, in its design, configuration and way of operating, a reflection of the priorities of the social system. That is, someone decides what control system is to be installed and for what reasons, someone decides what levels of light and temperature are deemed suitable or adequate and, of course, the designer inevitably incorporates a specific view of the user – whether they are to play an active or a passive role. Current practice is an overwhelmingly technology-centred, top–down operation in which the environmental system is installed and then people are expected to adjust.

We have not discussed here either the consequences for ill-health (see Bain and Baldry, 1995; Baldry, Bain and Taylor, 1997a) or worker responses to these consequences, and the degree to which they can contest undesirable and unhealthy working conditions (Bain, Taylor and Baldry, 1996). Yet our respondents' comments confirm that a crucial ingredient of a healthy and agreeable working environment is the degree to which the worker can exercise control over it. What we find in the contemporary office is either no control or, cynically, the deliberate provision of placebo controls, dummy switches installed in order to delude employees that they are actually able to affect some aspects of their environment (Wilson and Hedge, 1987).

This supports the proposition, at the beginning of this paper, that buildings must be seen as structures of control: this is, after all, *why* lots of people are brought together under one roof. But the control function of management obviously has several different dimensions – control over labour processes, over markets and over overheads and operational costs. Because, in a speculative property market, architects and developers will not know the precise nature of a tenant's work or work organisation, apart from the probability that it will involve IT, we have seen that they will concentrate their efforts on offering *cost* controls and the provision of flexible work space. We have seen in our three cases how the latter is used in the spatial configuration of work as part of the control process.

'Post-Mayoism' and the Death of Hawthorne

Clearly the physical environment *is* experienced by workers as part of the totality of the daily work process. Yet this experience remains unreflected in prevailing management and social science analysis. It is a tribute to the energetic self-publicising activities of Elton Mayo that the Hawthorne experiments have become enshrined in the academic pantheon as marking the death knell of theoretical interest in the influence of the physical environment over worker behaviour. It has of course not always been thus. Until the early 1920s the early industrial psychologists, in Britain personified by C.S. Myers and the work of the Industrial Fatigue Research Board, continued to investigate the relationship between aspects of the built working environment such as lighting and ventilation and the level of accidents, worker fatigue and productivity.

Myers' approach was the major influence in the thinking behind the first Hawthorne experiments – the lighting tests. Set up in 1924 under the aegis of the US National Research Council, on which leading industrial interests were heavily represented, the lighting tests were heavily promoted by the electrical companies, hoping to prove the proposition that artificial light would be shown to have significant productivity advantages over the then near universal reliance on natural lighting (Gillespie, 1991).

As we now know, the tests proved no such thing and so energetically promoted, in the pursuit of social science empire-building, was the 'discovery' of the social group that few people questioned the legitimacy of thenceforth excluding *all* environmental factors from analysis of work processes, on the basis of unsatisfactory tests carried out on one isolated environmental variable.

This chapter is an attempt to redress this long-standing and significant distortion in the focus of our understanding of the totality of the labour process in which, we would argue, the physical setting must be seen as a constituent and influential part. Ironically, one of the things about the Hawthorne Relay Assembly Tests was that the young women relay assemblers were actually given far more control over their working environment than their sisters on the shop floor. They were able to request alterations to the lighting and to ask for modesty screens on the front of their benches; more generally, they were regularly consulted and asked their opinion about working conditions. Their productivity, as we know, went up (Gillespie, 1991).

The case-study offices in this chapter are all recently constructed buildings which, from the outside, more than live up to the popular image of the office building as an icon of modernity. Some progressive architects (Laing, 1993) are currently keen to promote the concept of the 'office of the future' staffed by 'new professionals', in a variant of the New Middle Class thesis promoted by management writers such as Handy (1984). Despite their wholesale and enthusiastic adoption of the post-Fordist mantra of the flexible, flat organisation, actual analysis of what is going on in our offices does not support this proposition. If we combine office workers' experience of work intensification under Team Taylorism with their daily ordeal at the mercy of a malfunctioning built environment we can see that the total reality does not seem 'modern' at all but almost approximates to a Dickensian sweat shop.

References

Aronoff, S. and Kaplan, A. (1995) *Total Workplace Performance: Rethinking the Office Environment*, Ottawa: KDL Publications.

Atkin, B. (ed.) (1988) *Intelligent Buildings*, London: Kogan Page.

Bain, P. and Baldry, C. (1995) 'Sickness and control in the office – the Sick Building Syndrome, *New Technology Work and Employment*, 10:1, 19–31.

Bain, P., Taylor, P. and Baldry, C. (1996) 'Sick Building Syndrome and the industrial relations of occupational health' paper to *BUIRA Conference*, University of Bradford.

Baldry, C. (1997) 'Hard Day at the Office: the Social Construction of Workspace', *Occasional Paper No. 9*, Department of Human Resource Management, University of Strathclyde.

Baldry, C., Bain, P. and Taylor, P. (1997a) 'Sick Building Syndrome and Human Resource Management' in Rostron J. (ed.) (1997) *Sick Building Syndrome: Concepts, Issues & Practice*, London: E & F N Spon.

Baldry, C., Bain, P. and Taylor, P. (1997b) 'Sick and Tired? – Working in the Modern Office', *Work Employment & Society*, 11:3.

Crompton, R. and Jones, G. (1984) *White-Collar Proletariat: Deskilling and Gender in Clerical Work*, London: Macmillan.

Dohrn, S. (1988) 'Pioneers in a dead-end profession: the first women clerks in bank and insurance companies' in Anderson, G. (ed.) *The White-Blouse Revolution: Female Office Workers Since 1870*, Manchester: Manchester University Press.

Gillespie, R. (1991) *Manufacturing Knowledge: a History of the Hawthorne Experiments*, Cambridge: Cambridge University Press.

Gregerson, J. (1989) 'How LA's worst high rise fire spread', *Building Design and Construction*, February, 72–7.

Greig, J. (1988) 'Xerox: model for copying', *Architects Journal*, 20 April, 33.

Handy, C. (1984) *The Future of Work*, Oxford: Blackwell.

Klingender, F. (1935) *The Condition of Clerical Labour in Britain*, London: Martin Lawrence.

Laing, A. (1993) 'Changing business: post-Fordism and the workplace' in Duffy, A., Laing, A. and Crisp, B. (eds) (1993) *The Responsible Workplace*, Oxford: Butterworth.

Lockwood, D. (1958) *The Blackcoated Worker: a Study in Class Consciousness*, London: Allen & Unwin.

Manning, P. (ed.) (1965) *Office Design: a Study of Environment*, Department of Building Science, University Liverpool.

Marglin, S. (1976) 'What do bosses do?' in Gorz, A. (ed.) *The Division of Labour*, Brighton: Harvester.

Mill, M. (1988) *A Trivial Pursuit in Architecture? The Impact of Advanced Technology on Total Building Performance*, Centre for Building Diagnostics, University of Dundee.

Oldham, G. and Brass, D. (1979) 'Employee reactions to an open-plan office', *Administrative Science Quarterly*, 24, 267–84.

Smith, C., Knights, D. and Willmott, H. (eds) (1991) *White-Collar Work: the Non-Manual Labour Process*, London: Macmillan.

Vischer, J. (1989) *Environmental Quality in Offices*, New York: Van Nostrand Reinhold.

Wilson, S. (1987) 'Making offices work', *Management Today*, October.

Wilson, S. and Hedge, A. (1987) *The Office Environment Survey – a Study of Building Sickness*, London: Building Use Studies.

Wright, G. (1988) 'Federal building showcases advanced technology', *Building Design and Construction*, September, 73–7.

10 'Survivors' Versus 'Movers and Shakers': The Reconstitution of Management and Careers in the Privatised Utilities

Kate Mulholland

Introduction

This chapter examines the ways in which organisational politics in a climate of change shape the fate of managerial careers in the regulated utility business. The significance of organisational politics is that it is embedded in a corporate culture which is constituted in and through marketisation and shareholding expectations underpinned by particular efficiency strategies. In the context of widespread restructuring characterised by economic recession and privatisation, the search for efficiencies has largely been brought about by cost reductions in human resources. Since the utility business is unlikely to rely on the growth of their product markets in facilitating accumulation, there has been a shift of focus to the internal dynamics of the firm, such as ways of working and a concern with quality initiatives (Froud *et al.*, 1996). This strategy has given rise to an interesting contradiction relating to the role of managers as agents of capital (Armstrong, 1989 & 1991). While managers are the purveyors of change programmes and efficiency drives, they have become, paradoxically, the focus of attention because they also comprise part of the human resource cost. The delayering of middle managerial jobs is evidence of this development (Ferner and Colling, 1993; Heckscher, 1995). It will be argued that these series of events generated an organisational politics which dislocated established career patterns and gave rise to a new 'career' path resulting in a deep cleavage within managerial ranks. The chapter explores the way in which interprofessional rivalry and competition for the role of agency underpins such a cleavage.

The Study

The research for this chapter is based on a case study of a large water plc and an electricity company. The water company, the largest supplier of water in the UK, is located in the south-east and provides clean water and sewerage services for about twelve million customers. Since privatisation in 1989, it has developed consultancy and training programmes in overseas markets and has an annual investment programme of £400m. In a series of reorganisations pre- and post-privatisation it has shed more than a third of its personnel and presently employs about 7000 people. According to company documentation for the company, pre-tax profits for 1996 were £188m. UK located, the electricity supply company is American owned. It serves a customer base of over two million, providing employment for 4500–5000 people. In 1995 it had a £95.7m investment programme with pre-tax profits for that year of £218m. Sixty managers were interviewed, thirty in each company. They were dispersed throughout headquarters and sixteen regional locations and covered a wide range of functions including operations, finance, personnel and corporate strategy. Twenty of the managers were in senior and forty were in middle-management positions, and two also directors. This data source was supplemented by company documentation.

Managers as Agents of Capital

The issue of managerial work has been the subject of much debate within labour process analysis and Braverman's (1974) characteristic emphasis on the thrust of the capitalist imperative. Similar to subordinate employee categories, Braverman assumed that managerial personnel are subject to the rigours of Taylorism and scientific management, resulting in a detailed division of labour and hierarchy that culminate in a form of proletarianisation. Thompson and McHugh (1995) argue that the heterogeneity characterising management can be explained in the diversity of the capitalist enterprise, whereby functions are hierarchically delineated and delegated among the different professional competing managerial groupings. It is pertinent to ask however, how each of these functions is perceived by corporate management, and what role the different groups of professional managers play as the *global agents* in the circuit of capital. The dilemma for each stratum of management is that there may be a conflict of interest between themselves and corporate management, which arises from their function as the contenders for the role of global agents versus their interests as another employee group. At the same time, their status as employees suggests they endure some of the alienating employment conditions characteristic of waged labour. Consistent with these themes, writers such as Willmott (1997) focus on managerial subjectivity, while Collinson and Hearn (1994 & 1996) explore the boundaries of managerial identities and Scarbrough and Burrell (1996) highlight the lack of career prospects and job insecurity for managers. Although the focus on class and managerial identities offer interesting insights into the *condition of management*, according to Armstrong (1989 &

1991) the problem with this perspective is that it deflects attention from the aspect of control, the core feature of the managerial function.

Armstrong's (1984, 1986 & 1987) exposition of the genesis of the managerial function and interprofessional competition, and his more theoretical writing (Armstrong, 1989; 1991) offer a more fruitful framework in which to address the issues raised in this chapter. For instance, the theme on interprofessional rivalries identifies a particular form of competition between the engineering and accounting professions which, he argues, is unique to British capitalism, rooted in the 'prevailing conception of what management is about' (Armstrong, 1987:421). Since the 1920s perceptions of what constitutes managerial competence has been dominated by accounting expertise. Concern with raising capital and financial administration has superseded 'the intellectual component of producing goods and services (424). This means that engineering as a discrete strand of knowledge essential to the production process takes second place to financial concerns. In characteristic labour process tradition, Armstrong explains that financial management has been given the administrative task of extracting surplus value from the productive labour of manual and intellectual employees. This places managers with an engineering background as part of the production process, and although performing a control function essential to extraction of surplus value, they are a relatively subordinate managerial group. The view is that engineering interests, orientated towards a concern with productivity, may compromise agency goals should they be appointed to corporate boards. The 'role of agency' has been dominated by accountants since their ascendancy in the 1920s. The fact that they have been able to maintain the 'confidence' of corporate management has generated tensions and rivalries between the different professional disciplines (Armstrong, 1986).

The problematic character of establishing and sustaining the trust and loyalty of sections of management selected for the role of global agency is explored by Armstrong (1989; 1991). Agency theory assumes that utilitarianism and self-interest sustain the principal/agency relationship, and that the interests of both capital and management can be sustained through contractual relations, external monitoring, trust and loyalty. The logic of this relationship is that according to agency theory, capital 'the principal' delegates its responsibility to agency, the managers. Sisson and Marginson (1995), Armstrong (1989) and Thompson (1983) suggest that their primary responsibility is to manage employees and to behave in ways that are consistent with capital's interest.

Armstrong's (1991) critical reformulation of this notion, agency concept, draws on the theory of structuration and offers an explanation for social action conditioned by voluntarism. While this solves the problem of determinism, it does not solve the problem of contradictory principles, in the sense that utilitarianism assumes that behaviour is governed by self-interest, while trust assumes degrees of autonomy. Indeed Hyman's (1987) sentiments that the managerial role provides 'opportunities for managerial misbehaviour' illustrates the dilemma. Armstrong recognises that the reproduction of trust can be costly for corporate management – who may look for ways of reducing expenditure in a manner which impinges on their interests. As a consequence, the contradictory problem for corporate management is about how both to discipline and control managers, whilst securing their allegiance and loyalty (Armstrong, 1991).

Political Background

The privatisation of British utilities took place in a highly charged political background, and has resulted in large institutional shareholdings and foreign ownership, espousing a business ethos and a demand for large profits. Trenchant critics of the public sector are now willing to admit that privatisation had a political imperative (Kay, 1996). Paradoxically, post-privatisation management, apparently *independent*, is still subject to political intervention via increasingly powerful regulation through the mechanisms of price review and control foreshadowed by the regulatory regime and the RPI–X pricing formula. At the same time, there has been implicit pressure from the government for such management to be seen to be succeeding (Ogden, 1995). As a senior public relations manager at the electricity supply company reported:

> Part of what we are trying to do is to prove that privatisation works, that it is a good thing. And we spend quite a lot of time telling the public that prices have come down and that standards have gone up.

In order for privatisation to be seen to be working, companies must improve quality and reduce prices. The way this has been achieved is through controlling operational costs which centres on a reduction in head count and labour intensification combined with a tendency to lower wages, a strategy commensurate with the former Conservative Government's notion of efficiency based on a low wage policy but glossed over in ideologies about the sovereignty of the consumer. The logic of the argument is consistent with O'Connell Davidson's (1993) excellent discussion about the way in which marketisation has transformed and degraded employment relations in the water industry, and also in the electricity supply business (Ferner and Colling, 1993).

The particular pricing mechanism exemplified in the RPI –X[1] (and K in the case of water) formula insists that pricing must be cost reflective, while facilitating escalating profitability. Arguably, the usual means of achieving these combined aims through market expansion is limited in the case of the utility industries. The utilities operate in mature product markets, and although they are asset rich, the characteristic method of production is a combination of medium-level technology with labour intensity, which indicates that further demands for efficiencies from either shareholders or the regulator will result in a downward pressure on labour costs which must include managerial personnel. A comment from a senior manager in corporate strategy articulates the kind of pressure managers face while attempting to reconcile competing demands:

> Up until this round of price reviews we have had pressure from our major institutional shareholders and the City to drive costs down, but now it's coming also from the regulator. There is constant pressure ... And no one is safe, not even us.

This comment illustrates two parallel themes, the thrust of the market philosophy and the acknowledgement that management are also under scrutiny. The pace in which corporate management in the water industry embraced the values of the market is reported by Ogden (1993; 1995). At corporate level, he notes this translated into a marked shift in accounting practices 'from its previous concern with probity, compliance and control to one which focused on efficiency, effectiveness and cost savings' (1995:198). Cost savings certainly became the dominant concern, spurred on by stereotypes of over-fat public bureaucracies and City expectations. As another senior manager in corporate relations explained:

> The City has a lot of power over us. Aside from the government they wanted privatisation, and when we were floated, the view of us was that we were over fat, and there was a lot of money to be had from us. And they made sure we delivered it. Now if the City's view of us is one of poor management then that could potentially put our management out of work. So we have to be seen to be cutting costs.

According to industrial relations management, flotation precipitated a reaction at board level whereby in order to impress the City, companies engaged in a rather crude head-count reduction war which has depleted the core skill base among specific essential employee groups, and has left the traditional recruitment and managerial training schemes in disarray. Historically, one of the attractions of public sector employment was the security and the good working conditions it offered. By the beginning of the 1990s, managerial job markets had undergone dramatic reorganisation with a redefinition of employment relations for managers. The notion of 'delayering' glosses the eradication of middle-management jobs accompanied by a regrading of managerial job ladders. In addition, individually negotiated agreements offered a standardised package of salaries and benefits to remaining managers. Again, these changes were politically driven and signalled a break with, and the marginalisation of, trade unions. In the opinion of a senior manager in industrial relations:

> The senior managers too in the old nationalised days were collectively bargained for. When privatisation came that was the first thing to go. I think the underlying philosophy was that you had to get the people who were running the company to work with you ... that they are on your side and not allied to the trade unions. In any case being in a union has a blue-collar ring to it.

In order to be able to identify with the new enterprise culture all the senior managers in both companies were obliged to abandon trade union membership. Yet the research found a significant difference between the two companies in this respect. While around half of the managers in the electricity supply company still belonged to a professional association, only one manager in the water company belonged to a union.

This foregoing discussion provides some sense of the culture, pressures and concerns underpinning the management of human resources, notably that employees are viewed negatively as a cost, and in the current era of regulated marketisation, good management means reducing operational expenditure. This is not a new trend, and is more of a continuation of the restructuring strategies characteristic of the 1980s, when the mantras of the market not only dispensed with jobs but also challenged conditions under which people were employed. In further sections, this chapter will explore how the traditional career path for managers, characteristic of the public sector, has been displaced and replaced.

Public Sector Survivors and Movers and Shakers

Heckscher (1995) and Batstone, Ferner and Terry (1984) place all the managers they studied in similar categories. This research, however, identified two managerial groups: the *public sector survivors* and the newly recruited *movers and shakers*. Although both groups share some characteristics, there are marked differences between them related to work experience, training, skill profiles, career patterns, and their role as the agents of capital.

As argued earlier, Armstrong's (1984; 1987) work provides a framework in which to understand the dynamics of interprofessional rivalry, which in this case also masks a contest about changing values. The fate of professional groups is embedded in the changing patterns of political economy, in which these groups struggle for the prize of the 'global function of capital' by gaining the trust and confidence of the owners. The reward coveted by members of the different professional groups is either a job at board level, and/or being able to respond to capital's changing taste for different forms of expertise.

The first group of managers identified by this research are long-serving company or industry employees, and are older – in their late forties and very early fifties. They are company, or industry trained and many are engineers, which at the beginning of their careers was very important, because the utilities were developing an infrastructure. In order to survive they have broadened their skill base through part-time study and gained MBAs or other related business qualifications, so that now it is their 'managerial skills' that are appreciated.

The second group, the movers and shakers, have a shorter work experience, and in the private sector. They are younger (in their thirties) and have graduated from university in the 1980s. Often head-hunted, they are newly recruited managers who have established a reputation as efficiency drivers elsewhere. Though often business graduates, some are also engineers. They have been recruited into graduate management training programmes, are task oriented and have built reputations through *efficiency drives*.

Technical Competence Versus an Entrepreneurial Culture

The centrepiece of Armstrong's agency concept is embedded in issues of confidence, trust and loyalty – features which have characterised the relationship between management and corporate capital – and has resonance with the dynamics of this particular study. What is at the heart of the unhappy relationship between corporate management and the *public sector survivors* is in part a lack of faith on the part of those at the apex of the organisation, as well as a difference of opinion in terms of formulating a corporate strategy. It was with a degree of irony that the public sector survivors recognised and described themselves as *non-preferred managers*, although they formed the nucleus of the production process.

Technical/physical/manipulative and bureaucratic skills characterised the public sector survivors who formed the backbone of the substantive skill requirements upon which these businesses operate. Yet long-serving engineering-trained managers above operational level are excluded from strategic decision making:

> Well this is still a technically based industry and we are still the core of the business. But we as engineers haven't helped ourselves, because we haven't wanted to get involved in boring things like costing and accountancy. This is something we now have to recognise and operate within those constraints. Then you get sidelined and you are left with getting on with the engineering and you leave the management to someone else. I think that has happened ... What does worry me is the trend from engineers being represented at a fairly high level ... This is true at headquarters as well. People at the top of the business have no knowledge of utility engineering. This is a problem for us.

The concern is that the decline of the engineering influence has resulted in an absence of engineers at corporate level, which in turn has meant that operational engineering interests are overshadowed and do not inform corporate strategy. The public sector survivors thought that the engineers' opinions should be forefront in the formation of any business strategy. This view is sharply articulated in the following comment:

> The person running an organisation which distributes electricity – by preference he should be an engineer. You need some experience of the sharp end of the business in my opinion. That is not to say that I denigrate the administrators, but I question whether when the chips are down, that they have the necessary skills to make the

key decisions. It is a bit like when you start making the tea and you work through the organisation.

The exclusion of engineers and the devaluation of engineering expertise has generated resentment amongst this group who are expected to sustain the throughput of the service. Of course the marginalisation of the engineering influence is neither self-induced nor accidental and clearly mirrors a more general pattern observed by Armstrong (1987) whereby engineering values are curtailed within functional specialisms. It also reflects the dominance of accountancy values which replace engineering competencies, an ethos which has seeped through the organisation. Paradoxically, whilst engineers are operationally indispensable, their competencies within the industry have been marginalised and their status degraded. Instead of being the purveyors of global agency, they have become objects of control in the interests of corporate goals.

Yet the lack of appreciation placed on engineering expertise is all the more surprising given that at corporate level both companies had pretensions in lucrative overseas markets especially in some of the newly industrialised countries, where engineering knowledge could prove to be the acid test for success in the provision of water and electricity supply systems. Managers sent overseas in the quest for new markets were characteristically engineers but it was their marketing and communication skills that came to be appreciated. This illustrates the sense in which engineering as codified knowledge has been surpassed by market values. The trend is reflected throughout both organisations, when managers at operational – and surprisingly at corporate personnel levels – were concerned about the general dearth of engineering skills, which they argued should constitute a necessary component in making the companies global players in future product markets. As Armstrong (1984; 1987) argues this is not in opposition to the corporate goals, but rather a particular profession's perception about the best way to perform the agency role. This interplay around the politics of knowledge and commitment is illustrative of the divide between those managers who espouse the dominant accounting values and those who value engineering skills, and is also a deeply rooted argument about how best to manage a utility.

The view among corporate management is that *new blood* is needed in areas commercialised by privatisation: 'The new people have been brought in to do the things the nationalised industries didn't do, like public relations, treasury and company secretariat.' While there may well be valid grounds for the new expertise in such areas the following comment is more incisive:

> Obviously the people who came in to the industry background aren't carrying the baggage of forty years of nationalised industry culture. Therefore they find it surprising that the indigenous culture seems to require certain tribal customs to be gone through before anything is done. They are knocking aside the tribal customs for us.

The research found that both companies strategically placed movers and shakers in positions such as personnel, where they were able to control both redundancy and recruitment policies, wielding influence over change culture. Reminiscent of the *take-over man* characterising entrepreneurial models (Mulholland, 1996), such utility managers typically adopted a rugged individualism and perhaps a 'masculine' management style, and were prepared to identify and make 'essential' cuts in human resources, while promoting a reorganisation of internal labour markets on more flexible lines. For instance, the employee relations manager in the electricity company explained:

> Previously I worked for Arthur Andersen on mergers and acquisitions, where there was little sentiment about staff issues. I have been through all of that. They recruited me to help the newly appointed HRM director put together a new industrial relations package. We have now got down to a core of 4000 employees from 7000.

The goal of lean production, the mark of efficiency, signals an important departure from the traditional style human resource management, and translates into redundancies and cost-cutting exercises. There are two aspects to this strategy; the first one is concerned with reducing numbers, and the second is about changing the value system.

Changing the value system is intricately linked with the manner in which individuals 'volunteer' for redundancy.

> In the last spate of reorganisation they asked people over fifty years to volunteer, and a forest of hands went up. You can't tell me that is unconnected to the kind of changes that are taking place. We have lost a lot of our managers this way.

This trend mirrors Turnbull and Wass (1997) who show that voluntarism is a mere fig-leaf which glosses over the pressures that are brought to bear on those offering themselves for redundancy. 'Volunteering' for redundancy is precipitated by an inability to comply with an organisational ethos that is at variance with an established order. Under the guise of redundancy, new values can be introduced by filling vacated posts with carefully selected new recruits.

For those managers who remain in the organisation, the appropriation and ownership of change initiatives become the prize to be competed for, a contest that is fought out between the public sector survivors and the movers and shakers, especially in the water company. For instance, managers in operational functions faced a barrage of change programmes which included contracting out, contracting in, franchising and partnering. In addition, some operations, which some would argue work better as an integrated network, were set up as independent companies whose fate depended on the vagaries of the market. Managers in operational sections resisted these developments by forming alliances with other colleagues and thus were able to gain *some control* over change projects from the movers and shakers:

For instance we have gone from a small group in ... to a large group and it is very much taking over the ... area. The X ... thugs are just taking over ... and we have expanded. We did it strategically according to the Diploma in Management Studies criteria. We did it just as you would do a take-over. That was our strategy.

Other managers aptly described their growing weariness in response to such corporate policy as *change fatigue*. While O'Connell Davidson (1993) reported that water supply and sewerage, core features of the business, were to be regulated and not contracted out, this study found that the notion of 'core' had begun to be challenged by the movers and shakers. What is clear is that under pressure from the regulator for further cost reductions, what can be regarded as core labour processes essential to the central operational system and to be retained as part of the work of direct labour are now becoming increasingly contested. Operations as diverse as the training of personnel and the cleansing of the water beds – the latter a core feature of the production process – are being mooted for contracting out.

The tension between the two managerial groups hinges on two connected tactics. First, the proposal to extend contracting out advocated by the movers and shakers puts operational managers' jobs in jeopardy. Secondly, by highlighting the question of public health and safety, the public sector survivors cleverly construct a notion of risk for the movers and shakers should they dare further the contracting out of such functions. According to the public sector survivors, quality could not be guaranteed, and a mistake would undoubtedly call the competence and the jobs of the movers and shakers into question, seriously damaging their agency role as the trusted delegates of corporate management.

Traditional Professionalism versus Cost Effectiveness

The politics of continuous change is played out between the two groups in a number of ways. Movers and shakers promote further change programmes, such as business process re-engineering in the water company or a regional restructuring in the electricity company intended to achieve 'clearer lines of reporting, flatter structures, but broader jobs and more responsibility for our managers' linked to notions of efficiency. Indicative of this initiative is the emergence of the generalist manager posing a direct challenge to the codified knowledge associated with particular professions. They also argue that consumerism and the emphasis on quality can only be achieved through a technical productivist approach, the nub of engineering competence. Without engineering skills neither administrative nor financial competence could deliver on quality.

The chapter argues that despite these differences, both managerial types are bound together through organisational goals, the aims of which are to enforce efficiency drives in the interests of the shareholder and, more circumspectly, the consumer. From the perspective of agency, this is double-edged in the way it relates to the managerial function versus managerial self-interest in terms of careers and job security. Armstrong's notion of contradiction again helps to contextualise this paradox. For instance, as agents of capital, such managers are incentivised through shareholding including preferential options, investments in save schemes, performance-related bonuses, and individually negotiated but standard remuneration packages. This might suggest that it is in managers' interests to promote profit-driven innovations and efficiency drives. However, according to this research, labour costs, including management, account for about 60 per cent of the utilities' operational expenditure, an obvious target for cost reductions. This is so significant that Froud (1996) and her colleagues argue that the utility profits have largely come from cuts to labour. In reference to the two companies studied, this headcount reduction amounted to a loss of two-thirds of managerial jobs. Translated across functions it can mean, as a senior operational manager lamented, 'Our management team here has been decimated, we have gone from eighty to thirty managers and we have a bigger area to manage.' It is therefore in managers' interests to slow the pace of change.

Career Paths: Bureaucratic versus Portfolio

Consistent with these two groups, the research also identified two career patterns, the *bureaucratised career* and the *portfolio career*. The principal characteristics of the bureaucratised career path were a job for life, a career with a visible promotion ladder with professional expertise conditioned by a public service ethos and an enduring employment relationship founded on notions of loyalty and commitment. By contrast, the portfolio career is based on the notion of employability, individual responsibility, skill mix, limited promotion/sideways moving, market-driven values, individualism, a commitment to career and to capital in general with a silence about organisational insecurity.

The biggest difference between the two career patterns is the approach to promotion and future prospects. The job for life, the key feature of the bureaucratised career, more or less guaranteed promotion within the internal labour market provided that performance was reasonable:

> I started with this company in 1960 so I have been with them thirty-six years. I started as a craft apprentice electrician. I became an electrician and then I moved on to various training schemes. I became a commercial electrical engineer for the company on the contracting side ... then ... a District Commercial Engineer ... then became the Electricity Sales Manager for one of the Divisions ... then ... Customer Services Manager and basically I looked after the non-engineering side of the business. I then became Deputy Divisional Manager until now.

Although there were many hurdles to clear, there were excellent career opportunities facilitated by internal training and development. For those with ambitions, it was not unrealistic to assume that, as an employee relations manager reports, 'I'm going to start as a junior in accounting and I'll end up as Finance Director.' Supported by annual recruitment and company training schemes the bureaucratised career path also benefited the organisation by providing a pool of management personnel.

By contrast, the portfolio career is underpinned by the notion of employability, a reflection of human capital theory which rests on the idea of the enterprising self (du Gay, 1996), who takes responsibility for career development through seeking 'opportunities in the market':

> I did Geography at University. I wanted to join a fast-moving company, and my first job was a graduate trainee with Hewlett Packard. I moved to Andersen Consulting and did some consultancy there for them, and I was lucky to be involved here helping to introduce some change programmes. They were impressed with me and I was offered this job.

This woman, in her mid-thirties, is typical of the portfolio high flyer. Having been a consultant for the company, she was subsequently appointed as a director, but avoided formal recruitment channels. She is paid an undisclosed salary with inbuilt benefits. While the bureaucratic career can be criticised as merely a bureaucratic time-serving procedure, it was based on substantive experience and the notion of a plan, whereas there is a sense in which the portfolio career is based more on opportunism and 'luck' rather than on codified knowledge. Nevertheless, this path is also about career management, and is underwritten by a strategy which incorporates the development of social networks and the creation of a particular image.

The absence of a learning curve and a poorly developed career structure now characterise both companies, a situation which has negative consequences for the careers of the majority of managers. The policy of 'buying in expertise' combined with the reduction in managerial grades typically from 8 to 5, disturbs learning patterns and limits prospects for middle-management grades. The results are aptly described by Newell and Dopson (1996) as a muddle in the middle. Mobility for such middle managers is often associated with task accomplishment, whereby they are moved horizontally within the internal labour market.

Middle managers in operations were only able to protect their continuity of employment by accepting sideways job moves which translates into demotions, whereupon they are invariably required to brief the newly appointed movers and shakers. This is one of the ways in which corporate management exploit the skills and experience of such managers, while simultaneously denigrating them. Some of the managers are prepared to tolerate this situation, because they are nearing the age of eligibility for redundancy, but for other younger managers with little hope of promotion, the future is less clear. The situation is exacerbated by limited recruitment at both ends of the ladder. In terms of first-line management, the expectation was that this year's intake (the first for a number of years) of craft and technical apprentices would provide future managers for this grade, and contrary to past practice were not expected to progress any further. At the upper end for the future pool of top managers, there is very little evidence of graduate recruitment. Instead of training their own managers, the utilities have over the 1980s bought in new forms of expertise with the intention of bringing about a culture change.

However, in the opinion of some senior managers, the portfolio approach to recruitment is beginning to reveal gaps in managerial expertise in traditional disciplines. Up until now there was little appreciation of the wider and more negative implications of such a strategy:

> I do think that we need a greater emphasis on the training of engineers than is now recognised. I'm concerned that more people are not coming into the organisation as engineers. A lot of people from the production side are now doing ONC and HNC and they will become production leaders ultimately ... Now in terms of managers and senior managers we have done very little in the way of graduate recruitment. They are for the top, but we are recruiting in such small numbers that it is now questionable whether we will have enough people to occupy our natural wastage.

In the absence of a visible career ladder, managers and the movers and shakers in particular seek other ways of achieving the attention of corporate agency. From the latter's perspective, they are corporate management's natural choice because of their reputation and close association with the private sector:

> I joined in 1990 shortly after privatisation and up 'til then, managers tended to be people who were in the industry a very long time and worked their way through it. The view was that we couldn't operate the water industry any longer using that regime. They needed to bring people in with other skills. So I saw the company buying my skills. I had an engineering background, *but my skills were mainly in making change happen.* I was a bit of a change agent and trouble shooter in all the other jobs I had. I have gone into organisations that had low productivity, and turned the production operations around. I joined this company as a middle manager – I made a number of changes for the better, improving the efficiency of the operations which meant fewer people and a smaller operating budget. They looked to me to get rid of the 'Spanish' practices.[2]

Such enthusiastic cost cutters became the metaphor for good management. Invisible to corporate management this strategy encouraged informal organisational behaviour exclusive in character through the fostering of particularistic relationships. Such ambitious managers planned ways of gaining the attention and approval of key decision makers:

> Would I have been recognised if I wasn't aware of what was going on, and who were the right people to influence in the organisation? I mean lots of people do a good

job, but don't get recognised – so I'm suggesting that it is only those who are politically aware, and know who to influence are the ones who get on. In my case I was influencing some people at the top, and that was based on what I was doing. I invited people like the managing director down to see what I was doing. There were the reports from other key players who said: 'This chap is achieving a lot for the business.' Other people were horrified at the thought of the MD coming down but I relished the thought that he was to spend the day at the plant. In that way I got recognised throughout the company.

Promotion in this instance was achieved through playing the game of organisational politics, a practice reported by other researchers (Dalton, 1959; Pettigrew, 1985). The response of the public sector survivors was to question the morality of such behaviour:

Part of this wide-boy mentality is never mind tomorrow just think of today. Get what you want and win, win. And of course I have conspired in that because it is what I tell my people. I think some of these fellows are a bit short on ethics frankly.

Although considered disreputable, the public sector survivors realised they also were embroiled in it in other ways. Reminiscent of Armstrong's (1984) study this is a fresh illustration of how the role of agency is competed for among professional groups of managers.

The Portfolio Career: Employability or Job Insecurity?

A range of features of the 'new' forms of managerial work – budget holding, business planning, the management of cost and profit centres, enculturation programmes and the control function – are said to have enhanced autonomy. In the *entrepreneurial* organisation, the managerial role has been transformed from one of administration to one of innovation and enterprise. While O'Connell-Davidson (1993) shows such claims to be hollow, equally she observes enthusiasm among the Albion senior managers for the autonomy the market promised. Some years later, this study reports that experience has shown that the challenge of the market has proved disappointing:

I feel less free than I did five years ago, because let me define my freedom. I have very little control over my budget at all. I don't have the information. Before we had a breakdown in terms of how money was spent. That kind of information is now very difficult to get. The budget holders find it difficult to know where the odd £3000 comes from, and to know it in detail. And I can't buy anything from anyone I want to. I have to use a framework agreement which restricts me, when I know I can get better value. My boss is entirely command and control. His boss is command and control and the managing director is ... So where is the freedom there?

In the mimicking of market transactions through the selling and buying of services between departments, this comment is illustrative of the experience of managers in the regulated structures. The research shows that information concerning strategic decisions is released on the basis of 'need to know' to subordinate managers, as opposed to a sense of encouraging any wider understanding. It not intended to be power enhancing nor to encourage enterprise, but rather suggests the strict adherence to the administration and appropriate allocation of a specific sum of money. The difference is that in the days of nationalisation such managers were urged to spend up to the limits of their budgets, whereas under the constraints of 'efficiency' they must not overspend and must administer their budgets according to strict pre-determined criteria.

The autonomy associated with business planning is equally mythical, except in the independent subsidiaries such as civil engineering and construction. In addition to selling their services to the parent company, these subsidiaries also compete for other business. Subject to the rigours of the market, such firms are not protected by the parent and must realise a profit within a given period, otherwise their fate is sealed. The manner in which such companies are dispensed with is disingenuously conveyed by a financial director: 'we allow them to organically expire'.

On the other hand, current managers in the regulated units are required to anticipate their expenditure over a given period, which is then approved by seniors with a line role, who then monitor the targets set down in the plans. The managers are then held to the objectives set out in the plans. Business planning and budget holding are therefore mechanisms of financial control and limitations on managerial autonomy. Decision making remains centralised and goals translate into performance targets which are then passed down the hierarchy. The goals of the regulated regime, accommodated by the legacy of an authoritarian management style, coupled with a more transparent hierarchy, facilitate a greater degree of control over managers. Such managers cannot claim to have gained insights into enterprise as their tasks are limited to administrative duties and bureaucratic reporting, neither of which enhances the career portfolio nor furthers the quest for the role of agency.

On the other hand, managers reported an increase in work loads which has a number of possible explanations. First, the reduction in the number of grades has meant fewer managers which has led to a redistribution of work, whereby individuals have responsibilities for larger geographical areas and a wider range of responsibilities. Secondly, the whole issue of performance management, measurement and appraisal has much increased the control function of managers in their agency capacity, while drawing them into the framework of control. These developments raise questions about the purpose of appraisal which is so central to the role of management. Paradoxically, managers audit the performance of others, while they too are subject to appraisal.

The research found that managers at every level had some responsibility for enculturation programmes through regular team briefings when quality programmes, efficiency drives and performance targets are advanced. The statistical monitoring of quality programmes, particularly in areas such as customer service, has increased bureaucracy and work load for managers with line responsibility. A middle manager in a sewerage works explained:

> I go home on Friday and go out with one of my children. I get back at around 10.30 p.m. and I work until 2 a.m. doing my reports for Monday. But then I feel free and it is a kind of release until Monday.

Other managers reported similar patterns of work, which may be a consequence of having to increase the monitoring of employees and then having to report it. The task of managers with this particular agency role is to enforce and achieve performance targets set out for subordinates. However, such managers are subject to corporate surveillance in the form of targets, review and appraisal.

The Portfolio Career: Job Insecurity

Measuring and enforcing managerial performance is a prerequisite in the redefined agency role when the traditional basis of that bargain – good career prospects and job security – have been removed. The research found that job insecurity and uncertainty constitutes the dominant themes characterising the portfolio career. Organisational insecurity is continually played out according to the ideology of *employability* when the idea of labour market mobility attracts ambitious individuals, whereby they find they are simultaneously repelled by the absence of a clear career path, either with a particular employer or in the wider labour market. For instance:

> I'm resigned to the fact that I will lose the high flyers. If they are looking for opportunities they will have to look somewhere else. These are not going to portfolio. You know the sort of people who have got a clear objective: 'I want to become a Marketing Director.' It's no good saying we have got this interesting two-year thing in Research & Development, because these things simply get in the way of where they are going. You want to fast track the good people, but there again you have to be honest, the opportunity isn't with us. I have got this bloke and I'd like to keep him in my team and have offered him line management. But he is openly applying for other jobs ...

This illustrates the inherently contradictory character of a corporate policy based on the logic of the market, when clearly the unintended consequence is the loss of future candidates for the top jobs. The research found that both managerial groups were uncertain about prospects with their present company, and were equally unclear about alternative opportunities. The following comment is illustrative of the typical response: 'I really enjoy what I am doing now and we will see what challenges lay ahead.' Other managers were resigned to the fate of the market: 'I have long given up any thought that I can have any sort of plan. From now on it's random leaps and you take a chance on where you land.'

Although always ready to adopt the market rhetoric, the movers and shakers reluctantly admitted that they too faced similar uncertainties:

> 'No, no, I'm reasonably confident that something will come along and I can apply my skills and sell them on to somebody else.'
> Researcher: 'So you have no worries about that horrible job market out there then?'
> 'Well' ... very long pause ...
> Researcher: 'And have you taken any safeguards against the uncertainty ... ?'
> 'Well ... actually (long pause) my wife and I run a business, well she runs it.'

This shows that those who claimed to be believers in the market mechanism neither trusted nor depended on it. Many such managers were in the process of setting up businesses, or finding alternative employment – behaviour manifestly symptomatic of employment insecurity. The impact of the values of the market was reflected amongst those interviewed, when few envisaged progression to more senior positions within the company, or indeed having a job with the same company, echoing the uncertainty and insecurity reported by Heckscher (1995) and Newell and Dopson (1996) in their respective studies.

Conclusion

This chapter has drawn on Armstrong's work in order to show that efficiency drives primarily based on reductions in labour costs have included management, setting in motion an organisational politics in the companies studied which redefines the criteria of the principal/agency relationship. Corporate management (the principal) delegated its function down the hierarchy of subordinate senior and middle managers who, whilst being entrusted, were in the past also incentivised to further corporate goals by the provision of attractive careers and salaries. The problem is that, at this moment and in the present circumstances characterising the utility business, corporate management considers the securing of such levels of trust and loyalty to be too costly. As a result, expenditure is reduced by eliminating managers' jobs and shifting responsibility for career to individuals, except for an elite who could be expected to become corporate members, or to act directly in the role of 'global agency'. At the same time, corporate management's solution is to assume that senior and middle managers can be compensated for lost careers through remuneration, whilst simultaneously continuing the restructuring which compromises managerial loyalty.

Remuneration is also buttressed through the incorporation of managers into control systems. Evidence of this is performance management which, when subject to review and appraisal, tests managerial conformity and compliance. Fraught with a subjective tendency, appraisal underwritten by relations of power and authority as a way of measuring performance can sometimes be arbitrary (Gilman, 1997). If review and appraisal is introduced with the intention of reducing the managerial scope for misbehaviour, then the trust and loyalty in return for career and secure employment no longer form the basis of the relationship between subordinate managerial layers and corporate management in the privatised utilities.

The notion of contradiction (Armstrong, 1989 & 1991) contextualises the manner in which the issue of risk has become central to the rivalries and divisions between the managerial groups as they compete for the role of 'global agency'. However, in the light of the dramatic change characterising the privatised utilities, and by an attempt to bring about a new belief system, corporate management has merely recreated old divisions within the managerial hierarchy by favouring particular professional managerial groups over others. The relevance of Armstrong's well-established debate about the origins and contours of the struggle between engineering and accountancy values represents what is the deepest expression of the cleavage dividing the different managerial groups, here as the public sector survivors and the movers and shakers as they compete to appropriate change initiatives.

The movers and shakers are trusted by corporate management to implement a range of policies and working practices which has an uneven impact on the different professional groups depending on their location in the managerial hierarchy. There is a deprofessionalisation of the engineering function through the emergence of the generalist manager and the rise of 'skill-mix' which undermines particular forms of credentialism. On the other hand, the relationship between accountants and corporate management is more complex. Although accountants are regarded as the most appropriate group to further the agency goal, only a selected few can expect to win the coveted prize of promotion to corporate level, so the element of risk is a consideration for the majority of middle and older senior managers, manifestly evident in the portfolio career.

Other divisive factors come into play, such as difference in age and work experience. That a career and job security can be secured by being employable has been shown in this research to be unsustainable for older managers and those tainted with public sector values. This narrows the options for such groups, and the tendency is for them to want to remain with the particular company, although their seniority and status are compromised. This then translates into managers having low expectations and few envisage prospects other than a few years' employment with their present company.

On the other hand, while the 'challenge of the market' beckons the younger movers and shakers, it cannot guarantee them the coveted prize of a director's post, or a place on the board, nor indeed any job, a reality that is manifested in managerial ambivalence about prospects in the external job market. The other less frequent managerial response to the uncertainty of job markets is to find an alternative to employment and set up in business.

The picture painted by this evidence is that corporate management at institutional level no longer seeks long-term commitment from middle and some categories of senior managers, nor indeed from their relatively privileged movers and shakers. Arguably, corporate management no longer tries to sustain the loyalty and trust of its agents on the basis of either voluntarism, or utilitarianism alone, but rather through control mechanisms that attempt to enforce conformity and compliance to corporate goals. In this sense the terms of the principal/agency relationship have been broken, while the rules governing notions of trust and loyalty have been redefined and added to. In substituting employability for the job for life, corporate management has redrawn the terms of trust and loyalty to mean commitment to the goals of capital in general. This puts into context the transitional nature of the trust and loyalty underpinning the principal/agent relationship, suggesting that as defining relational terms, they are appropriate only in certain conditions of accumulation.

References

Armstrong, P. (1984) 'Competition between the Organisational Professions and the Evolution of Management Control Strategies' in Thompson, K. (ed.) *Work, Employment and Unemployment*, Milton Keynes: Open University Press.

Armstrong, P. (1986) 'Management Control Strategies and Inter-Professional Competition: the Cases of Accountancy and Personnel Management' in Knights, D. and Willmott, H. (eds) *Managing the Labour Process*, Aldershot: Gower.

Armstrong, P. (1987) 'Engineers, Management and Trust', *Work, Employment and Society*, 1:4, 421–40.

Armstrong, P. (1989) 'Management, Labour Process and Agency', *Work, Employment and Society*, 3:3, 307–22.

Armstrong, P. (1991) 'Contradiction and Social Dynamics in the Capitalist Agency Relationship', *Accounting Organisations and Society*, 16:1, 1–25.

Batstone, E., Ferner, A. and Terry, M. (1984) *Consent and Efficiency*, Oxford: Basil Blackwell.

Braverman, H. (1974) *Labour and Monopoly Capital*, New York: Monthly Review Press.

Colling T. and Ferner, A. (1992) 'The Limits of Autonomy: Devolution, Line Managers and Industrial Relations in Privatised Companies', *Journal of Management Studies*, 29:2.

Collinson, D. and Hearn, J. (1994) 'Naming Men As Men: Implications for Work, Organisations and Management', *Gender Work and Organisation*, 1:1, 2–22.

Collinson, D. and Hearn, J. (eds) (1996) *Men as Managers: Managers as Men*, London: Sage.

Dalton, M. (1959) *Men Who Manage*, London: John Wiley & Sons.

du Gay, P. (1996) 'Making Up Managers: Enterprise and the Ethos of Bureaucracy' in Clegg, S.R. and Palmer, G (eds) *The Politics of Management Knowledge*, London: Sage.

Ferner A. and Colling, T. (1993) 'Electricity Supply' in Pendleton, A. and Winterton, J. (eds) *Public Enterprise in Transition*, London: Routledge.

Froud, J. *et al.* (1996) 'Stakeholder Economy? From Utility Privatisation to New Labour', *Capital and Class*, 60:3, 119–34.

Gilman, M. (1997) 'Bank Co' in *Performance Related Pay: Organisation and Effort*, unpublished PhD thesis, University of Warwick.

Heckscher, C. (1995) *White Collar Blues*, New York: Basic Books.

Hyman, R. (1987) 'Strategy or Structure: Capital, Labour and Control', *Work, Employment and Society*, 1:1, 25–56.

Kay, J. (1996) 'The Future of UK Utility Regulation' in Beesley, M.E.(ed.) *Regulating Utilities*, London Business School.

Mulholland, K. (1996) 'Entrepreneurialism, Masculinities and the 'Self-Made Man' in Collinson, D. and Hearn, J. (eds) *Men as Managers: Managers as Men*, London: Sage.

Newell, H. and Dopson, S. (1996) 'Muddle in the middle: organisational restructuring and middle management careers', *Personnel Review*, 25:4.

O'Connell Davidson, J. (1993) *Privatisation and Employment Relations: The Case of the Water Industry*, London: Mansell.

Ogden, S. (1993) 'Water' in Pendleton, A. and Winterton, J. (eds) *Public Enterprise in Transition*, London: Routledge.

Ogden, S. (1995) 'Transforming Frameworks of Accountability: The Case of Water Privatisation', *Accounting Organisations and Society*, 29:2/3, 193–218.

Pettigrew, A. (1985) *The Awakening Giant: Continuity and Change in ICI*, Oxford: Blackwell.

Scarbrough, H. and Burrell, G. (1996) 'The Axeman Cometh: the Changing Roles and Knowledges of Middle Managers' in Clegg, S.R. and Palmer, G. (eds) *The Politics of Management Knowledge*, London: Sage.

Sisson, K. and Marginson, P. (1995) 'Management: Systems, Structures and Strategy' in Edwards, P. (ed.) *Industrial Relations*, Oxford: Blackwell.

Thompson, P. (1983) *The Nature of Work*, London: Macmillan.

Thompson, P. and McHugh, D. (1995) *Work Organisations*, London: Macmillan.

Turnbull, P. and Wass, V. (1997) 'Job Insecurity and Labour Market Lemons: The (Mis)Management of Redundancy in Steel Making, Coal Mining and Port Transport', *Journal of Management Studies*, 34:1, 27–51.

Willmott, H. (1997) 'Rethinking Management and Managerial Work: Capitalism, Control and Subjectivity', paper at the *15th Annual International Labour Process Conference*, University of Edinburgh.

Acknowledgements

I am indebted to Chris Warhurst and Paul Thompson for their editorial guidance and encouraging comments. Thanks also to Paul Edwards and Anthony Ferner for reading and discussing an earlier draft, and my gratitude to Catherine Waddams and Michael Doble.

Notes

1   The RPI–X system, which limits the average rate of growth of the Retail Price Index (RPI) – X (less X%). The + K in water refers to improvements in quality.
2   My emphasis.

11 Hospitals and New Ways of Organising Medical Work in Europe: Standardisation of Medicine in the Public Sector and the Future of Medical Autonomy

Mike Dent

Introduction

Citizens of all Western European countries have come to accept their right to 'cradle' to 'grave' health care provision. These 'socialised' arrangements contrast with the privatised arrangements that have characterised the US system. It is, therefore, somewhat paradoxical that in attempting to maintain citizens' entitlements to health care services many European countries have looked to North America for new ways of organising their systems. The focus of the chapter will be on the implications of these organisational innovations for the work of hospital doctors within Europe, in particular Britain and the Netherlands. Both countries have well-established and organised medical professions and both have adopted the regulated or quasi-market model for health care delivery originally developed in the US. However, whereas the British reforms reflected a right-wing Thatcherite programme, in the Netherlands the reforms have been explicitly shaped by corporatist priorities and interests.

The aim of the chapter is to explore the labour process of professionalism within medicine in various European countries. This will be discussed in the context of governmental rethinking of the welfare state and the implications this has for professional autonomy within the new managed and marketed systems of health care delivery. Within this broader framework I will compare the extent of changes to the organisation of hospital doctors and their work and the implications this has for professional autonomy in two European countries – Britain and the Netherlands. Both countries have well established and organised medical professions and both underwent a radical shift from welfare state to quasi-market models[1] of health care delivery:

Britain:[2] NHS hospitals have undergone major changes in their organisation since the introduction of the 'internal market'. The professional staffs have been reorganised into clinical directorates – headed by doctors and supported by nurses – which ostensibly have incorporated them within an integrated management system. This organisational model – an adaptation of the American Health Maintenance Organisation (HMO) – is one that has its parallels in Europe too.

Netherlands: According to Freddi (1989: 15) 'nowhere in the Western world is the classic definition of medical autonomy translated into practice more accurately than in the Netherlands'. Unlike Britain the health service is an insurance-based system with hospital consultants being paid on a fee-for-service basis. Like the new NHS system, however, doctors are expected to take a full part in hospital management and medical audit. They also have responsibility for clinical budgets.

A particular focus of this chapter will be the issue of medical protocols (including clinical guidelines and evidence-based medicine) within medicine, and their growing popularity in North America and Europe. These guidelines are examples of 'best practice' in medical care and represent a growing bureaucratisation and standardisation of medicine. 'Protocols' would appear to represent clear evidence of deskilling and proletarianisation, their introduction being commonly presented as necessary to the improvement of quality and accountability. Moreover – in a manner akin to TQM – doctors, it would appear, are now subject to the continuous surveillance of quality control systems. The question as to the extent to which these new control systems have actually led to a fundamental loss of autonomy and status for medical specialists in Britain and the Netherlands is a primary concern of this chapter.

The chapter starts with a discussion of labour process theory and medical autonomy. It is followed by a review of the basic 'types' of health care delivery systems within Europe and an indication of the general changes in the organisation of health care currently underway. These two elements are then brought together in a comparative discussion of the changes in the health systems in the Netherlands and Britain. It will become clear that quasi-markets are 'intolerant' of professional claims to autonomy and control over work processes. Instead these new health care arrangements assume the need for externally validated quality control systems. Parallels with TQM within industry will be drawn out as will the differences. The question as to whether doctors have been able to preserve or renegotiate their medical autonomy – and the implications for the future – will underlie the discussion.

Medical Work, Autonomy and the Labour Process

The term 'medical autonomy' refers, in part, to the legal monopolies members of the profession possess. The right to diagnose is central and the organised profession, in the form of its associations, colleges, and so on, take on the responsibility of ensuring doctors are properly trained and monitored. Part of the rationale for medical autonomy is the complexity of medical work processes. As Freidson (1994:87) has pointed out, underneath the ideology there has to be a skill base. It is because of the complex and uncertain nature of medicine (Calnan, 1984) that medical work seems to be resistant to extensive rationalisation. Doctors are expected to make decisions (clinical judgements) drawing on their medical education, socialisation and experience. This narrower version of 'autonomy' commonly referred to as clinical autonomy has undergone some subtle changes over recent years. As Harrison and Schulz (1989:203) following Tolliday (1978) have shown, while this 'autonomy' has altered and now includes consideration of budgetary as well as clinical information, this has not meant any loss in status or influence within the workplace.

Doctors, the evidence suggested, were now happy or tolerated working within set budgets. They were less happy, however, about the introduction of quality assurance systems which were viewed as limiting their freedom of how to treat individual patients. Despite the doctors' reservations, however, quality assurance systems began to be introduced within many European countries (Jost, 1992). This development suggests that a fundamental change had occurred in the nature of medical dominance and clinical autonomy. European doctors now appear able – although not necessarily willing – to accept that their work will be routinely subject to external scrutiny of some kind.

These modifications to the notion of medical autonomy reflect a response to a 'sea change' in health policies in a range of countries. Governments have tried to devise ways to sever the links between professionalism and politics as part of a more general package of health system reforms. These models are based on some kind of 'purchaser/provider' split. In Britain this is between the health authority and the hospital (or other service); in those countries funded by health insurance it is the health insurers who become the 'purchasers'. One of the outcomes expected of the introduction of market-like principles into the organisation of European health care delivery was that the work of doctors would become increasingly rationalised and their autonomy would become curtailed. Such changes, it is argued, will improve the efficiency and quality of the medical services. The question now arises whether these changes reflect any kind of 'proletarianisation' or 'deskilling' of hospital doctors; whether their pre-existing dominance within the health care division of labour and its organisation has been sufficiently eroded by quasi-market forces that they are now merely a group of skilled employees. To explore this possibility it is necessary to clarify labour process theory and its relevance (or otherwise) to public sector organisations.

Labour process and the public sector

The public sector is a critical case for labour process analysis because of its historically necessary legitimising role within all capitalist societies (Habermas, 1976; Offe, 1984). Moreover, the services provided have been premised on the production of use values, 'however distorted' more than exchange values (Thompson, 1990:110). Both these tenets of the welfare state have been seriously challenged in the 1980s and 1990s with the introduction of quasi-market principles. This has given rise to new discourses of a post-Fordist and post-modern kind (Lash and Urry, 1987; Burrows and Loader, 1994; Dent, 1995) and the suggestion that an alternative communitarianism might be a replacement for both the marketed and public sector provision (Giddens, 1994; Rustin, 1995). All these new debates reflect a reconfiguration of the relationship between the state and society and present labour process analysis with a number of challenges. The health services, as the key example, are defined primarily by political rather than economic criteria even when operating under regulated market conditions. This is so because it is the state, not the market, that ultimately makes the decisions on resourcing issues.

It is also within the public sector environment that we find the professions have developed a particularly distinct role (Dent, 1993). Without the market to dictate priorities it has been the professions, to a greater or lesser extent, which have been responsible for defining them. To some extent, the relationship between state and the professions would appear to parallel that of *responsible autonomy* as the following quote from Friedman indicates:

> [This] type of strategy attempts to harness the adaptability of labour power by giving workers leeway and encouraging them to adapt to changing situations in a manner beneficial to the firm. To do this top managers give workers status, authority and responsibility. [They] try to win their loyalty, and co-opt their organisations to the firm's ideal ... ideologically. (1977:78)

There are a number of parallels between responsible autonomy and professional autonomy not least because the occupational groups thus organised are differentiated from others because of their central role within the division of labour. There is, nevertheless, a crucial difference between the two types of autonomies (Dent, 1993): responsible autonomy is the outcome of deliberate management strategies whereas professional autonomy is not. It reflects instead the success of the occupational group's own strategy to gain control over the work and who is qualified to do it.

A key defence against bureaucratic encroachment by the medical profession has been the doctors' claim to clinical autonomy. The assumption is that clinical decision making is a complex process which can not be standardised because patients are not standard and disease processes are themselves highly variable. In sociological terms, clinical autonomy is the 'indeterminate' component of the indetermination / technicity (I / T) ratio. It is defined by its lack of definition by the profession (Jamous and Peloille, 1970:112). The distinction between a state-defined responsible autonomy and an independent (that is, autonomous) status might be said to be that which lies between organisational and institutional control. Organisational control refers to the rules imposed by management in order to control costs and / or quality. Institutional control, by contrast, refers to the ability of an organised profession to define its members' autonomy within the workplace. It is important to note, however, that the distinction between organisational and institutional control is, in reality, far from clear-cut. Both types of control can and do co-exist uneasily together. The autonomy of doctors is something that is constantly being renegotiated.

The introduction of quasi-market principles can be viewed as being partly motivated by the state wishing to exert greater organisational control over doctors in order to control the costs and quality of treatment. There is now a much clearer separation between allocative and operational decisions. As a consequence doctors are no longer able to commit additional resources as an outcome of their clinical decisions alone but have to work within predetermined budgets (Flynn, 1992). Doctors retain their control over their work (operational decisions), but allocative decisions are the preserve of management *qua* management. Nevertheless, the dividing line between doctoring and managing is no longer clear-cut and it is perfectly possible that some members of the medical profession will pursue careers as senior managers (and directors). These speculations are explored further within the Netherlands case study.

These changes in the profession / state relations do not, however, constitute any 'proletarianisation' of doctors, for as McKinlay and Arches have explained they still retain their 'control over certain prerogatives relating to the location, content and essentiality of [their] task activities' (quoted in Elston, 1991:63) even if they perceive themselves as suffering a loss of occupational status as Larson (1980), Derber (1982) and Derber *et al.*, (1990) have argued. Instead, doctors are increasingly coming under the organisational control of the state. This, however, has not been at the expense of the doctors' dominant position within the division of labour for health care. Nevertheless, they have had to accept the state exercising greater suzerain powers than they have been used to previously.

The fact that there are increased pressures to control costs and increase efficiency leads Ritzer (1996) to argue that there has been a McDonaldisation of health care provision. There are four basic dimensions to McDonaldisation (1996). It is true that one can identify elements of the four basic elements of the model – a concern with efficiency, quantification and calculation of tasks and product, predictability, and control through replacing human skills and knowledge with technology. In the classic service context, this system of control, however, is not exercised through any monolithic corporate or state hierarchy, but via a tightly controlled franchising arrangement.

There is a prima facie case that the purchaser / provider split associated with the quasi-market arrangements operates in a similar way. The health authority 'franchise' the hospital according to tightly defined contracts. On closer examination, however, one finds important differences: firstly, as with *cordon bleu* restaurants, general hospitals continue to remain dependent upon the medical expertise and autonomy of the doctors. This limits the extent to which standardised routines (protocols) and new technologies can routinise the work of the doctor. Secondly, measurement and assessment of the quality of service is not limited to the patients' or managers' evaluations. Medical staff, unlike those working at a McDonald's restaurant, will claim an ascendancy in judging whether their work is of a high quality or not. Thirdly, the organisation of hospitals is not directly determined by the quasi-franchiser as is the case with McDonald's restaurants. It is up to the staff and management at the individual hospitals to decide. There is, in short, more flexibility than is available to a McDonald's franchisee. These elements limit the rationalising impact of the reforms and provide hospital doctors with a new repertoire of opportunities to take on the leading role in the organisation and control of health care. We will now explore those developments in a broader institutional context.

European Health Care Systems

An important reason behind this matching of interests between the medical profession and the welfare state was that only the medical profession could offer a systematic model for the organisation and control of the health care labour processes. Historically, the other health care professions emerged in the shadow of the medical profession (Freidson, 1970), which had opportunely established itself in its modern form (in the nineteenth century) at just the time to provide the state with the means of managing health care (Johnson, 1995). Their autonomy as well as their dominance was based on their strategic claim to expertise and control over the division of labour. Nurses and midwives, dentistry, optometry and pharmacy as well as the professions allied to medicine (for example, dieticians, physiotherapists and occupational therapists) were variously constrained in the degree of professional autonomy they could achieve because of their subordination to the medical profession (Turner, 1995). The particular dynamics of this historical process of medical control included a strongly gendered element, for professionalisation reflected the patriarchal nature of the state and wider society (Witz, 1992). Thus it was that governments establishing public sector health care systems came to rely on the medical profession as the arbiters of the type and quality of care delivered.

These arrangements not only benefited the doctors. Governments were also reasonably content with the arrangements, as too were the majority of people who used the system. By the 1970s, however, the contradictions of the welfare state (Offe, 1984; Flynn, 1992) had become so pronounced that the nature of the 'partnership' between the medical profession and the state was increasingly called into question. This led to the emergence of new organisational arrangements which putatively involved constraints on medical autonomy. Many of these innovations were influenced by the US model of Health Maintenance Organisations (HMOs) including the prospective reimbursement system based on Diagnostic Related Groups (DRGs) (Flynn, 1992). It is important to note, however, that there are major differences between European countries. A principal variation is in the funding arrangements. Most European countries, including France, Germany and the Netherlands are insurance-based and some are centrally funded, notably Sweden, the UK and Italy (Ham *et al.*, 1990; McCarthy and Rees, 1992). There are, however, other equally important cross-cutting differences too. The German and Dutch health systems, for instance, are embedded within a corporatist political culture (Freddi, 1989) although this is not the case with all insurance-based systems. France, by contrast, is *etatist*, a tendency also found in Britain under the Thatcher administration. Here, in order to achieve the policy objectives of deregulation, privatisation and marketisation the government became increasingly *dirigiste* (Flynn, 1992). Conversely, the centralised SSN (Servizio Sanitario Nazionale), established in Italy in 1978, is dominated by the party system for it is through this mechanism that individuals are elected onto the management boards of the local health units – *unità sanitarie locali* (Freddi, 1989). The Swedish public sector health system, like those of Britain and Italy, is organised as a nationalised health service. In the initial post-1945 period it was financed by health insurance, but the Social Democratic Party's ability to stay in government over a long period of time meant they were able, in 1970, to introduce a centrally funded service known as the 'Seven Crowns' reforms[3] (Ferrera, 1989; Immergut, 1992). Doctors are now salaried and patients have little motivation to seek out private medicine because the public sector service is so cheap. The other distinguishing feature of the Swedish system is that it is a devolved one with the county councils and largest municipal councils effectively running the system. Within these arrangements the Swedish doctors have lost ground to the professional managers over the control of their work environment. There are also parallels here to the situation in Britain and in Italy where the health systems are devolved. In Britain, however, it is the health authority rather than the local authority that is responsible for organising the provision of health care according to principles of the quasi-market. Clinical autonomy for both Swedish and British doctors has been preserved to a far greater degree than is the case in Italy which is characterised by a strong anti-technocratic bias that peripheralises medical opinion (Freddi, 1989). Clearly, these variations in political cultures, coupled with the funding arrangements, create very different contexts within which doctors and their professional associations operate. What emerges from this review of European health systems is that the degree of medical autonomy is directly related to a country's political culture: corporatist cultures provide professionals with the strongest support, etatist the least, while the social democratic egalitarianism of the Swedish system, characteristic of the pre-marketised version of Britain's health service, lies somewhere in between. To illustrate this reconfiguration of medical autonomy it is useful to examine the recent reforms in the Netherlands' health care system in relation to that of Britain.

Introduction of Regulated Markets into Health Care: the Netherlands and Britain

The Netherlands' health system is a particularly useful one to look at in comparison to Britain's. Whilst it is a small country with a population of around fifteen million people it is a good example of the social insurance model commonly found in Europe and, along with Germany, embedded within a strong corporatist tradition. Moreover, it too has and is undergoing major reforms of an HMO-inspired kind in an attempt to control its health care costs. Under the Sickness Fund Act (ZFW) of 1964 more than 60 per cent of the population were compulsorily insured with a sickness fund. Subscribers' premiums were set at a uniform percentage of gross income. Employers also contributed 50 per cent. The Sickness Funds concluded contracts with health care providers (for example, hospitals) on behalf of their subscribers. The remaining population was mostly privately insured.

Until 1992 sickness funds had no discretion over what hospitals, clinics and so on with which to contract. Instead the terms were negotiated nationally. All this changed in the wake of the Dekker Committee set up in 1986 and reported the following year (Ham *et al.*, 1990). The Committee's recommendations bear striking resemblances to Britain's 1990 reforms although being an insurance-based system the 'purchaser–provider' arrangements are rather different. It is the health insurers and sickness funds who are the 'purchasers' for health services. This has given rise to different sets of problems and possibilities from those found in Britain. In order to provide some sense of a 'level playing field' the sickness funds were to become health insurers in their own right with freedom to enter contracts with providers selectively. The insurers' incentive – as is the case with health authorities in Britain – lay in contracting with only the more efficient providers, thus holding down costs. The providers' incentive was to find economies over and beyond that reflected in the prospective contract payments. It was also intended that the new system would lead to more emphasis being put on the primary care services and health promotion. In the longer term the aim was to reduce the number of beds and close the less efficient hospitals (Ham *et al.*, 1990).

The introduction of a quasi-market in the Netherlands was the outcome of a political consensus, following the failure of a previous programme of reforms, that cost containment was no longer to be solely a government responsibility. In future it was to be shared with the health insurers and sickness funds (Schut, 1995). A single national insurance system was to be introduced that would replace the pre-existing two-tier one of 'sickness funds' and private health insurers, and to do so in terms of a marketisation of the system. There was to be much greater flexibility within this new system with 'purchasers' free to select whichever 'provider' they preferred. It was intended that this would promote the development of HMO-type organisations and thereby improve efficiencies and the quality of the health services; though to date the new arrangements do not appear to have had the desired effect.

The British version the quasi-market was officially introduced with the 1990 *NHS and Community Care Act* with the introduction of competition by means of the 'purchaser–provider' divide. Hospitals, clinics, ambulance and other services were now known as 'providers'. These bodies would now have to compete for contracts from the health authorities who had meanwhile been transformed from being the next tier in the bureaucracy to becoming the 'purchasers' of health services on behalf of the local citizenry. The model, as in the case of the Dutch reforms, derives explicitly from the HMO type advocated by Enthoven (1985a; 1985b). What this means is that contracts are agreed prospectively at a fixed cost. The pressure on the hospitals (providers) is always to reduce costs in order to ensure contracts will be renewed. In the North American model costings are based on standardised DRGs – a patient's diagnosis allocates them to a broad diagnostic group for costing purposes. If the patient's actual costs are less than the average the hospital makes a 'profit', if not, then it loses money. The assumption of the proponents of the system is that the hospital and physicians will be motivated to reduce costs wherever possible in order to 'profit' from the system. Britain's variant of DRGs are the Health Related Groups (HRGs) which are organised on the same principles but are customised more to the requirements of the NHS (Dent, 1996).

The assumptions of the efficiency of HMOs, however, may be a little premature for as Freidson (1994) reports, in the US a new phenomena of 'DRG creep' has occurred which obviates the need to be super-efficient. What happens is that the physicians allocate a patient a DRG code that will provide them with the time and resources to manage the patient as they would wish rather than attempting to minimise the care given:

> [S]hould [the physicians] want their patient to spend more time in hospital than is the norm for one DRG, they select a diagnosis in another, related diagnostic group which provides the reimbursement that pays for such a length of stay. (Freidson, 1994:186)

While the original Dekker recommendations in the Netherlands had widespread political support, it has proven to have been as resistant to change as the British NHS, possibly even more so. Nevertheless, despite these implementation problems the generality of the Dekker reforms do appear to be irrevocable. As in Britain, the health system is to be subjected to the 'pulls' and 'pushes' of the quasi-market. The inherent assumption was that in pursuing their legitimate self-interest and responsibilities 'players' in the 'market' would create a 'virtuous circle' of continuous improvements in efficiency and quality. But this has not proved to be the case either in the Netherlands or in Britain as will be explained in the next section.

Medical Work, Organisational Change and Professional Accountability: the Netherlands and the UK

The Netherlands

In this section I will first set out the background to the organisation of medical work in the Netherlands and the principle changes in quality assurance introduced in the wake of the Dekker reforms (before turning to the situation in Britain). My purpose is both to present an account of the Dutch experiences and to explore the similarities to and differences from British arrangements. By so doing it should be possible to identify the implications for the medical labour process and the autonomy of doctors. The work of doctors is divided between general practitioners (GPs) and hospital specialists. The GP – as in Britain – acts as the 'gatekeeper' to the specialist hospital services. There are 190 acute hospitals plus eight teaching hospitals (McCarthy and Rees, 1992:44). The medical staff within general hospitals are ostensibly private practitioners who contract their services to a hospital. Hospital specialists, on qualifying, join established partnerships and provide both outpatient and inpatient care. The new entrant has to pay a substantial entry fee – approximately one year's earnings (Schut, 1995).

An important element of the reforms in the Netherlands, as in Britain and elsewhere, has been the increasing emphasis on quality and accountability. Until relatively recently the work of doctors did not come under public scrutiny. Good-quality doctoring was commonly seen as a function of training and socialisation. The ultimate sanction of the profession's governing body was to take away a doctor's licence to practice. Nevertheless, the medical profession in most countries have developed their own systems of peer review, commonly referred to as medical audit, which have been in operation over many years – although not necessarily with any great enthusiasm on the part of the doctors (Dent, 1996). With the introduction of the HMO-type quasi-market, however, quality assurance has become a much more central issue than in the past. In principle, doctors, along with other health professionals and workers, have to be seen to be delivering good-quality care as part of the contract between the 'purchasers' and 'providers'.

In the wake of the Dekker reforms the Royal Dutch Medical Association (KNMG) organised a conference, sponsored by the Government in 1989, to establish a national quality care policy attended by doctors and hospital managers ('providers'), and representatives of the patients' associations and insurers ('purchasers') (Casparie, 1993). Government officials attended, but only as observers. The official aim of the conference was to put in place quality assurance systems that would meet the World Health Organisation's (WHO) deadline which was set for 1990. There were also three other central concerns that lay behind this initiative:

- to assure good quality of care in the new quasi-market that had no government regulation;
- to ensure that cost containment would not be seen to be at the expense of the quality of care;
- to counteract any tendency on the part of insurance companies to disadvantage high-risk patients such as those with chronic diseases or serious disabilities.

There were two more conferences the following year which 'hardened up' on the general areas of agreement and identifying the key responsibilities for ensuring good quality care. The outcome was an agreement over the role the different parties would play in quality assurance. While the 'providers' (that is, institutions and professions) were principally responsible for quality of care, the insurers were to ensure the efficiency and organisation of care while the patient organisations would review the culture of care (Casparie, 1993). A key accord was that the external audit would only be to ensure that the internal systems of quality assurance were in place and working well and not the quality of care in itself. This reflects the logic of Total Quality Management (TQM), an approach which was introduced in some hospitals in the 1980s but not followed through. Within two years more than half of the twenty-three professional associations had introduced peer review although only three have adopted external review. Most, however, have adopted the use of clinical guidelines. Neither the insurance companies nor the patients' associations have become actively involved in any quality assurance initiatives. The Government is underpinning developments with a bill on quality of care which demands all health institutions set up internal quality systems and publish annual reports on their quality assurance policy.

The conferences of 1989 and 1990 were not the first time quality assurance had been introduced into the Dutch health care system. A national body – the National Organisation for Peer Review in Hospitals (CBO) – responsible for overseeing quality assurance development, had been set up by the medical profession in 1976 (Reerink, 1990; Casparie, 1995). It started work on the consensus development of explicit clinical criteria in 1982 (Klazinga, 1994): a common methodology used in the US and Canada (Scrivens, 1995) and one adopted because of the then growing dissatisfaction doctors had with peer-review within hospitals. In the Dutch context 'criterion audits' took the form of nationally set clinical guidelines or protocols and by the end of 1993, thirty-nine sets of practice guidelines had been introduced. This innovation reflected the traditional 'corporatist' political culture of the Netherlands. The problem in adopting this consociational approach, however, was that implementing and monitoring the agreements locally was a complex process. The procedure for the formulation of clinical guidelines nationally is as follows. Topics are first selected, a chairperson is appointed and experts are recruited through their scientific societies. The average expert group has ten members and meets twelve times each year. The expert group writes the background papers which are then discussed at a specially convened consensus conference of around 300 participants. The final text is published in an appropriate medical journal. The whole process fundamentally altered the role of the hospital-based peer review committees. This body now acts as the main channel for the dissemination of these clinical guidelines. Up until recently the whole process has been entirely a peer review process. Recently, however, there are signs that representatives of the health insurers and patients' associations are beginning to get directly involved. Rather than representing an erosion of the doctors' autonomy it appears to be a price that the profession is willing to pay in order to maintain credibility with the general public. Part of the problem is that even after the programme has been in existence for over twelve years it is still not possible to demonstrate with any great certainty that any health improvements relate directly to the introduction of the clinical guidelines (Klazinga, 1994). The guidelines seem to mean all things to all the interest groups. Doctors, insurers, managers, consumers and government, apparently, see them as the solution to their problems. Any conflict between goals is usually glossed over. The Dutch medical profession has become adept at using the guidelines to both defend its autonomy and demonstrate its accountability towards the other groups. 'Clinical guidelines' in Britain have appeared later and while also driven by concerns to protect medical autonomy have been based on a different rhetoric.

Britain

The medical profession in Britain operates within a rather different political culture from its Dutch colleagues. To quote Mishra (1984:108) from a decade ago:

> [T]he failure to establish viable forms of corporatism have left a depressing legacy of lame-duck welfarism and half-baked interventionism ... In English-speaking countries we have very little acquaintance and virtually no experience of a corporatist welfare state.

The Netherlands' strong corporatist political culture has enabled the medical profession to pursue an effective consensualist strategy in establishing 'clinical guidelines' not available to its British counterpart. The Thatcherite introduction of the quasi-market in Britain paradoxically produced a very centralised system of management. As Harrison and Pollitt have perceptively explained:

> [T]he quasi-market allows some of the possibilities of control provided by a hierarchy to be added to the pressures created by the market. The ... *purchasers* can still be

controlled by a hierarchical line of authority that runs directly from the Secretary of State. (1994: 118)

It was the 1990 *NHS and Community Care Act* that legally required doctors to carry out audit procedures on a regular basis. A reasonable expectation would be that hospitals would set up internal audits which would identify appropriate criteria or guidelines for good practice as occurred in the Netherlands. Yet despite a substantial injection of money little of this happened (Harrison and Pollitt, 1994). Instead, monthly audit meetings tend to focus on case reviews and morbidity and mortality reviews (Butterly *et al.*, 1994). Kerrison *et al.*'s (1993) King's Fund review of medical audit reforms appears, at first, to contradict this CASPE finding. They state '[m]ost of the audit being undertaken is *criteria audit ...*' (1993: vii).[4] But they add significantly that 'too often the criteria were implicit, and even when explicit, criteria were not always clearly research based or clearly justified.' In fact 'most audits sample sizes were small, based on case note reviews' (*ibid*). All of which should hardly be surprising given that medical audit was originally introduced within Britain by the medical profession to resist managerial encroachment (Dent, 1991).

But the medical audit strategy of the medical profession has probably gone as far as it can. In the short term they have been able to retain control over the audit process and procedures (*ibid*:104) but there has been little sense of closure to the issue. The doctors seem to have achieved this state of affairs by prevarication and apathy – a strategy they have often employed before (Klein, 1995). But to ensure their continued ascendancy under the new contractual arrangements necessitates the profession finding a new quality assurance candidate which will offer guarantees to managers, purchasers and patients at the same time as ensuring the doctors retain control over the clinical processes. This is what evidence-based medicine appears to offer (Eddy, 1990a; 1990b; Sackett *et al.*, 1996). It is, however, not the only candidate on offer. TQM and accreditation are also being advocated for consideration. Although not from within the profession, Morgan and Potter (1995:184) define quality assurance (including medical audit) in terms of 'the expertise and infallibility of the professional as arbiter of appropriate care' in order to distinguish it from management-led TQM. This is viewed as a multi-disciplinary approach 'that empower *all* staff at all levels' (*ibid*:184).[5] Whether TQM is really intended to achieve such results is dubious. Research by Sewell and Wilkinson (1992) within the manufacturing sector, for instance, has effectively disabused us of such an optimistic interpretation. TQM for these researchers is best understood as a latter-day version of the 'panoptic gaze' (Foucault, 1979). Reed (1995) is also critical of TQM, arguing that it leads to the 'management of blame' within the NHS. He observed that as a control technology TQM becomes particularly distorted by the 'heterogenous, rivalrous and recalcitrant' social environment of the public sector. Accreditation too can be viewed as a similar form of quality management (for example, King's Fund organisational audit). Neither approach has so far found much support within Britain or in the European context (Harrison and Pollitt, 1994; Scrivens, 1995).

As Shaw (1980) has shown, quality assurance can mean almost anything to anybody. In current parlance it can, broadly, be said to cover multi-disciplinary clinical audit, single disciplinary medical audit and organisational audit – or accreditation. There has, however, been a central tension between pressures for external accreditation procedures versus doctor-controlled medical audit. Criterion audit emerged in the US to placate the pressures from the accreditation authorities (Scrivens, 1995). It was out of this earlier experience with criterion audit that clinical guidelines (or protocols) emerged, initially in the US and later in Canada and Australia and more recently in Europe. This history does suggest that the whole issue reflects the '*contingent* nature of medical power' (Coburn *et al.*, 1997:19) for it suggests that clinical guidelines may be developed, paradoxically, not to erode medical autonomy but to protect it. In an influential article, Ellwood (1988) has presented a case for the medical profession to support clinical guidelines. He argues for the introduction of a new system of 'outcomes management' (*ibid*: 1551) based on four techniques:

- established standards and guidelines;
- systematic measurement of clinical outcomes;
- pooling of this data;
- data to be analysed and disseminated.

The process would become a 'clinical trial machine' (*ibid*:1552) of the kind advocated by Cochrane (1972)[6] and not part of TQM or any accreditation procedures. Ellwood recognises the contentiousness of his proposals and acknowledges that it might be seen as 'cookbook medicine' (*ibid*:1553) of the McDonaldised type (Ritzer, 1996), 'a bureaucrat's paradise' (Ellwood, 1988:1553). Moreover, the US Congress has attempted to make the innovation more acceptable to the US medical profession by referring euphemistically to the process as 'technology assessment' – a term adopted within the Netherlands (Klazinga, 1994:56), but not in common use within Britain. Nevertheless, Ellwood puts forward his proposal as a strategy for improving the quality of health care *and* enhancing the authority and autonomy of doctors (*ibid*:1556).

While he does not use the term, what he describes and implicitly advocates is the previously described system of evidence-based medicine (EBM). Clinical guidelines based on EMB are – as with the Dutch system – designed as a prospective system of quality assurance based on the assumption that the protocols will avoid mistakes and/or sub-optimal treatments before they happen. The approach, however, is more technocratic than the consensual model adopted by the Dutch. Under an EBM regime one can envisage doctors accessing computer-based medical records, entering the details of their patients and being informed or reminded of the necessary protocols or guidelines to follow in light of the most up-to-date evidence.[7] Indeed, there is much emphasis on the use of the Internet to access the most up-to-date research information. One can now access, for example, the 'Cochrane Collaboration' on one Internet site in Canada, the findings of RCTs throughout the medical world. Similarly, abstracts of research published in medical journals are summarised on the Internet too.

Comparisons and Conclusions

The introduction of HMO-type arrangements has not only been on the agenda of the New Right within European politics. Regulated markets are also supported by left-of-centre parties too. The latter, in the case of the Netherlands, offered such support following the failure of earlier policies for more planned provision. In adopting a marketised solution, however, there is also a consequence for the professions. In this chapter I have explored this dynamic in relation to medical autonomy and the introduction of clinical protocols, guidelines and evidence-based medicine in relation to a labour process theoretic.

This chapter has dealt primarily with hospital doctors in Britain and the Netherlands although mention has been made of other European countries as a way of contextualising these two cases. Here I return again to the wider picture before leading into the specific conclusions regarding the putative rationalising effects of marketisation on British and Dutch hospital doctors. The question lying behind this brief survey is whether or not those European countries without a marketisation strategy have any greater autonomy than those with. In the cases of Britain and the Netherlands this would seem to be overstated: the political culture and institutional context mediates the impact of the regulated market. Moreover, it provides doctors with new possibilities as well as challenges. In all European countries what protects the doctors from 'real subordination' to the medical labour process is partly the technical complexity and uncertainty of medicine and partly the political sensitivity of the issue of health care facilities. Politicians seeking office, for instance, have to be able to convince the electorate that the health services are 'safe in their hands' almost as much as they have to convince them of their ability to run the economy. During the 1980s Europe saw major changes in the organisation of health care delivery systems. Some states have embraced the market rhetoric with greater warmth than others. Britain has been something of a 'flag-ship' in this respect. Others have taken a more cautious approach. Sweden, for instance, with its social democratic traditions, has put more emphasis on decentralisation than marketisation. The doctor is much more of a public servant and reasonably content to be so. By comparison with the broader 'class-based' interest groups (for example, the Trade Union Federation [LO] and the Swedish Employers' Federation [SAF]) the profession's ability to significantly influence politicians on policy matters has been limited. Doctors do, on the other hand, have a legal monopoly which underpins their practical autonomy over all medical matters including recruitment.

France remains committed to a *dirigiste* approach and has preferred to rely on top–down budgetary reforms rather than marketisation in order to encourage efficiencies within the system (Griggs and Dent, 1996). Doctors for their part have been less reliant on their organised profession to protect and advance their interests. Instead, French doctors have long relied on direct political influence within the community as 'local notable', as a member of Parliament, or as an elite member of the profession (Immergut, 1992).

Italy, during the 1980s, chose to reject marketisation having implemented a centralised national health system (SSN) in 1978. It now appears to be following the British model of separating the local health units – including hospitals – from the Local Health Authorities. They are funded from the region and doctors are now able to practice private medicine from within the hospital. All this is the result of 1992 legislation which passed with 'total public indifference' (Niero, 1996:127). The Italians have been the least satisfied with their national health service of anybody in Europe despite general improvement in health. The organisational arrangements between 1978 and 1992 seriously constrained doctors' autonomy. Medical work was organised strictly by civil service rules with seniority being the key to promotion (Freddi, 1989). Hospital doctors were, however, able to opt for part-time contracts (as in Britain) and reclaim autonomy by engaging in private practice, although this is a most competitive activity given the highest ratio of doctors per head of population in Europe.

In sum, Sweden, France and Italy have relied in different ways on political strategies to manage their health delivery systems and medical professions. Italy probably has encroached on medical autonomy the most and France the least. The continued politicisation of health care in these countries does not seem to constitute a viable alternative to the marketisation strategy. Italy does seem to have exercised greater controls over medical autonomy than many countries and gained some measurable improvements in the country's health (Niero, 1996). However, there is no direct evidence that the two factors are directly linked as opposed to the general improvement in health care facilities under the nationalised SSN. It is important to note that I have not subjected either Italy or France's systems to any detailed analysis and therefore any conclusion needs to be treated with caution. The same is true of my comments on Sweden. Here the impetus has been on decentralisation coupled with experiments with the regulated market. This seems to be a more pluralistic and incremental set of strategies that is as much about consensus building as it is about improving the efficiency of the health services (and reducing their costs). It appears that there is little evidence of significant movement towards further limiting medical autonomy.

Returning to our case studies, within the Netherlands the professional associations are commonly viewed as an essential part of the 'organic solidarity' of society. The introduction of the regulated market has been robustly negotiated by the state with the medical profession. The doctors, in turn, have had to find a solution that not only protects their interests but is acceptable to the general public too. Consequently, the profession has gone down the route of introducing quality control measures such as clinical guidelines that are under their control but include some participation from patient groups. The profession here has been able to adopt a consensual, corporatist approach to 'clinical guidelines' in a way not open to Britain's profession. Whereas doctors in the Netherlands still function as independent contractors to the health service, UK hospital doctors are salaried and vulnerable to a greater degree of incorporation into the management of the service, at least at the local level (Harrison and Pollitt, 1994) although this process, in my view, represents a modification rather than an undermining of their professional dominance. In this respect there is more commonality between British and US doctors than with their Dutch colleagues. The latter are much less under threat from any incorporationist strategy of government. Doctors within the Netherlands are also less susceptible to the rationalising effects of cost containment strategies. The 'purchasers' (insurers) within the Dutch version of the quasi-market are far less motivated to drive down costs than are their equivalent in British health authorities.

It is for this reason, and in order to avoid even the threat of a 'McDonaldised' future, that the British medical profession will continue to explore the possibilities of evidence-based medicine. It acts as a means of countering managerial and state-sponsored control mechanisms. The imposition of protocols as part of contracting arrangement could lead to a deskilling of certain elements of medical practice and possibly a proletarianisation of some medical practitioners. Hospitals, for instance, could contract for high-volume procedures, such as hip replacement and cornea grafts – organised on something that resembles a Fordist production line. It is this kind of scenario that the British medical profession is keen to avoid and has avoided. Doctors in the Netherlands, by contrast, can continue to rely on the corporate, consensualist and consociational assumptions of the political system to limit any threats to their medical autonomy and rationalisation of their work situation. Their own privatised relations with the hospitals within which they work and the 'hands off' approach of government and the insurers limit their degree of vulnerability to the rationalising impact of marketisation.

The current generation of quality assurance systems reflects the new demands of the HMO-type organisation of health care in Europe. In examining the similarities and differences between the Netherlands and Britain it is clear that the medical professions in both countries have been able to avoid the imposition of external controls. But they have done so using different techniques that reflect their structural positions within their countries' political systems. The Dutch doctors have been able to rely on a collectivist and consensual response which has not, so far, been undermined by the introduction of market priorities within the public sector. The British welfare state, by contrast, accommodated the medical profession and provided doctors with a particularly strong version of professional dominance and the ability to block change (Klein, 1995). With the introduction of the quasi-market the doctors found their powers of veto undermined. They have had to reconsider their strategy for maintaining medical autonomy and dominance within the workplace. The evidence discussed here suggests that 'accommodation' is now giving way to an ambivalent form of 'incorporation' in which doctors accept the reality of financial constraints and their role as clinical directors. They also accept the unavoidability of quality assurance systems and will seek ways in which they can keep them under their own control. Whereas in the Netherlands the emergence of clinical guidelines represents a strategy of the organised profession to facilitate audit for their members, in Britain the process is more a strategy of inhibiting the encroachment of externally controlled procedures such as accreditation. Clearly the autonomy of hospital doctors is being reconfigured. At the same time it is hardly an unambiguous case of *responsible autonomy* any more than the work is being 'McDonaldised'.

In both countries, but to different degrees, the introduction of clinical protocols indicates a degree of rationalisation. They also, and significantly, serve to ensure that the profession has a means of legitimating its members' relative freedom from external scrutiny. Medical autonomy can be seen to be under revision and the *individual* autonomy of the physician is giving way to a *group* version.

Acknowledgements

I am greatly indebted to Ruud van Herk for his help especially relating to the literature on the Netherlands health care system.

References

Barnet, G.O., Winickoff, R., Dorsey, J.L., Morgan, M.M. and Lurie, R.S. (1978) 'Quality Assurance through Automated Monitoring and Concurrent Feedback Using a Computer-Based Medical Information System', *Medical Care*, XVI:11, 962–70.

Burrows, R. and Loader, B. (eds) (1994) *Towards a Post-Fordist Welfare State?* London: Routledge.

Butterly, Y., Walshe, K., Coles, J. and Bennet, J. (1994) *Evaluating Medical Audit*, London: CASPE Research.

Calnan, M. (1984) 'Clinical uncertainty: is it a problem in the doctor–patient relationship?', *Sociology of Health and Illness*, 6:1, 74–85.

Casparie, A.F. (1993) 'View from the Netherlands', *Quality in Health Care*, 2: 138–41.

Casparie, A.F. (1995) 'Medical Audit in The Netherlands: experience over 22 years', *Journal of Epidemiology and Community Health*, 49: 557–8.

Coburn, D., Rappolt, S. and Bourgeault, I. (1997) 'Decline vs retention of medical power through restratification: an examination of the Ontario case', *Sociology of Health and Illness*, 19:1, 1–22.

Cochrane, A.L. (1972) *Effectiveness and Efficiency: random reflections on health services*, London: Nuffield Provincial Hospital Trust.

Dent, M. (1991) 'Autonomy and the Medical Profession: medical audit and management control' in Smith, C., Knights, D. and Willmott, H. (eds) *White-Collar Work: the non-manual labour process*, London: Macmillan.

Dent, M. (1993) 'Professionalism, educated labour and the state: hospital medicine and the new managerialism', *Sociological Review* 41:2, 244–73.

Dent, M. (1995) 'The New National Health Service: a case of postmodernism?', *Organisation Studies*, 16:5: 875–99.

Dent, M. (1996) *Professions, Information Technology and Management in Hospitals*, Aldershot: Avebury.

Derber, C. (1982) 'The proletarianisation of the professional: a review essay' in Derber, C.(ed.) *Professions as Workers: mental labor in advanced capitalism*, Boston, Mass: Hall & Co.

Derber, C., Schwartz, W.A. and Magrass, Y. (1990) *Power in the Highest Degree*, Oxford: Oxford University Press.

Eddy, D.M. (1990a) 'Guidelines for policy statements: the explicit approach', *Journal of the American Medical Association (JAMA)*, 263:2239–443.

Eddy, D.M. (1990b) 'Designing a practice policy: standards, guidelines and options, *Journal of the American Medical Association*, 263: 3077–84.

Ellwood, P.M. (1988) 'Outcomes management; a technology of patient experience', *New England Journal of Medicine*, 318: 1549–56.

Elston, M.E. (1991) 'The politics of professional power: medicine in a changing health service' in Gabe, J. *et al.* (eds) *The Sociology of the Health Service*, London: Routledge.

Enthoven, A.C. (1985a) *Reflections on the Management of the National Health Service: an American looks at incentives to efficiency in health services management in Britain*, London: Nuffield Provincial Hospital Trust.

Enthoven, A.C. (1985b) 'National Health Service: some reforms that might be politically feasible', *The Economist*, 22 June.

Ferrera, M. (1989) 'The politics of health reform: origins and performance of the Italian health service in comparative perspective' in Freddi, G. and Warner, J.W. (eds) *Controlling Medical Professionals: the comparative politics of health governance*, London: Sage.

Flynn, R. (1992) *Structures of Control in Health Management*, London: Routledge.

Foucault, M. (1979) *Discipline and Punish*, Harmondsworth: Penguin/Peregrine Books.

Freddi, G. (1989) 'Problems of organisational rationality in health systems: political controls and policy options' in Freddi, G. and Warner, J.W. (eds) *Controlling Medical Professionals: the comparative politics of health governance*, London: Sage.

Freidson, E. (1970) *Medical Dominance: the social structure of medical care*, New York: Atherton Press.

Freidson, E. (1994) *Professionalism Reborn: theory, prophecy and policy*, Cambridge: Polity.

Friedman, A.L. (1977) *Industry and Labour*, London: Macmillan.

Giddens, A. (1994) *Beyond Left and Right: the future of radical politics*, Cambridge: Polity.

Griggs, S. and Dent, M. (1996) *Remodelling Public Hospitals in France and the UK*, Stoke on Trent: Knowledge Organisations and Society Research Unit, University of Staffordshire.

Habermas, J. (1976) 'Problems of legitimation in late capitalism' in Connerton, P. (ed.) *Critical Sociology*, Harmondsworth: Penguin.

Ham, C., Robinson, R. and Benzeval, M. (1990) *Health Check: health care reforms in an international context*, London: King's Fund Institute.

Harrison, S. and Pollitt, C. (1994) *Controlling Health Professionals: the future of work and organisation in the NHS*, Buckingham: Open University Press.

Harrison, S. and Schulz, R.I. (1989) 'Clinical autonomy in the United Kingdom and the United States: contrasts and convergence' in Freddi, G. and Warner, J.W. (eds) *Controlling Medical Professionals: the comparative politics of health governance*, London: Sage.

Immergut, E.M. (1992) *Health Politics: interests and institutions in Western Europe*, Cambridge: Cambridge University Press.

Jamous, H. and Peloille, B. (1970) 'Professions or self-perpetuating Systems? Changes in the French university-hospital system' in Jackson, J.A. (ed.) *Professions and Professionalisation*, Cambridge: Cambridge University Press.

Johnson, T. (1995) 'Governmentality and the institutionalisation of expertise' in Johnson, T. *et al.* (eds) *Health Professions and the State in Europe*, London: Routledge.

Jost, T.S. (1992) 'Recent developments in medical quality assurance and audit: an international comparative study' in Dingwall, R. and Fenn, P. (eds) *Quality and Regulation in Health Care: International Experiences*, London: Routledge.

Kerrison, S., Packwood, T. and Buxton, M. (1993) *Medical Audit: taking stock*. Medical Audit Series No. 6, London: King's Fund Centre.

Klazinga, N. (1994) Compliance with practice guidelines: clinical autonomy revisited', *Health Policy*, 28, 51–66.

Klein, R. (1995) *The New Politics of the NHS* (Third Edition), Harlow: Longman.

Larson, M.S. (1980) 'Proletarianisation and educated labor', *Theory and Society*, 9:1, 131–75.

Lash, S. and Urry, J. (1987) *The End of Organised Capitalism*, Cambridge: Polity Press.

Le Grande, J. (1991) Quasi-markets and Social Policy, *The Economic Journal*, 101:1256–67.

McCarthy, M. and Rees, S. (1992) *Health Systems and Public Health Medicine in the European Community*, London: Royal College of Physicians of London.

Mishra, R. (1984) *The Welfare State in Crisis: social thought and social change*, Brighton: Wheatsheaf Books.

Morgan, P. and Potter, C. (1995) 'Professional cultures and paradigms of quality in health care' in Kirkpatrick, I. and Lucio, M.M. (eds) *The Politics of Quality in the Public Sector*, London: Routledge.

Niero, M. (1996) 'Italy: right turn for the welfare state?' in George, V. and Taylor-Gooby, P. (eds) *European Welfare Policy: Squaring the Welfare Circle*, Basingstoke: Macmillan.

Offe, C. (1984) *Contradictions of the Welfare State*, London: Hutchinson.

Reed, M. (1995) 'Managing Quality and Organisational Politics: TQM as a Governmental Technology' in Kirkpatrick, I. and Martinez Lucio, M. (eds) *The Politics of Quality in the Public Sector: The Management of Change*, London: Routledge.

Reerink, E. (1990) 'Improving the quality of hospital services in the Netherlands: the role of the CBO', *Quality Assurance in Health Care*, 2:1, 13–19.

Ritzer, G. (1996) *The McDonaldisation of Society (Revised Edition)*, London: Pine Forge Press.

Rustin, M. (1995) 'The idea of community and the non-profit sector', *Renewal*, 3:2, 25–34.

Sackett, D.L., Rosenberg, W.M.C., Gray, J.A.M., Haynes, R.B. and Richardson, W.S. (1996) 'Evidence-based medicine: what it is and what it isn't', *British Medical Journal*, 13 January: 71–2.

Saltman, R.B. and von Otter, C. (1992) *Planned Markets and Public Competition*, Buckingham: Open University Press.

Schut, F.T. (1995) *Competition in the Dutch Health Care Sector*, Den Haag: Cip-Gegevens Koninklijke Biblitheek.

Scrivens, E. (1995) *Accreditation: protecting the professional or the consumer?* Buckingham: Open University Press.

Sewell, G. and Wilkinson, B. (1992) 'Someone to watch over me: surveillance, discipline, and the just-in-time labour process', *Sociology*, 26:2, 271–91.

Shaw, C.D. (1980) 'Aspects of Audit: 1 The background', *British Medical Journal*, 24 May: 1256–8.

Thompson, P. (1990) 'Crawling from the wreckage: the labour process and the politics of production' in Knights, D. and Willmott, H. (eds) *Labour Process Theory*, London: Macmillan.

Tolliday, H. (1978) 'Clinical autonomy' in E. Jaques and members of the Brunel Health Services Organisation Research Unit (eds) *Health Services*, London: Heinemann.

Turner, B.S. (with Samson, C.) (1995) *Medical Power and Social Knowledge*, London: Sage.

Witz, A. (1992) *Professions and Patriarchy*, London: Routledge.

Notes

1 Quasi-market, the term introduced by Le Grande (1991), refers to the arrangement where an agent (a manager) exercises choice on behalf of the patient/consumer as in the case of the National Health Service (NHS) in Britain. I will also use the term 'regulated market' (Saltman and Von Otter, 1992) which will be taken to cover any kind of simulated 'marketisation' within the public sector.

2 The term 'Britain' is a little misleading for there are some significant differences in the organisation of the NHS in Scotland and Northern Ireland as compared to England and Wales which will not be discussed here. Nevertheless, the general points about the quasi-market and the specific ones on medical autonomy do apply.

3 The 'Seven Crowns' refers to the charge to the patient of a hospital visit in Sweden.

4 Emphasis added.

5 Emphasis added.

6 Cochrane (1972) was a strong advocate of the idea that good medicine needs to be based on the best clinical evidence provided by randomised control trials (RCTs). His arguments are currently being employed to support the case for evidence-based medicine.

7 There was an early experimental version of automated clinical protocols designed on the principles of prospective criterion audit, based on the Massachussetts General Hospital's automated patient record system which was developed by Barnett *et al.* (1978) in the 1970s.

Author Index

Rose, N., 110
Rosenthal, P., Hill, S. and Peccei, R., 11
Routh, G., 3
Rowlinson, M. and Hassard, J., 67
Ruigrok, W. and Van Tulder, R., 68
Rustin, M., 207

Sackett, D., Rosenberg, W., Gray, J., Haynes,
    R. and Richardson, W., 216
Salman, R. and von Otter, C., 224
Salzman, H. and Rosenthal, S., 157
Sandberg, A., 8
Sauer, C., 155
Scarbrough, H. and Burrell, G., 15, 185
Schonberger, R., 43, 47
Schulein, J., 111, 116, 120
Schumann, M., Baethge-Kinsky, B.,
    Kuhlmann, M., Kurz, C. and Neumann,
    U., 106, 109
Schut, F., 211, 213
Scrivens, E., 214, 217
Segal-Horn, S., 5
Sewell, G. and Wilkinson, B., 40, 92, 216
Shaiken, H., Loperz, S. and Mankita, I., 31
Shapiro, S., 148
Shaw, C., 217
Simoleit, J., Feldhoff, J. and Jacke, N., 112
Sims, H. and Lorenzi, P., 113
Sinden, A., 20
Sisson, K. and Marginson, P., 186
Smith, C., Knights, D. and Willmott, H., 164
Smith, D., 16
Somerville, I., 146
Starkey, K. and McKinlay, A., 16
Stephenson, C., 65
Stewart, P., 71, 76, 78-9
Stewart, P. and Garrahan, P., 75, 78, 83
Stewart, P. and Wass, V., 76
Storey, J. and Bacon, N., 79
Sturdy, A., 84
Summers, D., 11
Swan, E., 86

Taylor, S., 5, 11, 98, 103
Taylor, W., Elger, T. and Fairbrother, P., 44
Terry, M., 78
Thomas, A., 16
Thomas, R., 32, 143
Thomas, W, 109
Thomasson, K., 144

Thompson, E., 130
Thompson, P., 60, 85, 99, 186, 207
Thompson, P. and Ackroyd, S., 10, 83
Thompson, P. and du Gay, P., 20
Thompson, P. and Findlay, P., 12, 83, 85, 100
Thompson, P., Jones, C., Nickson, D. and
    Wallace, T., 5
Thompson, P. and McHugh, D., 116, 118, 185
Thompson, P. and Wallace, T., 8
Thompson, P., Wallace, T., Flecker, J. and
    Ahlstrand, R., 8, 107
Tolliday, H., 206
Tomaney, J., 61
Townley, B., 112-13, 117
Toyota Motor Corporation, 51
Trautwein-Kalms, G., 115
Tudor, D. and Tudor, I., 162
Turnbull, P., 43
Turnbull, P. and Wass, V., 192
Turner, B., 209
Turner, S., 14
Tyler, M. and Taylor, S., 100

US Congress Office of Technology
    Assessment, 135
US Department of Labor, Bureau of Labor
    Statistics, 5, 32, 127

Vischer, J., 178
Vob, G., 11, 116

Waddington, J. and Whitston, C., 65
Walsh, K., 86
Watson, T., 100
Wilkinson, A. and Willmott, H., 86, 98, 103
Willcocks, L. and Fitzgerald, G., 162
Williams, K. and Haslam, C., 80
Willmott, H., 6, 85
Wilson, D., Petocz P. and Roiter, K., 156
Wilson, S., 167, 176
Wilson, S. and Hedge, A., 180-1
Wilson, T., 14
Witz, A., 209
Womack, J., Jones, D. and Roos, D., 28, 40, 187
Wood, S., 60
Wright, C. and Lund, J., 8
Wright, G., 166

Zoll, R. et al., 115
Zuboff, S., 27-8, 32-3, 125, 138

Subject Index